Quo Vadis Univer-Cities?

"The role that universities have played in the economic development of cities, regions and nations has been seriously underappreciated. From their origins in the medieval centuries in Europe and the Islamic world to their centrality in the growth of entire new industries in modern times, universities have played a key part in the evolution of urban and regional economies. The beneficial effects of clustering of research and entrepreneurship around great universities has radiated outwards and profoundly affected the course of the global economy. The editors of this Univer-Cities book are to be congratulated for producing a timely and prescriptive book that should be read by all those concerned with the intertwining of centres of learning with the improvement of mankind's material and qualitative conditions."

~ **Dr Ali Allawi**, former Senior Research Professor, Middle East Institute of National University of Singapore 2012–14, former Finance Minister of Iraq, Fellowships at Kennedy School, Oxford, Exeter, Princeton and the World Bank, and Author of *Faisal I of Iraq*.

"In our highly interconnected world, knowledge networks will play an ever-increasing role in fueling economic growth, societal development and interactions, as well as developing the engaged deep dialogues which are essential for communities around the world to understand and advance thinking on complex global issues. This is an area where Universities are uniquely placed to lead and contribute, and will be a growing part of the distinctive value that we can bring in a rapidly changing environment."

~ **Professor Tan Chorh Chuan**, President, National University of Singapore (QS 2014 Ranking: No. 1 University in Asia), Deputy Chairman, Agency for Science, Technology and Research, Singapore, and Chairman of the World Economic Forum's Global University Leaders Forum since 2013.

"A great university is where people with great minds gravitate to learn, explore, and contribute in solving important problems of humanity and in advancing the frontiers of knowledge."

~ **Dr Nam Pyo Suh**, former President, Korea Advanced Institute of Science and Technology (QS 2014 Ranking: No. 2 University in Asia) 2006–13 and Ralph E. & Eloise F. Cross Professor, Emeritus, MIT.

"Univer-cities are redefining the New Silk Road by posing new vistas of challenges for Asia's universities with multi-focussed approaches to the future. Interestingly, we are building upon half a millennium of West Asia-East Asia cross-links and can visualize these in Asia's emerging multimedia super-corridors."

~ **Professor Dato Dr Mohd Amin Bin Jalaludin**, Vice Chancellor, University of Malaya, and former President, Asia Pacific Academic Consortium for Public Health 2011–13.

"*Univer-cities will accelerate. University of British Columbia is an incorporated municipality porously contiguous with the garden City of Vancouver; and pioneered social embeddedness through private-public co-development which raised some $500 million for our endowment.*"

~ **Dr Arthur Hara OC**, former Chairman, Board of Governors, University of British Columbia.

"*When Professor Teo addressed the faculty and community leaders, including Alumna Governor Esther George of the Federal Reserve Bank of Kansas City, at a UMKC dedication event, he spoke about 'Univercities' which struck a chord with us. It does take a city and its universities to reinvent the emerging Univer-City in the 21st century as with the mid America frontier hub of Kansas City founded in 1854.*

Repositioned with state, city, public, civil society and a tradition of univercitizens in philanthropy from Vogel and his founding 41 acres to Hyde, Kauffman and Henry Bloch to co-create a global vibrant city with UMKC and Henry W. Bloch School of Management to pioneer entrepreneurship and innovation through experiential learning, attract talent, higher value jobs, businesses, research, start-ups and a by-product — an overarching spirit evoked by the peerless Kansas City Royals in World Series 2014 versus The Giants as destiny versus dynasty."

~ **Dr Henry W. Bloch**, Co-Founder of H&R Block and Benefactor of the Henry W. Bloch School of Management, University of Missouri, Kansas City, and **Professor Tan Teng-Kee** PhD. (Cambridge), former Dean and Harzfeld Professor of Technology Entrepreneurship and Innovation, Henry W. Bloch School of Management, University of Missouri, Kansas City.

The big Greco-Roman books have influenced learning at universities, cities and society. With the rise of China, Confucius is now making a comeback, anecdotally a preferred undergraduate course at Harvard.

25 centuries ago, my ancestor Zengzi (曾子) transmitted the teachings of Confucius to posterity. After 75 generations, I (曾繁如) at a personal level am amping up its essence to the West in selected Univercities.

~ **Dr Alan HJ Chan** (76th Zeng Generation), Director, Qufu Confucius Neo-Institute, Honorary Citizen of Qufu, Professorial Mentor, Zhejiang University, and Benefactor, Singapore Institute of International Affairs.

UNIVER-CITIES
STRATEGIC VIEW OF THE FUTURE FROM BERKELEY AND CAMBRIDGE TO SINGAPORE AND RISING ASIA

VOLUME II

UNIVER-CITIES
STRATEGIC VIEW OF THE FUTURE
FROM BERKELEY AND CAMBRIDGE TO
SINGAPORE AND RISING ASIA

VOLUME II

EDITOR
ANTHONY SC TEO

Published by

World Scientific Publishing Co. Pte. Ltd.
5 Toh Tuck Link, Singapore 596224
USA office: 27 Warren Street, Suite 401-402, Hackensack, NJ 07601
UK office: 57 Shelton Street, Covent Garden, London WC2H 9HE

National Library Board, Singapore Cataloguing-in-Publication Data
Univer-cities. Volume II : strategic view of the future from Berkeley and
    Cambridge to Singapore and rising Asia / editor, Anthony SC Teo. –
    Singapore : World Scientific Publishing Co. Pte. Ltd, [2014]
        pages cm
        ISBN : 978-981-4630-26-9 (paperback)

        1. University towns - Asia. 2. Community and college – Asia.
    3. University of Cambridge. 4. University of California, Berkeley.
    5. Nanyang Technological University. I. Teo, Anthony S. C., 1944–   editor.
    II. Inaugural Univer-Cities Conference (2013 : Singapore)

    LC238.4.A78
    378.103 -- dc23   OCN895007119

British Library Cataloguing-in-Publication Data
A catalogue record for this book is available from the British Library.

Copyright © 2015 by World Scientific Publishing Co. Pte. Ltd.

All rights reserved. This book, or parts thereof, may not be reproduced in any form or by any means, electronic or mechanical, including photocopying, recording or any information storage and retrieval system now known or to be invented, without written permission from the publisher.

For photocopying of material in this volume, please pay a copying fee through the Copyright Clearance Center, Inc., 222 Rosewood Drive, Danvers, MA 01923, USA. In this case permission to photocopy is not required from the publisher.

Typeset by Stallion Press
Email: enquiries@stallionpress.com

*To the idea of the New Silk Road re-defined
by Univer-Cities*

CONTENTS

Foreword	xiii
Acknowledgements	xv
About the Authors	xvii
Welcome Address *Bertil Andersson*, President Nanyang Technological University and Trustee, Nobel Foundation	xxxiii

Chapter 1 Univer-Cities: Strategic View of the Future — From Berkeley & Cambridge to Singapore & Rising Asia, Volume II
Anthony SC Teo 1

Chapter 2 Universities and Cities: The Future of Univer-Cities in Asia
His Royal Highness Raja Dr Nazrin Shah 31

Chapter 3 Berkeley: Campus and Community
Richard Bender, Emily Marthinsen and John Parman 39

Chapter 4 Cambridge: Beyond the Univer-City
Peter Carolin 67

Chapter 5 Universiti Kebangsaan Malaysia (UKM): East-West Views of Univer-Cities — UKM with Bangi, Kuala Lumpur and Tiger Malaysia
Sharifah Hapsah Syed Hasan Shahabudin 83

Chapter 6 University of Newcastle: Recasting the City of Newcastle as a Univer-City — The Journey from 'Olde' Newcastle-upon-Tyne to the New Silk Road
Nancy Cushing, Katrina Quinn and Caroline McMillen 93

Chapter 7 From Burnaby's Mountain Top to Vancouver and Surrey: The Making of an Engaged University
Andrew Petter, Richard Littlemore and Joanne Curry   119

Chapter 8 Modelling Good Urban (Design) Behaviour: University-led Neighbourhood Development, University of Manitoba
Richard Milgrom, David T. Barnard and Michelle Richard   139

Chapter 9 Carleton University: The Architecture of Knowledge and the Knowledge of Architecture
Roseann O'Reilly Runte   161

Chapter 10 KAIST: World-Class Innovations in Top-Notch Research University — Case of the On-Line Electric Vehicle (OLEV)
Nam P. Suh   175

Chapter 11 Cambridge: From Medieval Market Town to Univer-City
Gordon Johnson   205

Chapter 12 Tunisian Scientists' Experiences in Singapore: On the New Silk Road?
Lilia Labidi and Anthony SC Teo   231

Chapter 13 Univer-City of Melbourne: Case of Medical Regionality
Shane Huntington and Stephen K. Smith   261

Appendices   279

Appendix 1: Conference Programme   281
Appendix 2: Opening Remarks
    Anthony SC Teo   295
Appendix 3: Panel Session III: The Singapore Case
    Harold Guida and Andrew Donnelly   299

Index   305

FOREWORD

Universities and the cities in which they are located have a long history in driving economic development, educating leaders for society, and promoting cultural well-being. Their role in the contemporary world is widely recognized, particularly in Asia where such dynamic efforts are being made to found and develop institutions of higher education to meet the needs of rapidly changing societies. While there is often special attention to scientific and technological subjects, it is recognized that cities afford opportunities for enhancing the well-being of the whole person, and universities, by being open to all fields of knowledge, and sustain vitally the arts and humanities. Looking around the world, one cannot help but marvel at the differences between universities and the variety of the subjects they take for research and the culture they pass on to future generations through their teaching.

The Univer-Cities project is of particular interest. It seeks to promote consciously the development of networks between centres of knowledge across the Asia-Pacific and beyond. Previously such connections, and the beneficial transfer of knowledge that they brought about, tended to be serendipitous and random. Modern technology now makes possible the easy and considered exchange of information and the development of strategic collaborative inter-disciplinary and international programmes that prove so fruitful for research and understanding across the board.

The essays in this volume take up this theme from different perspectives and deploy different case studies. They contribute thoughtfully to an important debate: the concept of "univer-cities" linked as centres of excellence across the globe is an exciting one appropriate for our times.

Professor Sir Leszek Borysiewicz
University of Cambridge's 345th Vice-Chancellor
June 2014

ACKNOWLEDGEMENTS

Thanks to global pioneers whose contemplation and conversation to co-create strategic views of the future of Univer-Cities, the Inaugural International Conference 2013 was sparked off by a scholarly Royal Address by HRH Raja Dr Nazrin Shah, PhD (Harvard) in the presence of a most eminent audience. These included vice-chancellors, academic leaders, panelists, essayists, distinguished conferees and the Conference Advisory Council helmed by NTU President and host Professor Bertil Andersson with Chancellor Cham Tao Soon; Former Cambridge Deputy VC Gordon Johnson; Professor Lilia Labidi; Emeritus Dean John H. McArthur; Nobel Prize in Chemistry Professor Rudolph A. Marcus; VC Sharifah Hapsah; VC Professor Lap-Chee Tsui; and my Conference Co-Chairs Dean Barry Desker and Dean Stephen K. Smith.

Special thanks to the multi-disciplinary discoverers, creators and seekers of new knowledge — Richard Bender who despite cancer treatment flew in from Berkeley with Emily Marthinsen and John Parman to address the conference with Ali Allawi, Peter Carolin, Cham Tao Soon, Andrew Donnelly, Harold Guida, Sharifah Hapsah, Gordon Johnson, Caroline McMillen, Roseann Runte, Stephen K. Smith and Lap-Chee Tsui; and essayists David Barnard, Joanne Curry, Nancy Cushing, Shane Huntington, Lilia Labidi, Richard Littlemore, Richard Milgrom, Andrew Petter, Nam Pyo Suh; Katrina Quinn and Michelle Richard.

To World Scientific Publishing's Dr KK Phua and Max Phua my gratitude for turning thought-to-pen to print; and Chua Hong Koon and Triena Ong for astutely guiding and morphing these ideas into a magnificent volume.

Thanks to the generosity of NTU and the Lee Foundation and Chairman Dr ST Lee for funding this project. The Foundation's hugely generous benefaction of the NTU-Imperial's Lee Kong Chian School of Medicine has immeasurably strengthened the regional knowledge-research-medical nexus of Singapore.

And to my dear wife Swee Chee and our five grandchildren, Xuan, Jun, Wen, Yin and Kai, who are surprised that like them, we do still have homework to do. Their love and laughter are rewards enough.

To Janette Lau whose attention is intuitively uncanny; artist CK Yeo for the cover design and the signed original etchings; and S. Ang, Amy Au, T Bloch, Alan HJ Chan, HK Cheong, TP Chua, L. Cruz, Sir Richard and Lady Evans (Celebrating Wolfson@50th), R. Gamer, A. Hara, Chef Kathryn, BH Koh, KC Koh, KY Lam, C Lee, KW Lee, R Lee, CC Liew, CO Lim, P. Loon, Dean Mahubani, ADC Rajah, ADC Rosnan, MY Soon, Dean Tan, Ellice Tan, KY Teo, CH Tong, CL Yeo and CK Yun for their friendship and advice; and in prayerful remembrance of my late classmate, Emeritus Professor Mel Salazar, teacher and practitioner bar none — beloved by executives and captains of industry he inspired for four decades at the Asian Institute of Management. We miss his wise counsel and you will be remembered. And to all our fellow classmates at our 45th Re-Union this Autumn.

In happenstance, whilst writing this book, Gordon and I discovered that our colleague, Harvard Don Sugata Bose is now in academia with a public purpose — he was elected member for parliament for Calcutta's Jadavpur Parliamentary Constituency in India's Elections 2014. Recalling the saying of Hafiz of friends and pioneers, "Our hearts are very, very old friends."

ABOUT THE AUTHORS

Anthony SC Teo, is Adjunct Professor Lee Kuan Yew School of Public Policy, Chevalier of the Ordre des Palmes Académiques, Founder Management Board Member, Middle East Institute and Former Advisor, President's Office, Nanyang Technological University (NTU).

Anthony was NTU's Secretary to the University, an Ex-Officio member of the NTU Senate, and a member of the University Cabinet, until August 2010. He was in the troika of President, Provost and Secretary of the University to corporatize and reposition NTU. Anthony served as the Advisor on Special Projects to the President, NTU till June 2012.

In 2009, he became a Visiting Fellow at the Wolfson College, Cambridge University. He was awarded the Chevalier of the French Order of the Palmes Académiques in 2010. For six years, Anthony was a member of the Academic Committee for the Quacquarelli Symonds (QS) University Rankings and Asia Pacific Professional Leaders in Education Conference after co-hosting the first two QS conferences in NTU. He was Chairperson of the Univer-Cities Inaugural Conference 2013.

His Royal Highness Raja Dr Nazrin Shah ascended to the throne as the 35th Sultan of Perak Darul Ridzuan on 29 May 2014 and is now addressed as Paduka Seri Sultan Nazrin.

In the international arena, His Royal Highness represents the Government of Malaysia in his role as Financial Ambassador of the Malaysian International Islamic Financial Centre. He is also Malaysia's Special Envoy for Interfaith and Inter-Civilisational Dialogue.

His Royal Highness is Pro-Chancellor of the University of Malaya; President of the Perak Council on Islam and Malay Customs; Eminent Fellow of the Institute of Strategic and International Studies, Malaysia; Royal Fellow of the Malaysian Institute of Defence and Security; Member of the Chancellor's Court of Benefactors, University of Oxford; Honorary Fellow of Worcester College, University of Oxford; and Honorary

Member of Magdalene College, University of Cambridge. He is a Member of the Board of Trustees of the Oxford Centre for Islamic Studies, University of Oxford; Chairman of the Board of Governors of the Malay College, Kuala Kangsar; Royal Patron of the Kuala Lumpur Business Club; and Chairman of the Merdeka Award Board of Trustees.

His Royal Highness holds a BA in Philosophy, Politics and Economics from the University of Oxford; a Master in Public Administration from the Kennedy School of Government, Harvard University; and a PhD in Political Economy and Government from Harvard University. His research interests are in the areas of economic and political development in Southeast Asia, economic growth in developing countries and economic history. He has written articles and spoken on a wide range of issues including constitutional monarchy, nation building, Islam, Islamic finance, ethno-religious relations, education and socio-economic development.

Richard Bender is the former Dean of the College of Environmental Design and Chair and Professor of Architecture at UC Berkeley. He is a noted campus planner, with major involvement in university campus and related urban development in Asia, the Americas, and Europe.

Emily Marthinsen is Assistant Vice-Chancellor for Physical & Environmental Planning at the University of California, Berkeley. She graduated from the University of Chicago and earned a Master's in Architecture from UC Berkeley. Marthinsen is a licensed architect in California and has thirty years of relevant work experience at Berkeley and with design and planning firms in Berkeley, San Francisco, Washington, D.C. and Alexandria, Virginia.

John J. Parman writes on urban development for *Architect's Newspaper* and *Arcade*, among other West Coast publications. He co-founded and published the award-winning journal, *Design Book Review*, and is a founding editor of the San Francisco Bay Area-focused blog journal, *TraceSF.com*. He is a member of the Project Review Committee at SPUR in San Francisco.

About the Authors

Peter Carolin is Emeritus Professor of Architecture at the University of Cambridge where he was Head of the Department of Architecture 1989–2000. He worked on the British Library and other buildings, was Editor of *The Architects' Journal*, Head of the University of Cambridge Department of Architecture, and founding Editor of *arq* (*Architectural Research Quarterly*). He instigated and chaired the Cambridge Futures project 1997–2001 (the project director for which was Marcial Echenique). In retirement he has worked for CABE (Commission for Architecture and the Built Environment), advised several trusts and governing bodies, chaired the Cambridge design panel and co-directed a sub-regional visioning project. He is a Life Fellow of his college, Corpus Christi.

Sharifah Hapsah Syed Hasan Shahabudin is a medical graduate who has carved a name in the development of medical education, quality assurance and higher education in Malaysia. Her leadership as Vice-Chancellor of UKM (Universiti Kebangsaan Malaysia) since August 2006 has brought the university on par with leading research universities of the same age (40–50 years). Currently UKM is ranked 23rd in the world for universities below 50 years and 8th in Asia. She chairs the Vice-Chancellor's Committee and is credited with developing the Code of University Good Governance to facilitate the process of autonomy in public universities. As Chairman and CEO of the National Accreditation Board, she transformed the quality assurance system for higher education by formulating the Malaysian Qualifications Agency Act. Prior to that, she served as Director of the Quality Assurance Division, Ministry of Higher Education. Currently, she is President of the Association of Universities in Asia-Pacific and is a member of the Steering Committee of the Talloires Network of Engaged Universities. Sharifah promotes the idea that universities should be evaluated on their impact in raising the quality of lives of communities. The UKM transformation program aimed at raising the university's academic reputation internationally, also places a premium on knowledge and technology transfer for wealth creation and social wellbeing. Thus research, teaching and service excellence is supported by nurturing a culture of innovation and entrepreneurship as a means of developing entrepreneurial graduates, commercializing research output and activating social business as well as transferring knowledge for community development. She combines her social activist work as President of the National Council of Women's Organisation (NCWO) to strengthen community engagement projects at UKM.

About the Authors

Nancy Cushing is a senior lecturer in History at the University of Newcastle. Her interest in Newcastle's history began over two decades ago with the writing of her PhD thesis. She has since published on a variety of aspects of the city's past including its beaches, heritage and struggle against air pollution.

Katrina Quinn joined the University of Newcastle in April 2011. Prior to this, she worked as a Market Research Consultant across a variety of sectors.

Raised in Newcastle, Katrina has witnessed firsthand the city's remarkable transition from a coal and steel economy to a world-class innovation hub.

Caroline McMiller held senior appointments at Monash University, the University of Adelaide and the University of South Australia prior to joining the University of Newcastle in October 2011. She has served on national and international education and research review groups, and government groups focused on building innovation, climate change, and the resources industries.

Andrew Petter is President and Vice-Chancellor of Simon Fraser University (SFU) and Professor in the School of Public Policy. Prior to joining SFU in 2010, he was Professor in the Faculty of Law of the University of Victoria where he served as Dean from 2001 to 2008. He previously taught at Osgoode Hall Law School and practised law with the Saskatchewan Ministry of Justice. From 1991 to 2001, he served as a Member of the Legislative Assembly of the Province of British Columbia and held numerous cabinet portfolios, including Advanced Education and Attorney General.

Professor Petter holds an LL.B. from University of Victoria, where he was gold medallist, and an LL.M. with first class honours from Cambridge University. He is a member of the British Columbia and Saskatchewan law societies. He has written extensively in areas of Constitutional Law and Public Policy, including works on the *Canadian Charter of Rights and Freedoms* and Canadian federalism.

Since becoming President, Professor Petter has led the development of an exciting new Strategic Vision for SFU as "The Engaged University" defined by its "dynamic integration of innovative education, cutting edge research, and far-reaching community engagement".

About the Authors

Richard Littlemore is a writer/consultant who works extensively in the academic sector as well as a strategist, speechwriter, author and journalist with specialties in urban planning and sustainability, strategic planning and public consultation, climate change and other public policy issues. He has written academic plans and Visions for four universities in Canada and one in Kuwait. He also was the founding editor of *DeSmogBlog.com*, a climate-change website that *Time* magazine credits as one of the 25 most influential blogs in the world.

Joanne Curry is the Associate Vice-President, External Relations at Simon Fraser University (SFU) and is responsible for advancing community engagement at SFU's three campuses. Her 20-year history at SFU has included positions over a decade as founding Executive Director of the Surrey campus, Director of SFU's University/Industry Liaison Office, and Executive Director of a Canadian Network of Centres of Excellence in elearning. A recipient of the 2010 inaugural Surrey Board of Trade Women in Business Professional Category for her work in connecting the community with the university, Joanne has helped launch innovative initiatives such as SFU's India strategy and SFU Venture Connection to support student entrepreneurs.

Joanne has a Bachelor of Commerce (Hons.) with distinction from the University of Manitoba and a Masters of Business Administration degree from SFU. She is currently a candidate in a Doctorate of Business Administration programme in higher education at the University of Bath in the UK. Her thesis explores the factors in building successful university-city relationships for regional economic development.

Richard Milgrom is Associate Dean Research in the Faculty of Architecture at the University of Manitoba, and Associate Professor and Head of the Department of City Planning. His research interests focus on social and environmental justice in planning and design practices.

David Barnard became President and Vice-Chancellor of the University of Manitoba on 1 July 2008. He previously served as President and Vice-Chancellor at the University of Regina and prior to that, he was a Professor of Computing and Information Science and Associate to the Vice-Principals Research, Human Services and Resources at Queen's University. In 2005–08, he was COO of iQmetrix. He is currently the Chair of the Association of Universities and Colleges of Canada.

Dr Barnard holds a BSc, MSc and PhD degrees in computer science from the University of Toronto and a DipCS in theological studies from Regent College, University of British Columbia.

Michelle Richard, a Partner at RichardWiintrup & Associates, is an urban planner with experience in community and development planning, strategic policy and economic development. At the City of Winnipeg she coordinated the award-winning *"OurWinnipeg"* plan, and was Director of Campus Planning at the University of Manitoba responsible for over-seeing the Visionary (re)Generation international urban design competition.

About the Authors

Roseann O'Reilly Runte is President and Vice-Chancellor of Carleton University. She graduated with a BA summa cum laude in French from the State University of New York and obtained her MA and PhD from the University of Kansas. She has previously served as president of Université Sainte-Anne, principal of Glendon College, president of Victoria University and of Old Dominion University.

She has been awarded the Order of Canada and the French Order of Merit and is a Fellow of the Royal Society of Canada. She is a Chevalier of the Order des Palmes Académiques.

Dr Runte has served on numerous boards and commissions in both Canada and the United States. She was president of the Canadian Commission for UNESCO, president of the Humanities Federation of Canada, a member of the Royal College of Physicians and Surgeons, the Foundation for International Training, the Gardiner Museum of Ceramic Art, the Virginia Industrial National Development Authority, the Virginia Advanced Shipbuilding Integration Center, the advisory board of SunGard SGT, the non-profit LifeNet Health Board and the Ontario Quebec Private Sector Advisory Committee. She currently serves on the board of the National Bank of Canada, the executive of the Royal Society and Fulbright Canada-U.S., and on advisory committees of the Council of Ontario Universities and the Association of Universities and Colleges of Canada. She is a member of both the European and the World Academy of Arts and Sciences.

Dr Runte took up her duties at Carleton University on 1 July 2008 and was renewed for a second term which will conclude 30 June 2018.

Nam Pyo Suh was the President of the Korea Advanced Institute of Science and Technology (KAIST) from 2006 to 2013. He is also the Ralph E. & Eloise F. Cross Professor, Emeritus, MIT.

At KAIST, his goal was to make the Institute into a world leading research university. He hired about 350 professors, increasing the faculty size from about 400 to over 620, using mostly self-generated financial resources; constructed 14 new buildings; and increased the number of undergraduates to 4,000 from 3,000, while maintaining the graduate students at 6,500. He and his colleagues invented the On-Line Electric Vehicle (OLEV), which was selected as the 50 Best Inventions of 2010 by *TIME*, and as one of the 2013 Emerging Technologies by the World Economic Forum (WEF) in Davos. The ranking of KAIST was elevated to 60th overall and 24th in engineering from about 200th overall in 2006.

From 1970, he was the Cross Professor and the Head of the Department of Mechanical Engineering (1991 to 2001) at Massachusetts Institute of Technology (MIT). Under his leadership, the Department redefined the discipline of mechanical engineering from a physics-based discipline into one based on physics, information, biology, and design science. Many new endowed research and teaching laboratories were established to achieve this goal.

From 1984 to 1988, Professor Suh took a leave of absence from MIT to be at the US National Science Foundation (NSF), where he was the Presidential appointee in charge of engineering. He created the Engineering Research Centers and a new direction for the NSF Engineering.

He has received many awards and honours. He received nine honorary doctoral degrees, the 2009 ASME Medal, the 2006 Nicolau Award of CIRP, and the NSF Distinguished Service Medal in 1987 as well as many other awards and honors from US and international institutions. His scholarly contributions include the Axiomatic Design Theory, the Delamination Theory of Wear, complexity theory, friction and wear theories, microcellular plastics, On-Line Electric Vehicle, and Mobile Harbor. He has authored more than 300 papers and seven books. He holds about 100 patents.

About the Authors

Gordon Johnson has lived and worked in Cambridge since he arrived as a student in 1961. He is an historian. He was President of Wolfson College, Cambridge from 1993–2010 and has also served as Deputy Vice-Chancellor, Chairman of Cambridge University Press, Director of the Centre of South Asian Studies, and the founding Provost of the Gates Cambridge Trust. He was editor of *Modern Asian Studies* 1971–2008 and is the General Editor of the *New Cambridge History of India*.

Lilia Labidi, a Tunisian psychoanalyst-anthropologist, has been professor at the University of Tunis, co-founder of the Association of Tunisian Women for Research and Development and the Tunisian Association for Health Psychology. She is author of many publications on the Arab world, treating subjects such as gender issues, the feminist movement, the construction of identity, women and science, the aftermath of the Arab spring, etc., and has organized numerous international conferences and documentary exhibitions on women's movements and social issues. From January to December 2011, Labidi was Minister for Women's Affairs in the provisional Tunisian government, following the fall of the Ben Ali regime.

She has held fellowships at the Institute for Advanced Study(Princeton) and the Woodrow Wilson International Center for Scholars(Washington, DC) and has been visiting professor at the American University in Cairo(Egypt) and Yale University(US). She is currently Visiting Research Professor at the Middle East Institute, National University of Singapore, working on Arab women scientists and on the current situation in the Arab world

About the Authors

Shane Huntington is currently the Senior Policy and Strategy Adviser in the Faculty of Medicine, Dentistry and Health Sciences University of Melbourne. He also holds an adjunct senior research position within the School of Physics at the University of Melbourne. He is the Founder and Director of The Innovation Group Pty Ltd.

Stephen K. Smith is the Dean, Faculty of Medicine Dentistry and Health Sciences at the University of Melbourne. Formerly Vice-President (Research) at the Nanyang Technological University. A gynaecologist, he has published over 230 papers on reproductive medicine and cancer.

Harold Guida, is a Partner Guida Moseley Brown Architects. He has over forty years of international experience on a wide range of architectural, interior design and urban design projects undertaken in the United States, Australia, South-East Asia, and China. Originally from the United States, Mr Guida relocated to Canberra, Australia, in 1981 as Partner-in-Charge of Design Co-ordination for Australia's new Parliament House. He is currently senior design partner of Guida Moseley Brown Architects.

Mr Andrew Donnelly, is an Architect Guida Moseley Brown Architects. He is an architect with Guida Moseley Brown Architects in Canberra, Australia. He has extensive experience across a range of projects in both Australia and South-East Asia. His project portfolio includes master plans for two Universities, as well as architectural design work for a wide variety of academic, commercial and residential developments.

WELCOME ADDRESS

Your Royal Highness, Raja Dr Nazrin Shah, The Regent of the State of Perak;

Mr Anthony Teo, Chairperson of the inaugural conference on Univer-Cities;

Your Excellencies;

Honourable Delegates;

Ladies and Gentlemen,

Welcome to our beautiful garden campus at NTU, Nanyang Technological University!

Universities are an important cornerstone of modern societies. By 2050, it is estimated that three-quarters of the world's population will live in urban areas. Universities in the 21st Century will, therefore, play a catalytic role in pushing growth frontiers for major cities.

Inspired by the first Univer-City Symposium held in Lund, Sweden in June 2007 where the term *"Univer-Cities"* was first coined, we gather here today to present, discuss and debate on redefining the multi-faceted symbiotic relationship between universities and host cities in Asia.

As a fast-growing university with an international outlook, NTU is privileged to host today's significant conference. This comes just after we hosted two globally prestigious events early last month — the World Cultural Council's 30th Award Ceremony and the World Academic Summit, a strong indication that NTU is rapidly developing as the respected international venue where knowledge is debated and new ideas are born.

Today's conference that facilitates a continuing conversation on "Univer-Cities" is significant to NTU. Truly, Singapore is becoming a

'Univer-City' in which NTU, with its beautiful, tropical garden campus, is a university in a garden within the garden city state of Singapore.

As you make your way into our garden campus, you may have noticed a number of construction activities. Indeed, you are witnessing NTU's transformation under our *Campus Master Plan*, which aims to establish the right kind of physical, natural and social infrastructure to enable NTU to provide world-class education and research as we aspire to become a great global university.

In addition, being sited next to CleanTech Park, Singapore's first eco-business park which is currently under development by the JTC Corporation, allows for enhanced integration between NTU academia, our various world-class research institutes such as the Nanyang Environment & Water Research Institute and the Energy Research Institute @ NTU, as well as the business industry. This provides synergies for a full value chain, from R&D to downstream manufacturing. When fully implemented, our *Campus Master Plan* will transform the NTU campus into a "Univer-City" with varied spaces for education, research, recreation, and social and leisure activities.

NTU extends our "green" credentials into its major research programmes, which are dedicated to the idea of sustainability in all aspects. This includes some of the leading research groups in energy, especially renewables, and in water research working, not only in basic research but in applications, especially through our ongoing and close links to the industry.

For instance, the Nanyang Environment & Water Research Institute which was launched in 2008, represents NTU's efforts over the last two decades of being a committed and active participant in Singapore's Environmental and Water Technology R&D landscape. The institute continues to make a mark that can ultimately help improve lives with its interdisciplinary expertise in environmental science and engineering research in Singapore and around the region.

Our Energy Research Institute @ NTU, on the other hand, is well on its way to become a globally renowned research institute for innovative energy solutions. The institute strives to research and develop novel solutions to focus on the areas of sustainable energy, energy efficiency or infrastructure and socio-economic aspects of energy research, aimed at addressing the pressing energy needs of humankind. Already, the institute is collaborating with a variety of world-class blue chip leaders such as Bosch GmbH, ClassNK, DNV, Horizon Fuel Cell Technologies, IBM, Rolls-Royce and Sembcorp Marine.

All this research represents our efforts in putting NTU's global stamp on *Five Peaks of Excellence* by 2015 which include sustainability, future healthcare, new media, innovation and the best of the East and West. As a research-intensive university that ranks among the world's top 50 universities and is still going up, NTU remains committed to promoting interdisciplinary research excellence.

On behalf of the Advisory Council for this conference, I take this opportunity to thank our co-sponsor, the Lee Foundation, for making this conference possible. We are also privileged to have His Royal Highness, Raja Dr Nazrin Shah here with us today to deliver his Royal Address. I also understand that the co-authors and editor of *Univer-Cities: Strategic Implications for Asia — Readings from Cambridge and Berkeley to Singapore*, a book of the same theme of this conference are also here today to share their insights.

It is fitting for a major conference such as this to expound further on how universities can influence informed decision-making and contribute to fresh and valuable ideas that can benefit modern Asia. On this note, I wish all of you a productive and meaningful exchange today.

Thank you.

Professor Bertil Andersson
President Nanyang Technological University (NTU)
Singapore and Trustee, Nobel Foundation

About the Author

Professor Bertil Andersson is President, Nanyang Technological University, Singapore and Trustee, Nobel Foundation. He is a plant biochemist of international reputation and is the author of over 300 papers in photosynthesis research, biological membranes, protein and membrane purification and light stress in plants.

He was educated at Umeå and Lund Universities in Sweden. He started his research career at Umeå after which he became a Professor of Biochemistry. From 1996 to 2003, he became Dean of the Faculty of Chemical Sciences at the University of Stockholm. In 1999 he was the Rector (President) of Linköping University, Sweden until the end of 2003. From 2004 to 2007, he joined the European Science Foundation in Strasbourg as its Chief Executive. Prof Andersson was appointed NTU's first Provost in April 2007 and was installed as NTU's third President on 1 July 2011.

From 1989 to 1997, he was member of the Nobel Committee for Chemistry (Chair 1997), later becoming a member of the Nobel Foundation (2000–2006) and he is currently a member of the Board of Trustees of the Nobel Foundation.

He continues to hold academic appointments as Professor of Biochemistry at Linköping University and Adjunct Professor at Umeå University. He is also a visiting Professor and a Fellow of Imperial College London.

Bertil Andersson has been a member of the boards of several Swedish and international foundations and learned societies, including a member of the Royal Swedish Academy of Sciences, the Australian Academy of Sciences and Academia Europaea and holds honorary doctorates from several universities. He is also a member of the Science and Engineering Research Council (SERC) Board, A*STAR Singapore.

He is also a research adviser to the Swedish government and was, between 2004 and 2007, the Vice President of the European Research Advisory Board (EURAB) of the European Commission. He has also been an adviser to business activities in the area of biotechnology and pharma.

CHAPTER ONE

UNIVER-CITIES: STRATEGIC VIEW OF THE FUTURE — FROM BERKELEY & CAMBRIDGE TO SINGAPORE & RISING ASIA

ANTHONY SC TEO

> "... to solve important problems of humanity in the 21st century"
>
> Nam Pyo Suh, former President of KAIST 2006–13
> (No. 2 QS Asia University Rankings, 2014)
> and Ralph E. & Eloise F. Cross Professor, Emeritus, MIT

The Inaugural Univer-Cities Conference 2013 began with the Royal Address by His Royal Highness Raja Dr Nazrin Shah, PhD (Harvard). His Majesty Sultan Nazrin Shah ascended to the Throne as the 35th Sultan of Perak Darul Ridzuan on 29 May 2014 and is now addressed as Paduka Seri Sultan Nazrin. His Royal Address at the Conference was an engaging declamation that met with universal acclaim for engendering the conversation with such clarity that it ignited the initial discussions amongst academic leaders. The conference papers ranged from Berkeley, California, Canada's Carleton, Cambridge, Universiti Kebangsaan Malaysia, Newcastle in Australia, University of Hong Kong, Simon Fraser University in Vancouver to Manitoba of the 1870s at the time of the Morrill Act in America that started off Massachusetts Institute of Technology, Johns Hopkins University, and others. And, contextually from the historic Silk Road emanating from the Mahgreb, Middle East and West Asia, we had the benefit of thought leaders like Professor Dr Lilia Labidi and Dr Ali Allawi, academician-former ministers from Tunisia and Iraq respectively.

The multi-disciplinary tone was set by the vice-chancellors and academic leaders who brought to the conversation the needed richness of inter-continental and inter-institutional (Royal Society, 2011) expertise from architecture, anthropology, biochemistry, campus and city planning, engineering, genetics, gynaecology, information technology (IT), men of silk (legal counsel and attorney generalship, linguistics, medicine, politics) men of cloth (pastors, former ministers of advanced education, finance, defence and women's affairs, rulership) and others.

Frame of reference: The chapters in this book share multi-disciplinary and trans-disciplinary approaches. This introductory chapter brings management and strategic constructs, in order to sketch a frame of reference to further the conversation. Selections from the rich texts in this volume are referred to in this chapter as we navigate through this emerging body of work.

In an overall perspective, *structure follows strategy* led by the historian cum business researcher Alfred Chandler in the 1960s (Chandler, 1962). Others like Paul Lawrence and my beloved teacher Jay Lorsch refined it into the organizational design practice, but we do not need to go into those details at this stage.

Strategically: Beyond the generally accepted issues of competitive strategy of well-known Michael Porter and Clayton Christensen in the seeking, creating and knowing, institutions of higher learning must now contend with the new normal: to seek the strategic view or architecture of the future in order to prevail and preempt globally. Dynamically, the focus is on the four fulcrums of competition: within and between "coalitions" of institutions; "to shape the structure" of future univer-cities; for "core competence leadership" not product; and timed to "global preemption" not timed to market (Hamel & Prahalad, 1994). The case of Apple's radical iPhone is an industry experience; similarly, the Korea Advanced Institute of Science and Technology's (KAIST) disruptive innovation approach to proto-typing and implementing the On-Line Electric Vehicle (OLEV) (Time's 50 Best Innovations of 2010).

The trinity of Cambridge-Cambridge UK, Harvard-Cambridge MA, and Oxford-Oxford UK are leading examples in the last century of global preeminence; and the Berkeley-Berkeley CA, MIT-Cambridge MA, Princeton-Princeton NJ, and others, in the last half century are fast contending as the subtle changing distribution of Nobel Prizes might indicate.

Structurally: In the evolving theorems of structure, univer-cities individually and inter-univer-cities hubs evolving over 150 years as in Berkeley and Cambridge's 800 years, can be viewed in the multi-dimensional looking glass of Iansiti's structural systems of individual "keystone" and eco-system networks of firms (or our unit of discussion — univer-cities). In the author's view, the IT industries have the more complex keystone firms and eco-system of firms, in interdependent eco-systems (Iansiti & Levien, 2004). Welcome to univer-cities, a structure that promises to challenge the notion of complexity.

Structurally & strategically: We will approach by way of the "Regionality Continuum of Univer-Cities" and "Beyond Regionality & Emerging Strategic Architecture".

Caroline McMillen, Gordon Johnson and Sharifah Hapsah Syed Hasan Shahabudin at a panel discussion.

Regionality continuum of univer-cities: The first volume of *Univer-Cities* dealt with Cambridge, Berkeley and Singapore. This conversation explores the regionality continuum of "*Urbi et Orbi*" (Latin for city and world) — from the city to the global world with intermediate regions, countries, federations like the European Union (EU) and contending the case of the global University of Cambridge.

Historian Dr Gordon Johnson who was the former Deputy Vice-Chancellor of Cambridge undertook a historical analysis with emphasis on the 15th and 16th centuries with a view of the future of knowledge (Gibbons et al., 1994), marked by the founding of Cambridge University Press, circa 1584, some 375 years after the University's founding in 1209.

What Might Comprise this Regionality Continuum?

Towards the city end of the continuum is the case of the University of Manitoba at Winnipeg in Saskatchewan as described in Chapter 8 of this book. Written by VC David Barnard, his Associate Dean Richard Milgrom and Campus Planning Director Michelle Richard, it describes a change in the narrative. It looks at future opportunities to engage the City and university-industry partnership in the current development of its Fort Garry expansion which incorporates about 40 hectares of the Southwood Golf Club. It envisages enhancing walkability and co-creating "complete communities". Additionally, it addresses pedagogical issues and the wider societal impact of partnerships with indigenous peoples. Its history dates back to 1877 at about the time of the Morrill Act universities of the ilk of Berkeley, Johns Hopkins, MIT, and others.

Regionality from the city and its surrounding economy and its restructuring and change is the case of the University of Newcastle (UON) in Australia — from being a "gaol" (of a convict-colony in the words of VC Caroline McMillen in Chapter 6) to a coal-exporting harbour, then steel-works, to the emerging new economy.

Recognizing the emergence of the international steel industry restructuring as illustrated by global Korean POSCO (initially, Pohang Iron & Steel Company) coupled with its rising Pohang University of Science and Technology, Newcastle is in transition. The prime objective is to make "UON the talent magnet through education, research and innovation and as a partner of choice in driving world-class innovation. Today it ranks in the Top 50 universities under 50 in the world and as the best of Australia's universities under 50 years old."

Two projects are emblematic of UON. One is industry engagement — a world-first integration of solar thermal technology with coal-fired power generation which now produces 60 per cent of the state's energy supply. The other is innovation — the Jameson Cell for separating fine particles on the basis of density like cleansing coal created by a UON researcher, Laureate Professor Graham Jameson.

These projects reiterate UON's sense of place as attributed to Lord David Sainsbury: "The paradox is that while innovation is a global phenomenon, the role of regions as the critical nexus for innovation-based economic growth has increased."

In the field of medicine UON has been a *"disruptive innovator"* in creating the community-based practitioner by involving community from the outset and by new pedagogy in small group problem-based learning. This has a new societal impact across the country as this practitioner approach has "attracted indigenous students and UON now graduates more indigenous doctors than any other university, many of whom return home to work in their communities".

UON punches above its weight, an established role since the beginning of the Colombo Plan scholarships tenable in the British Commonwealth, training engineers and doctors, amongst other disciplines. Further afield, Newcastle, has a successful campus in Singapore and partnerships in Asia "realigning with a future captured by the reimagining of the New Silk Road".

Regionality from city to country is spearheaded by an inspiring academic and medical leader VC Tan Sri Dato' Seri Professor Dr Sharifah Hapsah at UKM, the fastest rising research-intensive university in Malaysia, as described in Chapter 5. Although based in Bangi, it is now connected within a half hour to the Federal Capital of Kuala Lumpur. It leads in medicine and medical specialties (with the only nuclear isotope facility) and research that has a national impact. Its geographic engagement complements a national innovation eco-system. This is strategically accomplished through its World Heritage GeoPark and local entrepreneurship and social enterprise extending from northwest Malaysia in the Langkawi Islands under the Patronage of His Majesty The Agong or King Abdul Halim Mu'adzam Shah of Malaysia, to the Medical and Public Health Research Centre in Perak under the Patronage of the Regent of the State of Perak, HRH Raja Dr Nazrin Shah, PhD (Harvard), the Eco-Sustainability Project at the largest inland lake of Tasik Chini; and the east coast Marine Research Centre at Mersing, Johor.

UKM has already attained the leading global rank in Malaysia. In its youthful 50 years, it is emerging as a keystone amongst the network of 20 state universities (Iansiti & Levien, 2004) in major and second cities (Florida, 2011). The impact is direct, with UKM coalitions internally in Malaysia and externally. The disruptive innovation was in implementing problem-based pedagogy which was radical in conservative medical education. Professor Dr Sharifah Hapsah was then head of medical education. The innovation in medical education influenced many, and some UKM academic leaders took that approach when helming a number of the young universities. More formally, Sharifah co-created the national benchmarking for institutions of higher learning when she headed the quality and standards agency of the country. The top five of the 20 state universities are being corporatized and the field is more open for the enterprising to develop and reinforce their own platform and hub network. Other examples like the venerable UM (University of Malaya), USM (University of Science Malaysia) in Penang and UTM (University of Technology, Malaysia) in Johor with the emergence of a new 21st century town, Iskandar, have hubs for industry, education, medical services, residences and sea access.

Regionality from city to city is seen in the case of Burnaby to the major metropolitan capital city of greater Vancouver as expounded by Simon Fraser University's VC Andrew Petter and his two colleagues in Chapter 7. SFU indeed adopted the nomen and idea of univer-city in the 1990s to describe how it moved down from the mountain top of Burnaby to the city of Burnaby through a strategic property swap with the city government. To become the "leading engaged university defined by its dynamic integration of innovative education, cutting-edge research, and far-reaching community engagement" in Canada, SFU secured a foothold in the centre of Vancouver, moving onto suburban Surrey and then back to the University of SFU-Burnaby in a foothill-mountain forestry swap.

Petter describes an "engaged univer-city" that made strategic inroads to engage the multiple cities (more than a "collect the earth" mode). The university expanded its constituency, specialties, and studentship to enrich the community whilst it rehabilitated and transformed abandoned properties of the city of Vancouver and Surrey — a robust form of low-cost urban renewal and high impact community equity. Uniquely it shapes a style of mixed development which is denser, highly liveable with walkable flow of community life towards deeper on-going engagement of university and city that he characterizes as "Vancouverism". The SFU Community Trust and the development of the Univer-City at Burnaby is more complex, and was sequenced after a strategically expanding presence and entry to Vancouver (now about ten acres) and Surrey. Univer-City Burnaby is more complex owing to the tighter municipal requirements and SFU's ambition to be a model of sustainability development befitting a research driven niche univer-city. Pleasingly, it yielded about C$30 million towards its endowment. This is beginning to be a proven avenue of strategy as UBC (University of British Columbia), a municipality in its own right. Pursuing a mode of isolating 99-year leases through its Trust during the leadership of Trustee Chairman and voluntary Chair of the Premier's Asia Pacific Trade Council from 2005–2008 Arthur Hara and Chancellor Robert Lee, reportedly accumulated significant additions to its endowment. Missions to study these experiences include the planners who are undertaking the major North West Cambridge development at the University of Cambridge.

This emerging eco-system with two major players, UBC and SFU, and a network of universities and community colleges in the greater Vancouver area deserves more study. Moreover, this diverse community with a large Asian composition reinforces links to Pacific-Asia — it is no coincidence that the federally chartered Asia Pacific Centre think-thank is based in Vancouver. To test the efficacy that univer-cities redefine the new Silk Road, the nature of this Pacific-Asia interdependency is a promising vein to tap.

Regionality beyond the univer-city, in a strict sense of the Univer-City of Cambridge is expounded by Emeritus Professor Peter Carolin in Chapter 4. The Univer-City of Berkeley is the focus of Chapter 3 by the doyen Richard Bender, Professor Emeritus of Architecture and Dean of the College of Environmental Design at the University of California, Berkeley; Emily Marthinsen, Assistant Vice-Chancellor for Physical & Environmental Planning at UC Berkeley; and John Parman, Editorial Adviser and contributor to *Architect's Newspaper* and a member of the Project Review Committee at SPUR in San Francisco. *Beyond the univer-city* implies Berkeley and Cambridge asserting themselves over the past 150 to 800 years respectively as regional hubs of univer-cities.

Panelists John Parman, Emily Marthinsen, Richard Bender and Peter Carolin being introduced by moderator, Anthony SC Teo.

I will address the historical analysis of the University of Cambridge by Dr Gordon Johnson separately as it extends the hub to global intent. So I posed to the Berkeley Trio: what is the comparative between Berkeley and Cambridge in the Conference deliberations? They explained:

> We shared our panel at the Univer-Cities Inaugural Conference 2013 with Cambridge Professor Peter Carolin, one of the prime movers of Cambridge Futures. This remarkable program, we recognized, applied a methodology similar to ours for the Berkeley campus to the entire city and its environs. Like ours, it explained the city to itself, clarifying how and why it works (or doesn't) as a physical place and social/economic space. And, also like ours, it then offered up a range of scenarios for the future. Unlike ours, it did polling, homing in on the future that was of greatest interest and attractiveness to citizens. We point to this as a logical development wherever campuses and communities intertwine. Given that they are relating to the same basic terrain and addressing the same people and resources, in a general sense, their futures are closely connected. They will "hang together or hang separately", as Ben Franklin said. It's an implication that's applicable

to Asian universities, including NTU (Nanyang Technological University in Singapore) and others, whether they exist as gardens at the city edge or as urban enclaves packed in among other uses or dispersed in their districts.

Univer-cities enrich their communities in countless ways. They prime the economic pump and provide the knowledge and talent to keep it growing. They provide employment and support housing and services. They often serve as urban parks. Their outreach programs serve the young and the old. In turn, they benefit from rising prosperity, able to attract faculty and students based on the city's drawing power as a great place. They have a common destiny, which argues for them to admit this and build on it. Berkeley, campus and community, is still a work in progress, but the signs are positive and encouraging. We look at Cambridge and feel we have a way to go, but as a younger university, admired in Asia, we may be better positioned to have influence. Certainly, Asian universities can learn from all of our mistakes! But there are positives to draw on, much as Cambridge Futures is a very successful initiative for us to consider in Berkeley.

Both Carolin and the Berkeley Trio take a long view: Cambridge to 2030 while the Berkeley Trio recommends a study group whose "focus would include the campus itself as a district of the city. That way, the 2030, 2040, and 2050 LRD (Long-Range Development) Plans will be not just the plans of the university, but increasingly of the city it shares."

Video presentation by Roseann O'Reilly Runte from Carleton University.

Beyond Regionality & Emerging Strategic Architecture

Regionality of univer-cities is one of at least five axes. The other four are Steve Jobs' technology to market, Clayton Christensen's disruptive innovation, Peter Drucker's talent, and Jay Lorsch's governance. Carleton's VC Dr Roseann O'Reilly Runte's chapter in this volume places emphasis on the univer-city, technology and talent. Emeritus KAIST President Professor Dr Nam Pyo Suh pointedly focuses on disruptive innovation told through the case dimension of their OLEV project. Gordon Johnson weaves all these factors into the mosaic of the history and heritage of Cambridge in a masterly historic analysis, "Cambridge: From Medieval Market Town to Univer-City" in Chapter 11. With the backdrop of the emerging free trade for global talent (Wildavsky, 2010), this could accelerate univer-cities to redefine the new Silk Road. Developed from his paper at the Kaufmann symposium on trends in higher education, he provides evidence that the great brain race is on and how global universities are reshaping the world.

Beyond regionality is Runte's conceptual framework of Carleton in Chapter 9 that expounds the physical and the quantum of "The Architecture of Knowledge and the Knowledge of Architecture" in the setting of a tale of the national capital of Canada Ottawa and Carleton, the two being in close proximity linked by road, a 15-minute skate away on a frozen World Heritage Rideau Canal in winter. Such proximity is one reason why both have not spent much on distance learning whereas elsewhere MOOC (massive open online courses) are more common. Canadians born with ice-skates can further cut perceived inter-campus distance and travel time connecting bi-cultural English-speaking Carleton University and the French-speaking Ottawa University.

Technology, the changing nature of work and the nurturing of entrepreneurship have impacted learning, innovation and the eco-system of interdependencies between the two universities. To optimize faculty teaching and research collaboration, students do not pay extra fees for courses in cross enrolment between the two universities and "together they bring to the City of Ottawa and the Province of Ontario, the second highest number and amount of research grants and awards in Ontario". Runte speaks of the rising high-tech crescent from Waterloo to Toronto, and Ottawa-Carleton. In fact, this is extendable to Ottawa-Carleton-Kanata and Montreal. This crescent is well known for the innovation that created NASA Space Shuttle's versatile "CanadArm", Sir Terry Matthews' Mitel and Newbridge Networks in Kanata and Bombardier, the answer to Boeing.

Just as Paris was the "City of Light" at the turn of the 20th century, Runte imagines a "Univer-City of Bright and Might" into the 21st century anchored in the National Capital where the architecture of knowledge and discovery brings to bear its intellectual and policy impact on the city, nation and global policies. We wonder why Canada escaped the toxic meltdown of the sub-prime crisis of 2008–09; has sound federal finance and central banking (former head of Canada's Central Bank, Bank of Canada Governor Mark Carney now heads the Bank of England), affordable healthcare, and a tradition of reconciliation via its long history in UN Peacekeeping; is a free trader as profiled by NAFTA (North American Free Trade Agreement) of Canada–USA–Mexico; and why its evolving social compact of a more just and more equal society since the Trudeau years, is an ongoing work in progress.

Moreover, this concept of the architecture of knowledge brings another dimension that research-intensive universities must constantly address besides the emerging strategic architecture of key nodes of univer-cities.

In a Socratic way, Runte asks: what shape will knowledge take? What will be the form of the ideal campus? How do we create the conditions necessary to promote the connections between and among institutions, locally, regionally and globally? Anecdotally, on an aspect of the architecture of knowledge impacting research, 1992 Nobel Prize in Physiology biochemist Edmond Fischer said that had he not chosen to study potato phosphorylase as any other specimen which possesses an added AMP factor, it would have taken him another half a dozen years to discover the breakthrough as the history of AMP discovery would have shown — of structure and serendipity (Fischer, 1992)!

Beyond regionality & the global University of Cambridge: One Cambridge with two interpretations — Gordon Johnson restates univer-cities and the lessons from history: "The present conference and emerging research project seek to explore, from a wide perspective, ways in which the contemporary university and city might be so nurtured and more ambitiously structured and led that it ensures it makes the best possible contributions to human progress, and is properly recognized for the service it renders to society and the city where more than half of humanity resides; and is a major engine for growth."

Then at Cambridge, circa 16th century: According to Gordon Johnson: "Cambridge contributed in major ways to the general good of society. The fact of having so many benefactions, the placing of so many Cambridge-educated men in positions of influence in church and state, its peopling of the professions, its promotion of scholarship and learning, testify to the importance of the University in English life."

Now, from Yale circa 21st century: Victoria Blodgett, Director of Graduate Career Services at Yale University states: "Academic institutions hold a responsibility to advance knowledge. ... People who take their Ph.D.s in humanities (Kagan, 2009) into other realms are not necessarily being hired for their content expertise, but for their process skills: the ability to do excellent research, to write, to make cogent arguments." These skills, it turns out, are in high demand (Segran, 2014).

Historic and New Silk Roads: Whereas the iconic medium of the old Silk Road was silk and other material and cultural benefits, Labidi and Teo in Chapter 12 explain how the New Silk Road is more complex though it underpins the commonality of the Boorstin proposition of discovering, creating and seeking new knowledge and understanding of our world (Boorstin, 1983, 1992 & 1998). The new Silk Road is engendered by rapid technological change, obsolescence, new innovation and discovery of knowledge beyond the cross and multi-disciplinary to the interstices of disciplines or trans-disciplinary modes. In their futuristic research on the "Race Against the Machine: How the Digital Revolution is Accelerating Innovation, Driving Productivity, and Irreversibly Transforming Employment and the Economy", the two MIT principal investigators show the growing diversion between these factors, creating more inequality and creative destruction of jobs by machines (Brynjolfsson & McAfee, 2011). Foxconn is reportedly expected in the next couple of years to install some three million robots to replace numerous workers. These threats also highlight some tough opportunities succinctly epitomized by an epigram from the unlikeliest, Havelock Ellis in 1922: "The greatest task before civilization is to make machines what they ought to be, the slaves, instead of the masters of men" (Brynjolfsson & McAfee, 2011, p. 53).

The Labidi-Teo essay on the anecdotal sojourn of Tunisian scientists in Singapore in the context of the multiple old Silk Roads, over land and seas, and the new Silk Road redefined by univer-cities is an added context to our conversation. Singapore is an island oasis, a multi-cultural first-world garden city, with a rich array of research and funding and two top ten rising Asian universities — might it be on the trajectory of a univer-city on the New Silk Road? Harold Guida and Andrea Donnelly discussed this in the 2013 volume on univer-cities but there is some skepticism as some fabled centres are lost in the sands of time like the city of Islamic scholarship and trade centred at Timbuktu; and about half a millennium ago, the Nalanda University of India that disappeared is now a world heritage project devoted to its resurrection.

Others have stood the test of time and tumultuous change for nearly 800 years like the University of Cambridge since 1209 (Pagnamenta, 2008). It exhibits the characteristics of an evolving twin *keystone platform and eco-system node* (Iansiti & Levien, 2004) of univer-cities with its dominance over the market town, and impact on the UK body politic. At the same time its reach extends to the wider EU and globally to other emerging keystone univer-cities and more strategically keystone eco-systems of univer-cities.

Over time it has the power of its alumni (as all universities in modern times do) to preserve its academic freedom and expansion as well as the disruptive innovation that is portrayed in the Cambridge phenomenon of the Silicon Fen.

Worldliness and Alumni: Besides convincing a skeptical King Henry VIII to preserve and enhance by creating a new and now most highly regarded Trinity College … "the king was persuaded not to send to the University an external committee of enquiry to assess the (financial) situation but to appoint a local body to do so. This committee consisted of three Heads of colleges who used their influence through men who had been tutors to the royal household, to gain the support of Queen Katherine Parr to preserve their endowments … The king accepted the report."

Disruptive Innovation and 50 Years of the Silicon Fen: "How universities interacted with the broader economy, what contribution their research made to immediate economic growth and how connected they were with business and industry, both locally and nationally. ... This 'phenomenon' is directly related to Cambridge being a 'University-City'.... By 2012, the number of companies had risen to about 1,400, employing some 48,000 people, accounting for almost a quarter of all jobs in the region."

Governance: "A further great shift in the past half-century has been the pressure to centralize and to manage resources in transparent and accountable ways. Here, the principal funders of the University — the state, either directly by way of annual grants or indirectly via Research Councils, philanthropic charities and wealthy individuals — have all been keen to see that the resources they provided have been well-managed and applied strictly to the purposes for which they were allocated."

Beyond the Silicon Fen and towards global engagement come the emerging challenges of identifying and nurturing the co-creation of keystone univer-cities and interdependent keystone eco-systems of univer-cities. This can be done by formulating and implementing, individually or collectively, the *strategic architecture of the future* to establish global knowledge (Hamel & Prahalad, 1994) and keystone eco-system nodes.

Gary Hamel and CK Prahalad focus beyond the usual competitive strategy, but include corporations. This strategy can be extended to the domain of univer-cities. For the University of Cambridge with its leading edge in low carbon process chemistry and research, its global strategic architecture chose the distant city state of Singapore (with the National University of Singapore [NUS] and Nanyang Technological University [NTU], both in the top 50 global universities). It did not choose India or China but the petrochemical processing centre of Singapore over rival centres like Rotterdam, Aruba and Houston. In competitive RFP (request for proposal), the C4T (Carbon Reduction in Chemical Technology), a joint Cambridge, NTU and NUS research project, was funded by the NRF (National Research Foundation) of Singapore.

Mobility and ubiquitous technology have sped up globalization in the international trade and "the brain race" for talent and minds and more particularly, "...the western research university being replicated around the world by societies that have realised that the road to economic success runs through college campuses" (Wildavsky, 2010). The question is which ones have the competitive edge as univer-cities with clear strategic intent, the timeless values and the will to act and sustain. Size may not be a defining factor. On an anecdotal level, in times of generally tighter research funding worldwide, researchers and scientists from well-known home bases have begun to "disappear" to such centres of higher research commitments (Stein, 2014). And those who prefer to benchmark with others have the benefit of post discovery and the matrix of known KPIs (key performance indicators).

Speed: Speed is a defining factor in advancing knowledge in the emerging univer-cities. To attain strategic preemption, speed and the eco-system of competence are needed to turn knowledge and strategic visions into concrete outcomes. The case of the Korea Advanced Institute of Science and Technology (KAIST) reflects this.

From the timeless Alexandria library, new knowledge, the ubiquitous internet and breakthrough technologies, we meet the frontiers that challenge humanity (McNeely & Wolverton, 2008). This volume includes the case of the inspired research and prototype created at KAIST and the eco-system of the Daejon "silicon valley" situated an hour south of Seoul, the capital of South Korea.

As a young top-notch fast rising engineering and technology university in Daejon, Korea, home of the reborn Samsung now rivaling Apple, Intel, Hitachi amongst others, KAIST responded to the call of the President of Korea to identify innovations that would become the next engines of growth in the 21st century. Inspired research as one of the tenets of the new gold standards for higher education, with the exemplar of Nobelist Pasteur's research and discoveries affecting human living ever since (Crow, 2007), Dr Nam Pyo Suh, President of KAIST, was in the thick of the cauldron of the university, the city of Daejon and the *single mindedness of Korea*. KAIST focused on the competence and commitment of some 3,000 scientists, thinkers and engineers and key industrial partners like Doosan and Hyundai across the nation. At KAIST, 100 faculty members and researchers turning innovation into prototypes through technology within a year, eight months to be sure, were tasked with and came up with the design and development of On-Line Electric Vehicles (OLEV). According to Dr Suh: "The first OLEV system was installed in Seoul Grand Park. The system, consisting of seven trolley-trams, operates daily and generates a profit. Since then, additional OLEV systems (buses and the underground power supply systems) have been installed in Gumi, an industrial city in Korea, on the KAIST campus, and at the 2012 Yeosu World Expo. Now, the basic core technology of SMFIR (Shaped Magnetic Field in Resonance) is being applied to develop other systems: an ultra-high speed train in Korea, wireless appliances, and others. The idea of shaping magnetic fields for transmission of large amounts of electric power using resonance to capture the transmitted power may find many new applications in the future."

Why the missionary zeal? Unlike mountaineer George Mallory who said because it's there, educator, scientist, engineer of engineers Dr Suh possesses a strategic view of the future and heroic leadership to accomplish it. For innovation has to pass the gauntlet of technology, market and preemption.

Dr Suh's strategic view of the future can be elucidated from his statement: "Leading world-class research universities must make significant major contributions to humanity through their scholarly, research, and educational activities. KAIST has adopted the strategy of solving some of the major problems that humanity has to solve in the 21st century as a means of elevating its educational and research capabilities." His assessment was that through OLEV, KAIST has achieved its distinction among world-class research universities. OLEV is also listed in *Time's* 50 Best Innovations of 2010.

Heroic leadership is needed. Dr Suh is an educator and scientist steeped in self-learning and commitment, challenging the status quo, leading by integrity, example, self reflection and renewal. Though he laughs a lot, it belies his seriousness and toughness. His leadership is akin to Jesuitical "heroic leadership" tested and survived through 500 tumultuous years (Lowney, 2003). It may not be dissimilar to the Cambridge 800-year experience that started from a monastic tradition. His leadership continually nurtured in-house leadership over about 2.5 years of service, renewing and reinventing itself. Only recently were vice-chancellors given seven-year appointments.

At his farewell speech at the KAIST Commencement ceremony 2013, Dr Suh addressed the graduates with a daring and vision — "You can change the history of human beings by using your knowledge and expertise in science and engineering" (Suh, 2013). He lead with conviction — he had changed tenures, injected almost 250 of new blood into the faculty, reviewed the curriculum, reinforced industry collaborations, raised endowments, testified and spread his message and created hands-on engineers who imbibe in the state of art of robotics design, and proto-typing, amongst others.

Additionally, a visit to the young and rising Shantou University (STU) in Shantou, PRC is an eye opener. Endowed generously by Asia's richest, Sir Dr Li Ka Shing and favourite son of Shantou, the provost and protégé of Dr Suh, STU revamped the curriculum in engineering and medicine. Such reinventing of the curriculum takes its cue from the classical Athenian scholarship: "The unexamined curriculum is not worth teaching" (Too, 2001, p. 16) expounded in the essay by the Honorary Spartan Citizen, Professor Paul Cartledge of Cambridge, a foremost scholar of Greek civilization.

At STU, contrary to the dominance of Chinese and its emerging ascendancy, English is a required second language (at KAIST, English is the medium of instruction as set by then President Suh). This added element of language helps its graduates to be highly sought after. STU's influence extends from Shantou city to farther in Guangzhou and beyond. This dimension is elaborated in the response of 1992 Nobel Laureate in Literature, Derek Walcott of St Lucia when asked to whom does the English language belong? "To the land of imagination, beyond just linguistics" (Plimpton, 1988).

What is the implication here? There exists a felt need to revisit and reinvent the curriculum in alignment with Asia-Pacific development and the New Silk Road.

Can the KAIST case be sustained and replicated? Two points are worth noting — KAIST is an outlier and has Factor X: succession & continuity.

Outliers have to continually sharpen skills (the idea of the needed 10,000 hours of practice) and strategy to meet the challenge. When skill matches challenge, the achievement seems fluid just as *"Outliers"* (Gladwell, 2008) and the *"Black Swan"* (Taleb, 2010) show that lessons are learnable, though with difficulty.

Malcolm Gladwell is more positive than Nassim Taleb. Gladwell states: "... outliers become outliers not just because of their own efforts. It's because of the contributions of lots of different people and lots of different circumstances — and that means that we, as a society, have more control about who succeeds — and how many of us succeed — than we think" (Gladwell, n.d.). This would support the efficacy of the eco-system of the univer-city — KAIST, Daejon, Seoul and Korea.

The case of core competencies leadership includes the Gladwell and Hamel-Prahalad propositions generally of leading the eco-system of competence of many. To be clear, at a specific level, Dr Suh brought to KAIST his thought leadership, developed when he was still at MIT. He "redefined the discipline of mechanical engineering from a physics-based discipline into one based on physics, information, biology, and design science. Many new endowed research and teaching laboratories were established to achieve this goal." Two influences merit mention: his mission to create engineers for the 21st century under the aegis of former US President Ronald Reagan's appointment at the National Science Foundation and serving with mission-driven MIT President Charles Vest. This dovetailed forward to his strategic view of the future and a proactive view to engage in two commissions of Korea's then President Myung Bak Lee innovations for the next phase of growth through the creation of new successors to Korea's globalists like Samsung and Hyundai. This had a basis during his earlier term in creating one of the first Korea national plans, learning from its success and shortcomings. Fast forward, the President deepened KAIST-industry partnerships with the likes of Hyundai, Doosan and others in the two KAIST initiatives, OLEV (as elaborated) and Mobile Harbour (mentioned). A detailed reading of the KAIST OLEV case in Chapter 10 of this volume will reinforce the impact of all of these factors in resolving technical and engineering hurdles.

Factor X: Dr Sung-Mo 'Steve' Kang succeeded Dr Suh. Dr Kang was the second Chancellor of the greenfield University of California at Merced, high in Yosemite. We were on an NTU Board mission to study campus planning strategies at the nuovo MERCED, and the historied Stanford, Princeton and Harvard. A hands-on missionary with a vision, Dr Kang knew every student we met. He exhibits great pastoral care of students and faculty and spoke of the future. Berkeley-trained Kang is an academic leader of accomplishment at Urbana-Champaign, KAIST Technische Universität München (TUM), UC Santa Clara in research, patents, inventions (32-bit chip at Bell Labs), entrepreneurship, author, refereed journals and successful startups like Sunnyvale-San Jose ZTI. Impressed, I wrote to the radical academic leader and thinker, Arizona State University (ASU) President Mike Crow to cyber introduce them. But to create a new univer-city remote and high in the mountains serving California's central valley and researching the snowpack and glacier hydrology of the Sierras near Yosemite is an interesting concept — many a bridge too far! Berkeley evolved over 150 years, and as my Berkeley authors opined: the Berkeley campus and community have grown up in parallel over the last 150 years. By the standards of Cambridge, England or Cambridge, Massachusetts, this is nothing, but those 15 decades were sufficient to bring Berkeley to the forefront of US public universities, the flagship of California's ten research university campuses and a world leader in the sciences and the arts, with numerous Nobel Prizes and other honours.

The University of KAIST with the eco-system of KAIST, Daejon, Seoul and Korea is more persuasive and imminent. Kang has that vision of the future. Korea-born, Kang shares that tension and intrepidity to co-create the post-Samsung engines of growth in the coming century. The race and free trade for talent has begun as per the Ben Wildavsky proposition. The centre of the IT hub of India's Bangalore has given forth the two new CEOs of Microsoft and Nokia in the persona of Satya Nadella and Rajeev Suri, respectively class of 1987 and 1989 from Manipal-Mangalore University (Sasi, 2014). All share a home-grown Asian heritage and global immersion in the global centres and cauldrons of innovation in East and South Asia, US, EU and emerging markets. They all face the tipping point in their mainstay leading-edge product. The choices are known — revamp, recreate to the holy grail of preemption, an ever changing new normal!

Ultimate speed & intrepidity: For ultimate real world speed and intrepidity, Silicon Valley pioneer Kang now knows what the co-founder of Apple and its legendary pioneering core competence leadership Steve Jobs' dictum was: *"Lay out a vision fast (in two weeks) or lose the project"* — this was Steve Jobs' ultimatum to his pioneer iPhone Team Leader Greg Christie (Wakabayashi, 2014). Proverbially, the rest is history, the birth of the iPhone revolution jumped sales like never before and amassed a mountain of cash!

Can univer-cities fail or too big to fail? Sir Karl Popper would search for the case that did not work out. One set that comes to mind is Detroit and Ann Arbor, Michigan respectively with Wayne State-Detroit (WS-D) and the University of Michigan-Ann Arbor (UM-AA), about 50 miles apart.

Univer-cities supposedly seem like a virtuous system. Universities and cities symbiotically evolve over time. Now over 50 per cent of the population is urban and cities are engines of growth. In the emerging knowledge economy, universities generate new knowledge and innovations. Univer-cities move into a virtuous cycle. Univer-cities redefine the brave new world on the New Silk Road. Detroit and Ann Arbor grew side by side over a period of some 175 years since UM moved away to Ann Arbor, within 50 miles of each other.

Detroit, once ranked amongst the top 20 cities in America, is the largest city bankruptcy and might go the way of Timbuktu in Mali, Africa. UM-AA is thriving.

Why? By all metrics, UM-AA is a leading public research-intensive university with academic leadership like James Duderstadt and Harlan Hatcher. It has also shared its success in core competence leadership. Charles Vest, its provost and vice-president, later invested 14 years as president of MIT and in his tenure made MIT the preeminent undergraduate engineering programme in America. So did Harold Shapiro to the presidency of Princeton and Lee Bollinger to Columbia. For resourcefulness, it captures a top tier of national research funding and awards and a built up endowment approaching US$10 billion. Wayne State is trending towards half a billion dollars.

Does size count? Detroit in its golden years was the Motor City or Motown capital of the world with engineering, new products, enterprise and talent. In the beginning of the 21st century, it ranked in the top 20 cities in America yet eventually went into Chapter 9 bankruptcy.

Does value count? Robert Fishman, a University of Michigan (UM) professor of architecture and urban planning and a historian of the city, when interviewed for his theory on why no great private university ever emerged in Detroit: "Detroit's business culture contained a deep suspicion of academia" (Pope, 2013). The big three auto corporations were silo-ed in their individual technical and vocational and research institutes. Gordon in his essay reflects this uneasy but important issue in the 16th century and a coping Cambridge, "that academics were disputatious and do not always support a correct establishment view of things". On being economic with the truth or economic in values, something's got to give — Detroit learns whilst Ann Arbor and the UM thrive and nearby across the river to Canada, Windsor-London and the University of Western Ontario also thrive.

It would be tough for a keystone eco-system to flourish in such a comparative environment driven by differing implied strategies of the future. Of a ranking research intensive UM-AA vis-à-vis an introverted industry research, vocational and employability-focused education whilst in inter-state competition rank low in the workforce with tertiary education. To be sure, the open community of scholars and society of UM-AA is a significant overall employer; and of note, is also a specialist employer at its highly patronized major regional medical centre.

Some 75 years ago, Detroit would be the no-contest winner over the parkland Palo Alto, the Seattle-Alaska trading harbour or the tobacco farms of North Carolina as to who would be an example of the future! Free enterprise bets on Stanford-Palo Alto, Duke-Durham and University of Washington-Seattle are shining examples of excellence with robust open-systems and the private endowment of the Lelands, Dukes and latterly, Gates. So too was it with the development of the University of Cambridge with the 16th century hugely generous benefaction of Lady Margaret Beaufort in creating the two colleges of St John's and Christ's colleges as told by Gordon Johnson in Chapter 11 of this volume.

These evolved to the I-5 technology corridor from Silicon Valley to "silicon valley north" of Microsoft, AMGEN, Amazon, and others the Durham-Raleigh-Chapel Hill research triangle; and the Silicon Fen, respectively of Stanford-Seattle, Duke and Cambridge.

Five Observations

Firstly, a twin observation: at the most basic level, size does not count but values do! For WS-D, structure and order prevailed over strategy! There was a silo-ed structure distrustful of academia yet the auto industry was facing an ever and rapidly changing world. The earlier 2008–09 bailout of the auto industry neither helped nor prevented the ignominy of being America's biggest city bankruptcy. How can it happen in the land of the free and home of the brave — and centre of the auto universe since Henry Ford's revolutionarily mass produced Model T Ford? At the same time, in building a strategic view and architecture of the future, Detroit had it backward-forward: new product leadership trumped core competence leadership where the old auto model and mentality were at odds.

Secondly, is UM-AA made more deficient? A keystone eco-system with nearby WS-D does not seem to work, let alone exist. If this interdependence is weighed against UM-AA, it would only make sense to act if there is a strategic fit in responding. If there is not, other options are possible that are *concentric* to or *distance neutral* from UM-AA and intermediated by technology or reputation. Coalitions forming strategic keystone nodes can be leveraged.

Being concentric with neighbouring states like Ohio as *"place"* remains a factor (Quelch & Joic, 2012). This is more likely to yield when venturing with Ohio's high quality set comprising Oberlin, Urbana, Western Reserve and Wesleyan to name a few. There of course are stakeholder issues in the commonwealth of Michigan. In that case, low-cost but high-impact expertise of a consulting kind or expeditionary economics (Schramm, 2010) of an entrepreneurial nature to spur the multiplier effect are worth considering. Schramm formulated this enterprising economic planning approach, whilst at Kauffman Foundation, for post-conflict rebuilding in Iraq and Afghanistan. Such an approach is quite applicable in recovery from trauma of economic disasters of a big city like Detroit to avoid being a failed city. JP Morgan has committed US$100 million to help revitalize Detroit. It has some of the features of expeditionary economics.

Distance neutral: New York once was near the throes of bankruptcy. New York was saved. It remains a leading global financial centre. Of note is the enterprise of leading universities in the legacy of Mayor Michael Bloomberg's vision of the "Univer-City of Roosevelt Island" with Cornell, New York University (NYU), Columbia and Technion.

Thirdly, there are at least five factor axes — regionality of univer-cities, Steve Jobs' technology to market, Clayton Christensen's disruptive innovation, Peter Drucker's talent and Jay Lorsch's governance. WS-D does not rate highly on any of these axes. Bankrupt cities have a chance to recover, but the jury is still out. Univer-cities may explain a part of the reality. But other questions arise. Did free enterprise capitalism as we know it fail Detroit? Is the emerging oligarchic capitalism easing out democratic capitalism and contributing to the worsening inequality? Was the succession of Mayors within the existing political system of city management dysfunctional? The deadly comparison remains — why the solidity of UM-AA?

A positive point, however, is that Detroit cars are rising in profile via the JD Power 2014 ratings. But General Motors is presently facing a new issue of trust in the US Senate with respect to malfunctioning GM ignition switches over the past decade. If speed is important as the KAIST OLEV project shows, the Ralph Nader-speak of "unsafe at any speed" isn't.

Fourthly, can a strong new university be created in an emerging univer-city eco-system in contemporary times? The answer is to look at the case of NTU as told by founder-president Emeritus Professor Cham Tao Soon in his book, *The Making of NTU: My Story* (Cham, 2014). In 1981, when he was 41 years of age, he was tasked with building a university to serve Singapore's industrial development anchored in the original beginnings of the Jurong Industrial Estate later Jurong Town Council, effectively Jurong City now with over a million population and a global manufacturing hub. "In 1985, NTI [Nanyang Technological Institute, NTU's predecessor institution] was named one of the best engineering institutions in the world by the Commonwealth Engineering Council, a distinguished council of engineers.... At that time, NTI was just four years old. But the council placed us among the top, after a four-year study of similar engineering institutions around the world" (p. 55). In 2013, NTU was ranked 41st globally (QS, 2013); and in 2014 retained 2nd position amongst the world's top universities below the age of 50 (QS, 2014). The challenge from Dr Tony Tan, President of Singapore: "How many people have had the chance to build a university from scratch?" (p.153). Cham shaped his vision: "I had all along thought that engineering students should ideally be taught like medical students in theory and practice with teaching hospitals, and budding engineers with industries."

NTU was able to serve the burgeoning industrial development with the "Jurong Engineer", the "Regional Engineer" and now the global "Renaissance Engineer" of tri-lateral capabilities of engineering, management and humanities. Its journey to become a comprehensive university with business, communications, art-design-media, and now a medical school completes its transformation to serve Jurong, Singapore, the region and beyond.

Professor Cham's ambition to create a comprehensive university with a medical school came to fruition after his 21-year tenure combining teaching-research in medicine and surgery with engineering, health-care management and humanities to nurture well-rounded and versatile health-care professionals, not just general practitioner doctors.

The Lee Kong Chian School of Medicine (LKCMedicine) was set up in a venture with the Imperial College of London, generously endowed with a gift of S$150 million from the Lee Foundation. It extended the NTU-Jurong City to NTU-Singapore City in the regional medical hub of the Singapore General Hospital, NUS Medical School (Yong Loo Lin School of Medicine), National University Hospital, Duke-NUS Graduate Medical School, Mount Elizabeth Hospital and TTSH or Tan Tock Seng Hospital (NTU's teaching hospital). With the occurrence of low probability high impact viruses like SARS, Bird Flu and MERS, the LKCMedicine link with TTSH famed for its research and practice in treating tropical disease is a specialty entity whose time has come.

Fifthly, speed, intrepidity and disruptive innovation. Two generations ago, South Korea was in tight fiscal straits. Today, it is one of the G-20. Samsung Group is Korean and giving Apple Inc a hard time. Hyundai Motor is Korean giving Toyota Motor and the Detroit Big Three (General Motors, Ford Motor and Chrysler group), a hard time.

KAIST and OLEV reflect the Korean spirit as they strive to be the next global core competence leaders like Samsung and Hyundai who compete and collaborate with competitors in complex interdependencies, sometimes ending in litigation. KAIST profiles speed, intrepidity and disruptivity enabled with an eco-system of competence of turning innovation to prototype within a year, eight months to be sure, as in the design and development of OLEV.

Importantly, lest we be carried away, we need to ask whether this disruptive innovation is just too difficult to be an outlier strategy to consider? The disruptive innovation encompasses the strategic choice of univer-city leadership and strategy (and there was a fair share of doubters and opposing views who wanted to curtail the leadership strategy at the university and legislative levels); as well as the disruptive innovation of OLEV itself. Petter best puts it: "A university that never produced unsettling ideas or disruptive technologies would be failing its community in a fundamental way. But a deep, mutually beneficial integration of university and community interests can go a long way towards safeguarding the univer-city relationship."

Yet the outliers gained recognition. QS Asia University Rankings 2014 released on 12 May 2014 ranks KAIST as No. 2 (QS, 2014). Dr Suh from his Sudbury home, nearer to MIT, on a phone call cheekily remarked "Pity, missed by one." "OLEV is running in three different places in Korea. I am trying to introduce it in the US (initially, Boston's Logan Airport). The technology is so versatile that it can be used in many applications other than automobiles, buses, etc. In Korea, they are extending the technology to high speed trains." With Asia and its universities rising, Cambridge's choice of NUS and NTU as partners in its strategic view of the future has panned out so far — NUS was ranked No. 1 Asian University 2014 and NTU No. 7 (QS, 2014).

To be sure, KAIST-Daejon-Seoul-Korea strives for all the five factor axes — regionality of univer-cities, Steve Jobs' technology to market, clear and present exemplar vide Clayton Christensen's disruptive innovation, Peter Drucker's talent and Jay Lorsch's governance. When the body of ensuing research from these cases and themes demonstrate efficacy, it might be said that univer-cities are a game changer in the 21st century.

In the brave new world, the surviving and strong univer-cities will redefine the New Silk Road.

Restating building theories from case studies: These dozen cases, initially of Cambridge, Berkeley and NTU, lend themselves to the Stanford Professor Kathleen Eisenhardt's proposition first expounded in the *Academy of Management Review* that in a new topic of conversation, building theories from case studies is a potentially productive avenue of pursuit (Eisenhardt, 1989). I had the opportunity to co-host Professor Eisenhardt at NTU's "The Chua Thian Poh Annual Distinguished Speaker Series 2012" which added inspiration to this enterprise.

Concluding Remarks

This chapter poses an initial and enabling frame of reference to a broad range of choices and dynamics described in the papers submitted for the Inaugural International Conference. The time scale stretches over 805 years from medieval to contemporary times — year 1209 in the case of Cambridge to 1981 in the case of NTU. They present the trajectories envisaged by the academic leaders and pioneers in the conversation on univer-cities. May it spark as much light as heat on some new disruptive pathways of the possible and "outlier" impossible! It is pleasing to note further direct conversations continue between the academic-leader conferees; and exchange visits made, like Berkeley's AVC Marthinsen and UKM's VC Sharifah with VC Mcmillen's UON.

This chapter is written in a conversational style whereas Chapter 12 coauthored with colleague Dr Labidi is in a more formal mode. The essay submitted past the deadline by Dr Shane Huntington and Dean Stephen K Smith is the final Chapter 13. It addresses the impact of a medical school on the evolving univer-city over 160 years at Melbourne. At the same time, it raises the question: does a strong medical school build a unique sinew and robustness to this univer-city and all univer-cities? Remember the University of Michigan and Ann Arbor.

Onwards to *Univer-Cities International Conference Kuala Lumpur 2016 at the University of Malaya*: A second conference, planned for 2016, aims to continue the conversation, engage the authors and share new research with academic and administrative leadership of universities, city officials, practitioners of campus and city planning, and thinkers who share the imagination of the strategic view and architecture of the future of univer-cities redefining the New Silk Road.

References

Brynjolfsson, E. & McAfee, A. (2011). *Race Against the Machine: How the Digital Revolution is Accelerating Innovation, Driving Productivity, and Irreversibly Transforming Employment and the Economy*. Lexington, MA: Digital Frontier Press.

Boorstin, D. J. (1983). *The Discoverers*. New York, NY: Random House.

———. (1992). *The Creators*. New York, NY: Random House.

———. (1998). *The Seekers: The Story of Man's Continuing Quest to Understand His World*. New York, NY: Random House.

Cham, T.S. (2014). *The Making of NTU: My Story*. Singapore: Straits Times Press.

Chandler, A. D. (1962). *Strategy and Structure: Chapters in the History of the American Industrial Enterprise*. Cambridge, MA: MIT Press.

Crow, M. M. (2007). "Enterprise: The path to transformation for emerging public universities". *The Presidency* 10, no. 2, pp. 24–28.

Eisenhardt, K. M. (1989). "Building theories from case study research". *Academy of Management Review* 14, no. 4, pp. 532–550.

Florida, R. (2011). *The 25 Most Economically Powerful Cities in the World*. Retrieved 18 May 2014, from <http://www.citylab.com/work/2011/09/25-most-economically-powerful-cities-world/109/>

Fischer, E. H. (1992). *Edmond H. Fischer — Biographical*. Retrieved 29 April 2014, from <http://www.nobelprize.org/nobel_prizes/medicine/laureates/1992/fischer-bio.html>

Gibbons, M., Limoges, C., Nowotny, H., Schwartzman, S., Scott, P., & Trow, M. (1994). *The New Production of Knowledge: The Dynamics of Science and Research in Contemporary Societies*. London: Sage.

Gladwell, M. (2008). *Outliers: The Story of Success*. New York, NY: Little, Brown & Company.

———. (n.d.). *Outliers: Q & A with Malcolm*. Retrieved 17 May 2014, from <http://gladwell.com/outliers/outliers-q-and-a-with-malcolm/>

Hamel, G. & Prahalad, C. K. (1994). *Competing for the Future*. Cambridge, MA: Harvard Business School Press.

Iansiti, M. & Levien, R. (2004). *The Keystone Advantage: What the New Dynamics of Business Ecosystems Mean for Strategy, Innovation, and Sustainability*. Cambridge, MA: Harvard Business School Press.

Kagan, J. (2009). *Three Cultures: Natural Sciences, Social Sciences, and the Humanities in the 21st Century*. New York, NY: Cambridge University Press.

Lowney, C. (2003). *Heroic Leadership: Best Practices from a 450-year Old Company that Changed the World*. Chicago, IL: Loyola Press.

McNeely, I. F. & Wolverton, L. (2008). *Reinventing Knowledge: From Alexandria to the Internet.* New York, NY: W. W. Norton.

Pagnamenta, P., ed. (2008). *University of Cambridge: An 800th Anniversary Portrait.* London, UK: Third Millennium Publishing.

Plimpton, G., ed. (1988). *Writers at Work: The Paris Review Interviews.* New York, NY: Viking.

Pope, J. (2013). *Could a Private University have Made a Difference in Detroit?* Retrieved 12 May 2014, from <http://www.theatlantic.com/national/archive/2013/07/could-a-private-university-have-made-a-difference-in-detroit/278148/>

QS. (2013). *QS World University Rankings 2013.* Retrieved 14 May 2014, from <http://www.topuniversities.com/university-rankings/world-university-rankings/2013>

QS. (2014). *QS World Rankings 2014.* Retrieved 15 May 2014 from <http://www.topuniversities.com/university-rankings/world-university-rankings/2014>

Quelch, J. A. & Jocz, K. E. (2012). *All Business is Local: Why Place Matters More than Ever in a Global, Virtual World.* New York, NY: Portfolio.

Royal Society. (2011). *Knowledge, Networks and Nations: Global Scientific Collaboration in the 21st Century.* London: Royal Society. Retrieved 17 May 2014, from <http://royalsociety.org/uploadedFiles/Royal_Society_Content/policy/publications/2011/4294976134.pdf>

Sasi, A. (2014). *After Microsoft's Satya Nadella, a 2nd winner for Manipal Institute: Rajeev Suri is Named Nokia CEO.* Retrieved 12 May 2014, from <http://indianexpress.com/article/india/india-others/after-microsofts-nadella-a-second-winner-for-manipal-institute-suri-is-named-nokia-ceo/>

Schramm, C. J. (2010). *Expeditionary economics.* Retrieved 12 May 2014, from <http://www.foreignaffairs.com/articles/66207/carl-j-schramm/expeditionary-economics>

Segran, E. (2014). *What Can You Do with a Humanities Ph.D., Anyway?* Retrieved 12 May 2014, from <http://www.theatlantic.com/business/archive/2014/03/what-can-you-do-with-a-humanities-phd-anyway/359927/>

Suh, N. P. (2013). "Charge to Graduates" [Transcript]. President of KAIST, Commencement Address presented at the 2013 KAIST Commencement, Daejeon, South Korea.

Stein, S. (2014). *America's Top Young Scientists Warn of Systemic Brain Drain: Colleagues 'Sort of Disappear'.* Retrieved 12 May 2014, from <http://www.huffingtonpost.com/2014/04/16/science-brain-drain_n_5161295.html>

Taleb, N.N. (2010). *The Black Swan: The Impact of the Highly Improbable* (2nd ed.). New York, NY: Random House.

Too, Y. L., ed. (2001). *Education in Greek and Roman Antiquity*. Boston, MA: Brill.

Wakabayashi, D. (2014). *Apple Engineer Recalls the iPhone's Birth*. Retrieved 12 May 2014, from <http://online.wsj.com/news/articles/SB10001424052702303949704579461783150723874>

Wildavsky, B. (2010). *The Great Brain Race: How Global Universities are Reshaping the World*. Princeton, NJ: Princeton University Press.

About the Author

Anthony SC Teo is Adjunct Professor, Lee Kuan Yew School of Public Policy, Singapore; Founding Board Member, Middle East Institute, National University of Singapore; and Chevalier of the Ordre des Palmes Académiques.

CHAPTER TWO

UNIVERSITIES AND CITIES: THE FUTURE OF UNIVER-CITIES IN ASIA

HIS ROYAL HIGHNESS RAJA DR NAZRIN SHAH

It is a great pleasure to be invited to Nanyang Technological University (NTU) and to address you at this conference. NTU has been, and is, an integral part of the Singapore story, and its global reputation for creativity, innovation and excellence is well deserved. If there was ever any doubt that NTU is a leading-edge institution, this august gathering of architects, planners and academics should dispel the notion. The reason we are gathered here is to have a conversation on the topic of "univer-cities", something that is clearly not idle wordplay but a frontier-moving subject.

Basically, we are invited to consider how two organizational entities, cities and universities, can combine to produce a result that is larger than the sum of the parts. And we are invited to consider real life examples of the mutually beneficial interactions between them. I believe that the future of our educational institutions is one of the central challenges that we all must grapple with, those in the East and West alike. We have a lot riding on our universities and they deserve the sharpest and most experienced minds to think, plan and manage them. In this regard, I must say that the thought leadership behind this conference is exceptional. But then with Anthony Teo helming the conference, one could hardly have expected or settled for anything less.

Before I share some thoughts on this subject and the strategic implications for Asia, let me first say that as a student of political economy and development, I will share my thoughts and ideas primarily from this angle. I hope this approach will open up another line of productive discourse to complement the ones already being taken. I will begin by briefly highlighting the role of cities in economic growth today and then universities. I hope to show that the economic view of cities and universities is not only consistent with, but highly complementary to, the ideas that will be exchanged in this room. I will then conclude by focusing on the strategic implications for developing states in Asia.

Cities as Economic Drivers

In the field of economics, the idea of placemaking has attained — or, more accurately, re-attained — currency. Paul Krugman is credited with his pioneering work in new economic geography, something for which he was awarded the 2008 Nobel Prize in Economics. In new economic geography, cities and regions with the most production are also the most profitable because of the increasing returns and positive external economies that exist. They therefore tend to attract more investment, the best talents and grow even richer as a result.

To underscore its practical importance, the 2009 World Bank Development Report entitled *Reshaping Economic Geography* provided evidence from around the world that cities are critical determinants of economic success. Policymakers were urged to think and act in "3-D" — the three "Ds" being density, distance and division. To put it succinctly, the authors found that countries that had been successful, and those that would be in future were the ones that increased urban densities, shortened distances and removed divisions thereby fostering specialization and integration.

That the recipe for economic success can be reduced to three relatively simple generic variables is, of course, debatable. That they are important, however, even extremely important, is less in doubt. Much of how economic development manifests itself is exactly in these three ways, from high-rise buildings to high-speed trains and highly seamless electronic commerce. Greater proximity reduces transaction costs, promotes network interactions and produces other positive growth-inducing externalities. Policymakers are therefore urged to renew their interest in urbanization and capitalize on these agglomeration economies.

Density characterizes the most significant cities in the global urban hierarchy. At the top, a handful of world-class cities such as New York, London and Tokyo act as primary agglomerations where a wide range of knowledge-intensive industries come together to produce complex systems of competitive advantage, often linked through financial and business services.

Below them, a tier of internationally significant capitals, such as Singapore, Chicago, Frankfurt, Seoul and, increasingly these days, Shanghai, occupy strong positions. Under these are a flight of aspiring cities, and here I would place Kuala Lumpur, Dubai and others that aim to leverage on their strengths.

As a brief aside, let me say that Malaysia takes the 3-D concept seriously. The Greater Kuala Lumpur/Klang Valley is one of twelve National Key Economic Areas in the country's Economic Transformation Programme. Greater KL/Klang Valley accounts for 20 per cent of the country's population and over 30 per cent of national gross domestic product. Efforts are currently underway to improve connectivity, notably through the construction of a Mass Rail Transit, while urban redevelopment and provision of quality affordable housing are helping to improve the quality of urban space and liveability.

Of course greater urbanization can also have drawbacks. Economists believe that past a certain size, the costs of urbanization will outstrip the benefits. Overcrowding, gridlocked traffic, crime, poverty, homelessness and environmental pollution are seen as symptoms that cities have exceeded their carrying capacities. In the past, policymakers imposed planning restrictions and imposed high taxes to control urban sprawl. They pursued regional diversification by relocating national or state capitals, often at a very high cost. They also offered generous incentives for companies to locate in areas where there were little or no economic activities. Naturally, takeup rates were less than encouraging.

Today, the costs of urbanization can be substantially mitigated even if not completely offset and the virtues of city size and increasing density are once again being extolled. Technological advances in transportation, for example, allow intra-city and inter-city mobility at a speed, comfort and convenience that would have been difficult to imagine in the past. Buildings can be built higher, more safely and cheaply with new construction methods and materials. Falling telecommunication costs and increasing broadband speeds are accelerating the growth of the digital economy and making the tyranny of distance much less of a factor. Renewable energy and energy efficient systems are reducing the carbon footprints of cities, while water harvesting and vertical farming in cities are conserving this vital resource.

Importantly, lessons have been learned about how to plan for better cities. Critical to this is the engagement of stakeholders through initiatives like Local Agenda 21 which seeks to ensure that cities are not just more prosperous but environmentally protected and resident communities are socially better off. In short, we are much less susceptible today than in the past to the negative consequences of density and distance, provided, of course, that adequate forethought is given and far-sighted action taken.

Universities as Change Agents

Let me now turn to universities. Economists have recognized the role of education and universities in raising national productivity and welfare since the late 1950s. Their contributions to improving human capital, advancing knowledge frontiers and catalysing technological change are well appreciated. Cases commonly cited include Silicon Valley in California, the Research Triangle of Raleigh-Durham-Chapel Hill in North Carolina, the Silicon Fen in Cambridge, UK and Bangalore in India, to name a few.

Universities, however, have evolved over time and, even today, are not all cast from the same mould. It is important to appreciate their differences, which are often the result of competing philosophies and policy priorities. They have undergone marked revolutions since they began as cloistered or reclusive communities of religious scholars. In 19th century Germany, for example, universities were enlisted to support state-making and nation-building through rational, secular and scientific scholarship. An élite professoriate was established and teaching and research linked for the first time. Towards the late 19th century, the American civic university appeared, shifting teaching beyond the professor to the development of disciplines and, with them, entire departments.

After World War II, younger demographics led to increasing demand for university entrance and a greater social mix of students precipitated "democratic mass universities". Then, driven by weakening state funding and increasing competitive threats from globalization, universities were forced to seek alternative funding sources, to innovate in their managerial structures, to engage with business and government and to become entrepreneurial and import private sector models into the academy. The "virtual" or "e-" universities continue this trend of evolution and change.

Various authors have suggested a number of archetypal forms, from the entrepreneurial university, through to the virtual university, the engaged university, the ethical university, and the useful university. Rather than being just one or another, it is likely that the universities of the future will have to be several or even a composite of all of these attributes.

Of course many have lamented the fact that as the mission of universities shifts away from service to the production of scientific knowledge, they do not address broader societal challenges. There have been calls for scholarship that also pursues knowledge that contributes towards solving pressing socio-economic problems at the national and local levels. Others have complained that the de-emphasis on the humanities, with the closing of whole departments, lessens appreciation of human and civilizational influences. Virtually all complain that competition for finance, staff and students are forcing reductions in standards of student quality, scholarship and teaching.

These different competing claims on universities are no doubt going to be around for some time. I believe that we will continue to need a range of institutions to meet these claims, from élite to mass participatory and from specialized to more generalist. Given the increasing importance of universities in producing and disseminating knowledge content of all kinds, I remain optimistic that policymakers and university managers will make responsive decisions, according to global and local imperatives and conditions.

Univer-Cities as Institutions

If cities and universities are both drivers of economic growth, then their close interactions should make them more than doubly potent. In this regard, there are at least three kinds of benefits that universities' broader campus development activities can offer to the development and competitiveness of cities. First, they can help create new knowledge-intensive spaces, either new knowledge districts or within existing ones. Second, they can contribute to improving the quality of urban governance. Third, universities can directly contribute to place branding while also becoming involved in strategic urban projects that can assist in repositioning the city's profile to external investors and knowledge workers.

While I have no doubt that the potential is there, we need to understand their dynamics in detail in order to ensure that this potential can be unlocked. We already know that the intrinsic relationship between the university campus and the city demands not just dialogue but active participation among a large group of stakeholders ranging from policymakers and planners to corporations and businesses, civic groups and service organizations and, of course, the public. How effectively stakeholders are able to dialogue, participate and jointly manage outcomes are important considerations. Holding townhall meetings alone is not sufficient to ensure that there is meaningful participation. Even if productive ideas and viewpoints are aired, it does not always follow that these are shared or have stakeholder buy-in.

The reality is that the interests of universities are also not always aligned with that of local and national authorities and may, at points, even diverge. Given the competing claims on cities and universities, a central question then will be how to ensure that stakeholders' inputs are received, internalized and accommodated. This places a great deal of dependence on systems of governance, namely, whether they are representative, fair and efficient and perceived to be so. Trust is one of the most powerful motivations for collective action, while distrust can be one of its most powerful deal-breakers. Unless processes are well established, transparent and robust, particularly in being able to handle a diversity of views, productive interactions between city and university may end up being more apparent than real.

Formal laws, rules and procedures can only go so far. They can often help to prevent conflict but they are not much good at creating the conditions for voluntary cooperation and collaboration. In this regard, I would emphasize the importance of facilitative social rules and norms-making, organizational arrangements, hierarchies, information dissemination, credible commitment, and transaction and monitoring costs. Given the wide variety of actors involved, these are critical in making univer-cities a success.

Strategic Implications for Developing Asia

I would now like to close by contemplating some of the strategic issues associated with univer-cities for developing Asia. Let me preface this with the general observation that throughout Asia, governments are typically the largest financiers of universities. Private institutions do exist but generally only a few have managed to reach critical mass and weight. As organizations that are funded through the public purse, the needs of national education, unsurprisingly, tend to be of paramount importance. Policies are largely made and implemented in top-down fashion and there are often strict lines of reporting and accountability back to bureaucrats.

The ability of these institutions to adopt the kinds of open system values and interactivity is, as a result, greatly restricted. Most lack the autonomy to redefine roles and respond to local needs because their mandates and modus operandi remain largely traditional in nature. Appointments and promotion are usually handled internally but, in many cases, may not be commensurate with competence and tangible results. Performance, especially in the form of course content and quality research publications, is frequently not up to par. Attempts to institute reforms can be blocked by regressive organizational cultures.

For brevity, I have grouped the strategic implications under three categories. The first category is institutional in nature. The ability to create univer-cities will require a desire for global best practices and then implanting a leadership team that can change fundamental values, norms and attitudes in this direction. But there must also be policy space. A degree of boldness and vision on the part of government will be needed to provide managers the autonomy to initiate, plan and direct their teaching courses and research agenda. These, I think, are the basic first steps on the road to linking universities with cities.

The second category of implications is interactivity. If universities are to be at the forefront of innovation, ideas about education must change. In order to be world class, universities must be truly collaborative and cease to be closed systems. The idea that knowledge is to be found within the walls of the lecture theatre or purely in books is outdated and more experiential learning and service orientation must be embarked on. Some Asian universities have managed to make this transition but quite a number still remain bound to outmoded notions of education. Faculty attachments and student internships abroad, for example, are important practical ways to help acquire knowledge as well as influence beliefs and behaviour. It is only with more open learning and research that univer-cities can be realities.

The third category is urban governance. In many Asian capitals, rates of urbanization are running ahead of the capacity of its governors to manage them. As a result, planning tends to be reactive, rather than proactive, and interactions with universities are not accorded the priority they deserve. As indicated earlier, universities can be a part of the solution towards constructing better systems of city administration, planning and development. Faculty and graduate students, for example, can be co-opted via industrial training schemes to help out in overstretched engineering, power, transportation, water and sanitation departments. In this way, the mutually beneficial linkages between universities and the urban populace can be strengthened.

Concluding Remarks

I hope that you find these thoughts helpful. I am certain that with the outstanding speakers here, there will be a very deep and meaningful conversation as to how universities can contribute to urban development and vice versa. I look forward to hearing your deliberations and sharing them with my fellow Malaysians.

About the Author

His Royal Highness Raja Dr Nazrin Shah is the Regent of the State of Perak, Malaysia. He is also the Pro-Chancellor of the University of Malaya; Eminent Fellow of the Institute of Strategic and International Studies; Member of the Chancellor's Court of Benefactors, University of Oxford; President of the Perak Council on Islam and Malay Customs; and many more.

CHAPTER THREE

BERKELEY: CAMPUS AND COMMUNITY

RICHARD BENDER, EMILY MARTHINSEN AND JOHN PARMAN

From early days, universities and their cities have had relationships marked by synergy and hostility. If the idea of a university has two archetypal models, then one of them — Cambridge or Oxford — is about universities distancing themselves from the city, while the other — Bologna or Paris — is about embracing it. Berkeley, the university and the city, grew up together. Today, the campus is set within a relatively urban context, but it is still recognizably a real campus.

This chapter reprises their development, noting that the university's steady expansion overflowed its original campus boundaries and, as it grew, influenced the sometimes cooperative, sometimes resistant community around it. Today, it is unavoidably clear that they are joined at the hip — not just where they overlap, but in the larger sense of mutual dependence.

Concluding that it is not too early to look out to a new mid-century and speculate what both might become by 2050, we end our essay by considering how the campus and the community might evolve. This takes the form of three scenarios that look out towards futures that we characterize as *small*, *large*, and *slow*. The first two reflect ongoing disputes over density between the advocates of preservation and of "smart" growth, while the third attempts reconciliation. The campus is not precisely a park, but it anchors the city with park-like open space, making it easier to add density around it. In 2011, a referendum in Berkeley endorsed the city's plan to redevelop the transit-served downtown area west of the campus at a higher density. As the plan is implemented, it will be important to give this and other campus edges breathing room, weaving together buildings, pedestrian and view corridors, and open space to make for a desirable and complementary whole that is not simply a response to regional density targets.

UC Berkeley Campus

(Source: Archive of the Campus Planning Study Group, College of Environmental Design, University of California, Berkeley)

Introduction

This era — the second decade of a new century — is an interesting time to reflect on the flagship Berkeley campus of the University of California (UC) and its city. Some 90 years after it was founded, spurred by state and federal largesse, UC Berkeley took on the highly specialized nature of a 20th-century research university in the American sense. The colleges that formed or grew in the initial post-War boom spawned new programmes and institutes. After 2000, as public funding declined, private donors stepped in to finance major new buildings, sometimes as part of research and other initiatives.

Fragmentation was the price that the campus paid for specialization. In an era of relative austerity, the overlap among these disparate parts has exacerbated an unwieldy and inefficient structure that is hard to sustain. When the Great Recession hit in 2008, no one could say for certain how long austerity would last. The initial response was to cut across the board, reducing salaries, eliminating lectureships, and trimming staff; five years later, it is clear that a return to business as usual is impossible. What Schumpeter called "creative destruction" may be the most fruitful way to look at the opportunity this crisis presents.

The city government of Berkeley has a comparable dilemma, having built up a structure dependent on revenue flows that are way below their high-water mark. Like the University of California, it has to secure voter approval of new tax measures to avoid continued deficit spending. In the view of some of their critics, these measures are temporary fixes that merely postpone the more radical rethinking and restructuring that both need to shift their respective models of higher education and governance. As the phrase "relative austerity" implies, neither the campus nor the city lacks for money. Their budgets are substantial by most of the world's measure. The university's budget is growing, although its sources have changed. Both still have considerable room to restructure and transform. Indeed, they have every possibility of doing so together, recognizing the extent to which their fates have always been entwined.

All of this points to the pregnancy of this moment. Over its history, California has often shown the way forward for others, with Berkeley — the campus and the community — among the leaders. The campus is legendary for its "reserved parking" signs for Nobel laureates, so valuable today that the winners joke that the monetary prize pales in comparison. UC Berkeley economists are credited with helping turn Indonesia around, among other countries. Now their attention is focused on Washington, D.C. and Sacramento. The city is bound up with this. Despite bouts of antagonism, there is mutual pride and influence.

The Campus and the Community

That there are tensions in the relationship reflects not only the steady growth of the campus beyond its original boundaries, but also the fact that the university is constitutionally independent from local control, addressing constituencies that are regional, national, and even international rather than local, with a student body that, while mostly transient, votes in local elections and often sways their results. While their proximity will always add tensions to the relationship, their issues and challenges are remarkably similar. The diminishing role of state funding puts them both at an interesting crossroads. Despite the financial pressures of their current situations, they have inherent advantages which position them well for the future, if they can see it and capitalize on it.

Not the least of this is the Bay Area's long-term prospects. The region is doing better than many others in the US, owing especially to its high-tech and social-media clusters in Silicon Valley and San Francisco. The economic challenge is to diversify from there — a shift in which UC Berkeley is likely to have a strong role. In the absence of strong regional government, the Bay Area has evolved a coalition of public agencies, institutions, and business interests that often coalesce around issues of regional, economic and environmental importance. UC Berkeley is part of this. The governmental challenge is to make a real regional government of this coalition, preserving its checks and balances but not the local veto power and the many regulatory lacunae that dog it now.

Within the region, Berkeley — campus and community — enjoys the advantages of a physical location of considerable beauty and amenity, directly accessible by transit to the main regional destinations and two of the region's three airports. If the university is an urban campus with a park-like setting, the city around it combines a relatively dense centre and arterials with residential neighbourhoods. Good bus transit to Oakland gives students access to housing beyond the city's borders in newly vibrant areas. (The campus is the biggest generator of bus trips in the East Bay, according to AC Transit.) As this implies, the university and the city together have brighter futures than their current challenges suggest. Both stand to benefit if they address them in tandem and work towards joint solutions whenever possible.

The Evolution of the Berkeley Campus

John Galen Howard's plan for the Berkeley campus exemplifies the strategy of creating a setting for architecture. It was a beaux-arts plan that reflected the way popes and kings built. It leveled the land. Although the campus was organized as a series of steps, Howard treated it as if it were flat. He designed buildings for it that had no relationship to the local materials and climate. Bernard Maybeck, whose work and planning for the campus was more organic, was pushed aside. The idea of making the plan for a grand campus largely came from Maybeck, but after the competition that he put together was held, the dreams and ambitions of others took precedence. Hearst and Stanford, vastly rich San Franciscans and US senators from California, had to change trains in Chicago when they travelled east. They would have seen Chicago's World's Fair, with its "White City" modelled on imperial Rome. This image, which reflected America's budding imperialism, appealed to these patrons of the "Athens of the West".

Maybeck, respecting the natural influence on the campus, crept in at the edges. Howard set the beaux-arts pieces down between the two branches of Strawberry Creek, at a distance from riparian nature. These remnants were where Maybeck designed the Men's Faculty Club and the original architecture school. Howard's shingle-style Women's Faculty Club and Naval Architecture Building demonstrate his acceptance of — indeed, his endorsement and participation in — a leitmotif of informality that almost from the beginning formed a counterpoint to the beaux-arts grandeur of the campus' inner core.

Remarkably, this framework had held — partly formal, rooted in classicism and expressive of California's sense of its own destiny, and partly organic, rooted in the land itself, predating Howard's interventions. The principal legacy of the Campus Planning Study Group (CPSG), with which all three authors were associated, was to draw attention to it often enough — and to stress the responsibility of stewardship that rested on successive campus administrators, deans, and academic entrepreneurs — to give it both currency and acceptance. Thus the campus, which was in real danger of being paved over by unplanned, outsized growth in the 1970s, has in fact been developed more thoughtfully. The results are far from perfect, but the setting that Maybeck and Howard in their different ways envisioned is still palpable.

John Galen Howard UC Berkeley Plan

(*Source*: Archive of the Campus Planning Study Group, College of Environmental Design, University of California, Berkeley)

Origins and Growth: 1860–1970

The history of the founding and growth of the flagship campus of the University of California reflects the wider history of California. If the Gold Rush brought temporary prosperity and a surge in population to the state, the railroads, large-scale agriculture, and urban-scale development of its metropolitan centres positioned it as the wealthy western anchor of America's economic expansion. As the ranking families sought to make their mark, higher education benefited from their largesse. If Stanford University was the privately funded rival of Harvard and Yale, the University of California was the public, populist riposte. That this image of public service persists — Berkeley as the model of a great public university — is a tribute to the power of a 19th-century optimism about the future that still animates California in the early 21st century.

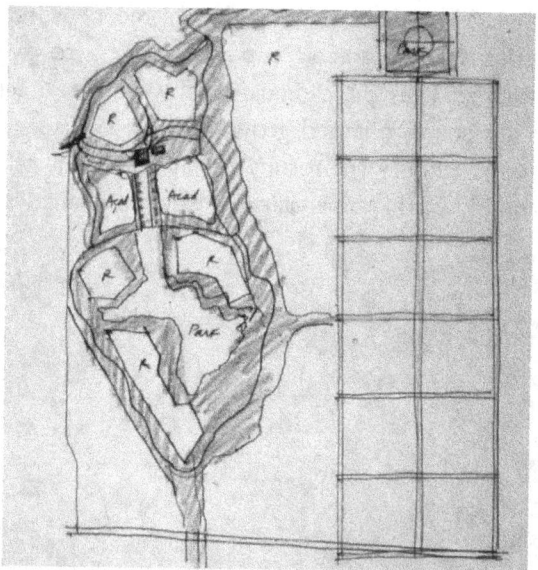

Olmstead Plan Sktech 1863

(Source: Archive of the Campus Planning Study Group, College of Environmental Design, University of California, Berkeley)

The formal history of the University of California's Berkeley campus begins in 1860, when the College of California, then located in Oakland, took over 160-acres of farmland between the north and south branches of Strawberry Creek as a new campus. In 1864, the College Homestead Association was formed to acquire and sell lots around the campus. In 1866, the Association bought an additional 320 acres for speculative residential development to benefit the college, and its trustees hired Frederick Law Olmsted to plan the future development of these combined holdings. The Morrill Act of 1862 had established federal land grants to the states for colleges of agriculture and "mechanics" (engineering). Four years later, in 1866, the California legislature founded a new Land Grant college on a site north of the College of California's campus. In 1867, the trustees of College of California offered its campus as the site of a merged public institution, the University of California.

A series of campus plans followed. The 1870 plan of San Francisco architect David Farquharson updated Olmsted's plan to reflect the university's ambitious building programme. One of the first two new buildings, South Hall, built in 1873, still exists. The Farquharson plan clustered the new buildings where Olmsted had originally placed them, with the view corridor towards Golden Gate as the organizing axis. The influential philanthropist Phoebe Apperson Hearst funded an international competition in 1897, based on a programme developed by Regents and lawyer Jacob Reinstein and the architect Bernard Maybeck. The winner was the eminent French architect Emile Bénard, who subsequently came to Berkeley to adapt his beaux-arts plan to the campus' realities. His plan shifted the Olmsted axis to the north, lining it up with the emerging street grid of the town. It left Strawberry Creek free to meander through campus.

UC Berkeley Campus circa 1873

(*Source*: Archive of the Campus Planning Study Group, College of Environmental Design, University of California, Berkeley)

Bénard declined the position of Campus Architect in 1900. The Regents then resolved that only an advisory committee, consisting of the original competition jury plus three prominent architects, could modify his plan. Outside member John Galen Howard became Supervising Architect for the University in 1902, immediately taking the position that the Bénard plan was more of a suggestion than a template for how to proceed. Designing the Hearst Memorial Mining Building, the first of his many buildings for the university, Howard aligned it with the existing campus nucleus, a legacy of Olmsted and Farquharson. He modified the Bénard plan in 1908, adopting their Golden Gate axis, and again in 1914 by orienting many of the new buildings towards this central axis rather than towards the city-facing edge.

George Kelham, a San Francisco architect who also planned the UCLA campus, succeeded Howard as Supervising Architect in 1927, extending the campus south to Bancroft Avenue. He was succeeded in 1938 by San Francisco architect Arthur Brown, Jr., who departed from the beaux-arts style of his predecessors to build in a stripped-down classical style affordable in the Depression years. He also commissioned a modern-style dormitory complex, Stern Hall, designed by William Wurster. Brown's 1944 plan relegated dormitories to sites off the main campus, made Strawberry Creek the armature of campus open space, and sited new development, limited to four stories in height, along a new axis extending south from the Hearst Mining Building.

Surging post-War enrolment at the university, along with new prosperity and growth in the city, shifted both towards a more urban context. When Brown stepped down as Supervising Architect, the Regents established the Office of Architects and Engineers (OAE) in 1949 to replace him. In 1955, they created a Committee on Campus Planning. Berkeley Chancellor Clark Kerr, Architecture Dean William Wurster, and Regent Donald McLaughlin worked with OAE Chief of Staff Louis DeMonte to produce the 1956 plan. It contemplated a modern campus with at least 25,000 students, to be accommodated "without sacrificing the beautiful physical setting". The 1956 plan increased the density of the central campus through redevelopment, removing some obsolete and temporary buildings, and increasing the size of new ones. Building coverage was set at 25 per cent. The plan increased close-in parking, sought to limit on-campus development to uses requiring campus access, and called for consultation and cooperation with the community through the City of Berkeley Liaison Committee, headed by Wurster until 1957.

The space race inaugurated by the Soviet Union's launch of the Sputnik satellite in the late 1950s, led to a surge in public investment in higher education, particularly in science, mathematics, and engineering, in the US. The University of California's 1960 Master Plan for Higher Education in California called for the student population of the Berkeley campus to rise to 27,500, 45 per cent of which would be graduate students, a level of enrollment reflected in the campus' 1962 Long-Range Development Plan (LRDP).

To preserve the 25 per cent coverage limit, the 1962 LRDP accepted the need for taller, mostly mid-rise buildings. Academic clusters were maintained, but major new campus buildings were added, along with multi-level parking structures at the periphery. In the ten years following the 1962 LRDP, two million square feet of buildings were added, bringing total campus building development to seven million square feet. (The issues of the campus' population and the balance of undergraduate and graduate student enrolment have persisted as points of contention between the university and the city. It arose most recently in relation to student housing in the Southside district adjoining the campus. The current enrolment breakdown is about 25,000 undergraduate students and 10,000 graduate students.)

Campus Revival: 1970–90

People only become aware that something is amiss when clear evidence of the fact is unavoidably in view. This truism proved true on the Berkeley campus when Evans Hall, a nondescript highrise building, was allowed to block the view corridor towards the Golden Gate envisioned early on in the beaux-arts campus plan. Then the threatened demolition of Howard's shingle-style 1914 Naval Architecture Building brought the Berkeley Architectural Heritage Association out in protest. In response, Chancellor Albert Bowker turned to Dean Richard Bender to establish and lead an initiative to understand the history and current situation of the Berkeley campus. From its vantage point on the ninth floor of Wurster Hall, the faculty and student staff of the Campus Planning Study Group (CPSG) set to work.

One of CPSG's decisions was to compile an inventory of the large number of historic buildings and places on the campus and protect them by nominating them for the National Register of Historic Buildings and Places. Another was to revive and update the campus' planning framework as a guide to stewardship and future growth. This meant understanding the framework that Howard and Maybeck had put in place and going beyond it to identify the individual precincts that had grown up as the campus evolved. These two efforts were complementary in that the National Register nominations established that the clusters of buildings around landscaped settings were the real source of the campus' significance. Both were carried out in collaboration with the city and the Berkeley Architectural History Association.

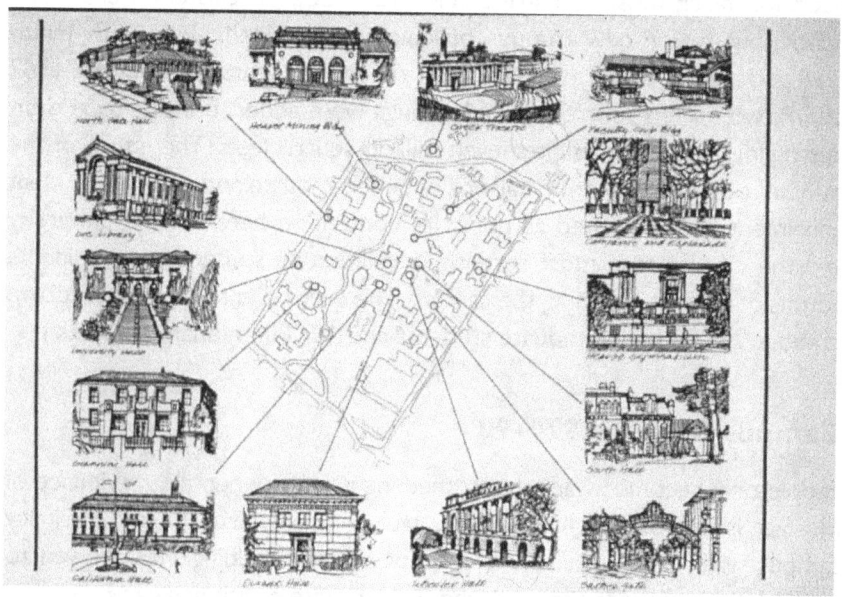

Historic Buildings Nominations of UC Berkeley
(*Source*: Archive of the Campus Planning Study Group, College of Environmental Design, University of California, Berkeley)

The CPSG produced guidelines for developing new buildings within the classical core and around the informal landscape, around and beyond the two forks of Strawberry Creek. The CPSG also defined and carried out studies of the individual campus precincts, in an effort to project how each could densify without losing the spirit of the place. The CPSG also addressed the development of the areas adjoining the campus, including the Downtown and Southside areas. These studies influenced decision-making about specific new building projects. They also informed the deliberations of the newly formed Campus Design Review Committee. Finally, the CPSG provided a "Plan for a Plan" that summarized its findings and suggested a future development framework. This led the Berkeley campus to tie the LRDP process to environmental impact review, now the norm for all of the UC campuses.

The CPSG had several kinds of influence, but the most important was a kind of moral suasion: thanks to its work and the active support and involvement of Chancellor Bowker and his successor, Ira Michael Heyman, it became harder, even with abundant building funds in hand, for would-be builders to ignore the fabric of the campus, because more and more people understood it and valued it. This is not to say that the fabric was not sometimes ignored, but the trend was positive. Over time, the campus became a better client, too, getting better results from the architects, landscape architects, and planners it hired.

The other important result of the CPSG's efforts was to point to the settings of the campus as the more important means to understand and preserve its essential qualities. This began with the broad sense of the classical core and natural edges, but it took into account the way the different precincts were anchored and activated by larger and smaller open spaces, by pathways, by views, and by buildings of a certain type and scale. This fine-grained understanding of what existed set the stage for a more sophisticated, more nuanced consideration of how it might evolve.

The CPSG's understanding of the campus was urbane and the value it placed on urbanity has survived, persisted, and grown. While every subsequent campus plan at UC Berkeley reflects it, the most important legacy may be to have communicated this understanding. By helping ordinary people, untrained in planning, design, or history, to grasp how campus buildings and settings contribute to the quality of life of the university community and its neighbours, the CPSG made the process of design advocacy easier for a generation of campus planners — not only at Berkeley, but at the other nine campuses of the University of California, each of which has benefited from the early and strongly positive example that the CPSG provided.

Sather Gate UC Berkeley (Courtesy of Professor Richard Bender)

Planning the Future Campus: 1990–2010

In the early 1990s, the Regents of the University of California began formally to require each campus to prepare a Long-Range Development Plan (LRDP) that would define its specific planning, development, and academic goals. UC Berkeley completed a 15-year LRDP in 1990 and began work on the 2020 LRDP less than ten years later. Certified by the Regents in 2005, it provided an integrated, contextual framework for UC Berkeley's future.

That the 2020 LRDP was conceived as a framework rather than a vision is the key to its effectiveness. The LRDP identified and addressed critical issues facing the UC Berkeley campus. It is an institution- and site-specific document that provides both a conceptual physical planning context and an academic context for making a wide range of decisions about the future of the campus and its environs. Unlike its 1990 predecessor, the 2020 LRDP addressed how the university and the city could work together.

The critical question answered for UC Berkeley through the 2020 LRDP planning process was: how can we support both development and stewardship of our campus? The LRDP process provided an approach to stewardship, defined a direction for campus development, and provided a framework for understanding the physical character of the campus. One of its important tasks was to identify appropriate future building sites and decide on their development capacities. The 2020 LRDP used campus history to understand these opportunities and put a structure in place for growth and change.

In considering the campus' future, it was clear that the 2020 LRDP would have to address where the campus would grow. How much growth and what types of programmes would be important to understand; but, for the purposes of the plan and its on-going effectiveness, specific growth and programmes became less important than establishing a consistent and overall approach to that development — including not only the campus proper, but also the Southside, Downtown, and Northside areas of the city that border it.

The 2020 LRDP viewed the campus as part of the region and thus one in a series of interconnected plans. Although the campus edge remains clearly defined, elements of the campus — people, buildings, and activities — would move into adjoining neighbourhoods. UC Berkeley facilities and activities would also be located elsewhere in Berkeley and other East Bay cities. While the historic campus remains a source of identity for town and gown alike, the 2020 LRDP envisioned the university being more fully integrated, physically and economically, with both the surrounding community and the region as a whole.

Even in 2005, it was clear that mobility was a factor of growing importance for the campus. The 2020 LRDP recognized that many people on the campus lived beyond its immediately adjoining neighbourhoods. While they may not need to be on campus daily, they still needed to connect with it — in reality and virtually. The 2020 LRDP responded to this by considering the transportation issues affecting the city and the university. Today, mobility's implications are more visible and much more pervasive. In 2005, it looked like virtual connectivity would reduce the demands placed on the campus as a physical setting. What has happened instead is that the use of the campus has stretched out to fill nights and weekends.

Interestingly, the technology-based industries that dominate the Bay Area have embraced place, even as they leverage mobility to use it more intensively than before. Often preferring to repurpose the buildings of the previous generation rather than build new ones, the fastest-growing tech companies pair high-density work settings with an array of curated amenities, from art to food trucks and carts. The spaces are "hackable", inviting users to shape and reshape them without having to rely on facilities staff. These urban and suburban campuses are not bad precedents for any campus, including Berkeley's.

Engaging the City: 1990–2010

The 2020 LRDP reflects the changed political context that had led, a few years earlier, to a joint Southside planning effort by the City of Berkeley and UC Berkeley. The City Southside Plan, adopted by Berkeley City Council in 2011, was informed by an understanding and acceptance of the ideas of this joint planning effort. Of particular importance was the principle that the Southside is an area the city shares with the university, with a physical and social character that is shaped by both. The idea that the Southside is an area with fluid boundaries and integrated campus/city spaces and activities is new, although its realization has been slow in coming. A similar impulse has led to greater campus/city cooperation in the Downtown area, which provides a model for the Southside area in the future. Despite its broader view, the 2020 LRDP stopped short of considering how the university and the city might share resources in the future. Since 2004, though, their cooperation has pointed more and more in this direction, as the university has had a growing role in using and developing the edges of the campus.

Downtown Berkeley adjoins the west edge of the campus and is its main gateway. Since the CPSG studied the area, the university has acquired and leased significant amounts of space there, but neither the 1990 nor the 2020 LRDP looked closely at how the area relates to the campus. After the Regents certified the 2020 LRDP, the City of Berkeley sued the University of California, arguing that proposed mitigations for the impacts on the city of UC Berkeley's future development were inadequate. In settling the lawsuit, the university and the city agreed to co-develop a plan for downtown Berkeley. The resulting Downtown Area Plan (DAP) reflects changes in the way the university views the downtown. The UC Berkeley-specific uses in plan are envisioned as settings in which flexible, mixed uses of all types can coexist. In particular, the importance of the economic relationship between the university and the city is stressed. The plan recognizes their shared interest in a viable downtown, with each having a role to play in achieving it.

At the same time that it provides a framework for the stewardship of the campus' rich landscape and building resources, the 2020 LRDP anticipates some basic changes in the way the campus is used. For example, it reserves campus buildings and future building sites for key academic activities, including instruction and research. Administrative and auxiliary activities, including athletics, recreation, and parking, are pushed beyond the edges of the campus park. This step posits an essentially car-free campus and proposes to locate new student housing based on travel time from the centre of campus on foot, bike, or transit. The city favours a car-free downtown, but the community is divided on the issue. Giving bikes more priority over cars, as is happening now in San Francisco, has been piecemeal and inconsistent. Yet cooperation and joint initiatives between the university and the city on these issues are growing.

The DAP and the Streets and Open Space Improvement Plan both suggest ways to link the physical campus and the downtown. Using scale, massing, and landscape, these plans define ways in which the university's growth in the downtown preserves the character of both. The DAP also supports economic connections between the campus and the city, particularly related to university uses and spin-offs in the downtown. Technology transfer — drawing on university-based research and development — plays a key role in such economic initiatives as the Green Corridor, which seeks to develop green technology as an industrial base for the East Bay. While the 2020 LRDP does not address these activities, they are one of the main considerations now in campus planning for new development.

The 2020 LRDP anticipated greater cooperation between the university and the city. A good deal of this was already implicit in the plan as it considered transportation, the co-development of the campus edges, and other issues and possibilities. Its authors could not foresee that only a few years later, a recession of unprecedented depth and length would dramatically change the funding picture for the public sector of which they were both part, setting the stage for a reappraisal of how each might operate, separately and together, to deal with consequences of a severe reversal of California's fortunes.

Campus Rally (Courtesy of Professor Richard Bender)

Facing up to the New Normal

"A crisis is a terrible thing to waste" — this memorable phrase by Rahm Emanuel, President Barack Obama's then chief of staff, was applicable to Berkeley, campus and city, in 2012. The University of California as it exists today is still very much a product of the "long boom" that saw the development of a number of new campuses and the consolidation of UC Berkeley's reputation as a public university of global reputation. The realities of a post-Great Recession world have understandably been slow to sink in. This is not to say that economic stringency will last forever, but that real recovery will not occur until the public sector undertakes the kind of fundamental restructuring that the private sector has undergone on a more regular basis since the end of the initial post-War boom in the early 1970s.

Although public support for higher education has ebbed and flowed in the decades since then, the University of California was largely insulated from it. Today, it is not — although California's recovery and higher taxes have eased the immediate crisis. US politicians prefer a crisis to "boil over" sufficiently to provide political cover for long-delayed action to acting in advance to forestall the crisis, which goes some way to explaining why the state, the university, and the city are pushing hard to restore their revenues through added taxation. Yet the real benefit of the crisis, which is to reconsider each of these institutions in a fundamental way — an act of imagination, not simply of political will — remains unfulfilled.

The University of California and the Berkeley campus have at least expressed a willingness to tackle the problem. How they will do so is not yet clear — understandably so, since it is not yet clear what will be required, even in the short run, as the state struggles to balance its budget. Still, the outline is visible. At the macro level, greater rationalization is needed among the three systems of higher education in the state, eliminating redundancy among facilities and programmes in order to preserve the most viable components and heighten their synergy. Across the board, there is a need to leverage resources far more effectively, to apply Buckminster Fuller's principle of "doing ever more with ever less". There is also pressure simply to do less — to focus the university on its strengths. Easily said, but Berkeley is comprehensively strong, so the debate about "less" often pits political and business priorities against academic and cultural ones.

Reforming a university is not for the fainthearted. At Berkeley, experiments in collaboration among departments still founder over jealousy and asserted prerogatives, despite an oft-stated commitment to it. As in previous eras, it will probably take a broader, transformative vision, imposed from above or without, to lift the university off the shoals of its current predicament and reposition it for the future. This is essentially what happened in the early 1960s, when the University of California took concrete steps to embrace the future as a public mega-university, with Berkeley as its flagship. The results would probably be unrecognizable to its planners, but they secured a pride of Nobel Laureates and a global reputation.

For its part, the City of Berkeley's situation is more like that of the healthcare "industry" in the region. After years and years of expansion and rising costs, healthcare providers have run into mounting resistance from the public and private sectors that ultimately fund them. To cope with falling revenues, insurers and providers initially penalized physicians and patients, starving the former of revenue and the latter of services. Today, however, insurers and providers are finally leveraging digital tools that are absolutely common in most of the private-sector economy. The City of Berkeley is belatedly showing signs of interest in doing the same thing, having first tried to maintain the status quo through myriad new fees and steadily diminishing services that it continued to provide in "customary" ways to preserve staff.

Campus Today

(*Source:* Archive of the Campus Planning Study Group, College of Environmental Design, University of California, Berkeley)

In our view, the Great Recession was really a turning point, an impossible-to-ignore signal that an era — the post-War era of US hegemony and California expansion and largesse — has ended. To revive and thrive, the campus and the community need to accept that the road to 2050 will be fundamentally different than the one that brought them through the post-War era to 2008. It is a challenge, but it is also a huge opportunity.

Three Mid-century Scenarios

Even today, it is possible to imagine Berkeley at mid-century. Forecasts are notoriously inaccurate, tending to overestimate current trends and underestimate the future's potential to surprise. A comparable forecast for 2012 would have been made in the early 1970s, around the time of the oil embargo. Reality reflects some of what might have been predicted for it, but a great deal was missed. To sidestep this dilemma, let us consider two scenarios, small and large.

Berkeley Small

In this scenario, the campus and the community accept the 2012 economy as the new base and begin to organize around it. The university reconsiders its size and its approach to education and research. With state funding no longer tied to enrolment, UC Berkeley targets the world's "best and brightest" students, ending or diluting its current role in helping to create a leadership meritocracy for California alone. Instead of being known as a leading public university, it is now considered as one of the world's leading research universities. Professional school enrolment shrinks significantly, and the undergraduate programmes are recast to compete directly with the top-tier private colleges, with little or no preference for in-state students. Emphasizing advanced research, the campus would shed its role as an R&D partner and training ground for industry. By 2050, campus enrolment would drop to a third of the current level — around 12,000 students. The campus would continue to modernize, mainly through renovation and reuse.

The community around the campus continues to grow "organically", with the downtown gaining modest density, but the residential districts largely maintaining their existing character. Buildings and settings that are seen as intrinsic to the city's sense of place are preserved. Growth is not proscribed, but it is no longer actively encouraged. Density targets set by regional government are resisted on the grounds that Berkeley already absorbs and houses a large student population, so it has already done its part.

Berkeley Small is about "less is more". Its antecedents include the preservation movement, opposed to growth "for growth's sake" and interested in preserving much of the existing fabric of the community, including the campus proper, to maintain a sense of continuity with the past and a sense of place that is closely identified with buildings and settings "of significance". It is less clear that the value placed on tradition would extend to redefining Berkeley as a smaller and essentially private institution, out of reach of many California families. By using some of the strategies outlined in the next scenario, the university could conceivably support higher enrolment without having to bulk up its programmes and facilities.

Berkeley Large

In this scenario, the campus and the community hitch their wagons to the global economy. The university expands on all fronts. Using new technologies and in response to worldwide demand, it transforms its curriculum and research programmes in an effort to offset diminished state funding. Financial aid is focused on the most promising students in need of it; everyone else pays full tuition. While advanced research is maintained, the bulk of university research addresses current federal, state, and industry priorities. The scale and diversity of this research attracts a sizeable cohort of enterprises that see it as a source of new products and talent, spawning an R&D corridor centred in Berkeley that stretches north and south. While the growth of jointly developed satellite campuses continues, the campus proper sees considerable new development, with the "park" redefined to take in specific open spaces and corridors, while other areas see historic and other older buildings removed to make room for larger ones better suited to current needs.

Meanwhile, the city follows through on its 2012 vision of a denser downtown and a "new and knowledge economy"-focused West Berkeley. Wholesale reform of transit infrastructure revives the city as a regional destination. Joint redevelopment of the main transit corridors increases their density, resulting in a much more urbanized city with a 2050 population of 200,000 people, including 50,000 UC Berkeley students. Smart growth policies, closely tied to regional government targets, anticipate 250,000 people by 2075.

Berkeley Large is about "more is more". Its precedents include the Smart Growth movement, which sees growth as inevitable and aims to accommodate it sustainably by adding density around transit hubs and limiting or prohibiting ex-urban sprawl. Another precedent is the mega-/multi-versity envisioned by California Governor Pat Brown and University of California President Clark Kerr during the state's post-War boom. Leveraging of technology, mobility, and synergy with the California State

University and Community College systems would thus be expected to support maximizing total enrolment at UC Berkeley, even if it simultaneously sought to mitigate its physical impact. More recently, the appearance of enormous tech campuses like Apple and Facebook, housing thousands of employees, reverses the trend of older tech companies to leverage mobility and technology to cut their real estate footprints. If this new trend takes hold, the campus might be expected to revive open-plan, studio-type settings — Wurster Hall is an example — because students expect them. Alternatively, these settings may find their way into the community, with the campus proper preserved for a different type of experience.

Berkeley Slow

The word *slow* reflects the influence of Slow Food and its offshoots, like the Slow City movement, on the Bay Region. Coined in opposition to the *fast* of fast food and mass tourism, the word suggests to us "careful, deliberate, and attentive to the nuances the local". It is about tempering the push and pull of these larger forces, whether global or regional, to preserve and foster the unique qualities of each community. Applied to the campus and the community, Slow seeks a middle ground that recognizes that both have unique qualities that warrant a more thoughtful and nuanced approach, responsive to the pressures of growth, but also determined to reinforce these qualities rather than sacrifice them. Berkeley Slow also recognizes that Berkeley is unique. As Michael Pollan puts it, "The University is so much bigger than the little islands of buildings that we think of it as." The same is true of the community: they both stretch out across the country and across the seas, cosmopolitan in spite of itself, with a corresponding impact.

In this scenario, UC Berkeley re-imagines the way that students, faculty, and staff interact and the places and spaces, real and virtual, where collegial interaction occurs. The idea is to leverage its human, physical, and technological resources more effectively to serve more students affordably and well. This may involve limiting their tenure on the campus, but it also focuses on making the on-campus experience richer. Whatever and whoever can be shifted to other institutions, to purpose-built learning and research centres (some potentially shared with the city), and to virtual learning.

The result is that while the campus grows, its growth is tempered by countervailing efforts to increase building utilization — a 24/7 campus — and limit its use to activities that uniquely benefit from it. So while the campus population reaches 50,000 students, they are accommodated in ways that limit their actual impact. Some density is added, some older buildings are removed and replaced, but the spirit of the campus as a park is preserved. New construction is reserved for truly new needs that cannot easily be met by the existing buildings.

Barriers to cooperation and joint development between the university and the city diminish. There is a mutual recognition that each benefits from the other, and that both have an obligation to live up to their importance and influence in the wider world. That resolve begins to guide how they think about their growth. The campus and community increasingly look for opportunities for shared use. The university joins forces with Berkeley High School and Berkeley City College to establish an East Bay Learning Commons that complements the Downtown Arts District now anchored by the Berkeley Art Museum and theatre. The revival of Telegraph Avenue, long identified as an important priority, is achieved through joint effort. People's Park becomes a shared open space, comparable to Live Oak Park in North Berkeley.

The city sensibly continues to emphasize transit-oriented development, but it helps push for regional reforms that link density with quality of life. More attention is paid to the role of the existing fabric in creating a sense of place and to the need to "build up" to the changes in density that occur around transit and transit corridors. By mid-century, the city has grown to 150,000 people. The downtown is thought of as a model of urbanity. Its neighbourhoods are recognizable as themselves, but new transit options have increased the density of their walkable commercial centres. The city looks better and works better.

A big part of that "working better" reflects the combined efforts by the campus and the community to secure the benefits of regional and statewide investment in transit infrastructure and in making the transition from private cars to a hybrid model that uses an array of strategies to reduce car trips and get people to walk, bike, and ride. Local transit, better attuned to its customers, replaces the cumbersome and underutilized bus routes of old. A fundamental rethinking of the street grid makes the city safe for bikers and pedestrians, while micro-cars and car-sharing hubs dramatically reduce the number of cars on streets. Moving goods follows transit's lead, aiming for low impact and convenience.

Classical vs. Rustic (Courtesy of Professor Richard Bender)

What the 2050 Scenarios Imply

These three scenarios have a degree of overlap in their aims and outcomes. We pose *Slow* to suggest the likelihood of a hybrid, partly unpredictable process — dialectal, perhaps — that moves towards a future that will not please all comers, but builds in enough deliberation, reconsideration, and recalibration to push the future of the campus and the community in a positive direction. Implicit in *slow* is a sense of the value of both as actual places with characteristics, such as the integration of communal open space and the fostering of a sense of community through a whole range of means that blur the boundaries of town and gown and maintain settings and features that have been in the picture almost from the start.

Today's concerns about the cost of higher education and the need to move it into the 21st century are skewing consideration of the university's future. The best analogy is probably to healthcare, which in the US is in the midst of a similar crisis of access and affordability. Both have lagged other sectors in leveraging technology. Doing so opens up new possibilities for using the campus more effectively, connecting it more seamlessly to the broader public education system in California, and making greater use of the resources, human and otherwise, within the University of California system itself.

The campus and the city both operate on the "long clock" that Stewart Brand described. The Berkeley campus has roots in both historic models of the university: Cambridge and Oxford on the one hand, and Bologna and Paris on the other. The city, brought into the 20th century by a remarkable cohort of activists that viewed their Athens as a people's democracy, also looks back at a much older tradition. Both stress the importance of supporting the community. Neither precludes integrating the innovations of modern life, but the people and settings that uniquely define them take precedence.

The university and the city have clear reasons to restructure, but if they do not rethink how they interact with and support their constituent communities, it will not make much difference. *Place* — the collectivity of buildings, settings, and connecting elements that the university and the city encompass and share — is essential. Most people think of place as "hardware", but it engenders the "soft" activities that fall outside the planner's calculus. A useful planner's word here is *armature*, which considers place as occasioning activities over time that are increasingly hard, even impossible, to predict. The useful life of a given place before some kind of intervention is required is determined by its innate openness to this unfolding.

As the flagship campus of one of the world's leading public universities, UC Berkeley has a responsibility to redefine for a new century the land grant tradition of public universities of which it is part. That idea, now 150 years old, retains at outsized importance, as exemplified by Cornell University's development of a second campus in New York City to serve one of the economic engines of the state, region, and nation. Along with it is the willingness of major universities, public and private, to share course content with the whole world, giving institutions and individual scholars and researchers across the planet online access to world-class curricula and teaching. Finally, prodded by current limits of public support, there is a desire to reform and streamline the streams of public and private education across the state. Cornell, which is both a private university and a public land-grant university, suggests a possible model for UC Berkeley.

Campus in the Region (Courtesy of Professor Richard Bender)

The campus is still best understood as a real place. Despite the attractions of online learning, everyone recognizes that time spent with a cohort of fellow students has intrinsic value. Graduates from the 1970s, visiting the campus, note that the language lab is gone and students gather in wireless-equipped cafés and other gathering places. They see, however, that there are still seminar rooms, studios for hands-on work, and places for lectures and concerts — opportunities to see and hear campus and visiting luminaries as real people. Much of what happens on campus is not really new, but the changes that have occurred, particularly in the way information is conveyed, has made some settings obsolete.

The Road to 2050

The CPSG explained the campus to a new generation. A similar impulse has guided successive LRDPs. The implementers rarely get everything right, but they manage to avoid the worst missteps of their predecessors. As this suggests, the university is further down this path than the city. A comparable understanding of its districts and neighbourhoods and, at another scale, its regional context and connections would, if it reflected broad agreement and shared understanding, help set the terms for discussion and decision-making about the city's future as a place. Right now, that's missing.

Planning a campus or a city has a strong and necessary element of stewardship. This is probably more honoured at UC Berkeley than within the Berkeley city government, but then the city's critics are almost exclusively focused on preservation, providing a check that may eventually lead to a better balance. The role of steward is to find a way forward that reconciles complex and often contradictory motives for growth and preservation. It comes down to keeping tradition in view while asking, again and again, how best to maintain tradition given changing needs, problems, and constituents. Part of being a steward is simply to pose the questions, "Is this really worth doing?" and "Isn't there a better way?"

The university is a better steward than the city because it has a longer institutional memory and less pressure, or fewer incentives, to embrace change for short-term, sometimes self-interested reasons. It also moves slowly, which gives it more time to reflect on the desirability of the "big ideas" in plans that need time to temper and improve. While the university's partnership with the city is a pragmatic one, not universally welcomed by the city or its citizens, it reflects a basic truth about their shared role and fate: they constitute a single community — and a unique one in the eyes of the world — like a univer-city.

The work of the CPSG a generation ago is a useful precedent for a planning process that lets the university and city find shared common ground with each other and with their respective constituents. Making use of Berkeley's district-based government, the two could sponsor an analogous effort to understand and do an inventory of the existing conditions of the districts and neighbourhoods, pointing to strengths, weaknesses, opportunities, and threats. Like CPSG's initial groundwork on the campus, the results of these efforts would be less of a plan for the future and more of a consensus about the broad framework within which such plans would unfold. Plans have a way of being subsumed by the immediate interests of politicians and organized "neighbours". Calling the effort a study and focusing on understanding the elements and how they add up to a framework would help to avoid this outcome.

We believe that the university is better positioned than the city to lead this process. Moreover, its involvement in spearheading it would acknowledge their mutual dependence — the extent to which the failure of either one to sustain itself and thrive would constitute a growing disaster for the other. The university would have to overcome lingering suspicion of its motives within the community, but it is the senior partner in the relationship, with greater resources and more staying power.

What we are proposing is really a new study group — an ongoing commitment to engage the community. We believe this will be better received and have a more lasting impact than a study or a plan on its own. Ideally, the study group's focus would include the campus itself as a district of the city. That way, the 2030, 2040, and 2050 LRDPs will be the plans not only of the university, but also increasingly of the city it shares. That way, any and all plans that these intertwining two communities make will reflect a collective sense of what matters — of the qualities of place, broadly understood, that are intrinsic, vital, valued, preserved and enhanced.

The redevelopment of Lower Sproul Plaza as envisioned in master planning. The project will activate a key place on the south edge of campus where town meets gown. John Eshleman Hall and additions to Martin Luther King, Jr. Student Union designed by Moore Ruble Yudell Architects and Planners. (Courtesy of Moore Ruble Yudell Architects and Planners)

About the Authors

Richard Bender is Professor of Architecture and Dean of the College of Environmental Design emeritus at the University of California, Berkeley.

Emily Marthinsen is Assistant Vice-Chancellor for Physical & Environmental Planning at UC Berkeley. **John Parman** is an editorial adviser and contributor to *Architect's Newspaper* and a member of the *Project Review Committee at SPUR* in San Francisco.

CHAPTER FOUR

CAMBRIDGE: BEYOND THE UNIVER-CITY

PETER CAROLIN

The form or idea of the univer-city can be interpreted in many ways. It might be a city that happens to contain one or more universities in it; or a relatively new city in which, by design, a university occupies a strategic location; or an older city in which academia, business and local government work together for the greater social, civic and economic good. There are many variations. This chapter shows how the last variation, collaborative action, is working in Cambridge. But to appreciate why this has come about one has to understand something about the unusual organizational and physical form of the University of Cambridge and its relation to its host city.

A Relationship Shaped by History

Cambridge, like Oxford, is a collegiate university. The University has at present thirty-one constituent colleges, each of which is an independent financial and administrative entity. Every student and most of the faculty are members of one of these multi-disciplinary colleges. Formal teaching is conducted on University premises, informal in colleges which also provide living accommodation, meals and social facilities. There is intense rivalry between colleges striving to attract the best students and faculty.

Since its foundation in 1209, the gradual, 805-year long development of the University and its colleges has meant that University and city buildings have become inextricably mixed. Two centuries after its foundation, during the dissolution of the monasteries, many of the town's religious houses, with their inward-looking court buildings, were taken over as new colleges for the University, further strengthening this haphazard physical integration. Indeed, until this century, there has been only one attempt to consider the formal physical relationship between university and city — Nicholas Hawksmoor's 1712 plan for Cambridge (he did one for

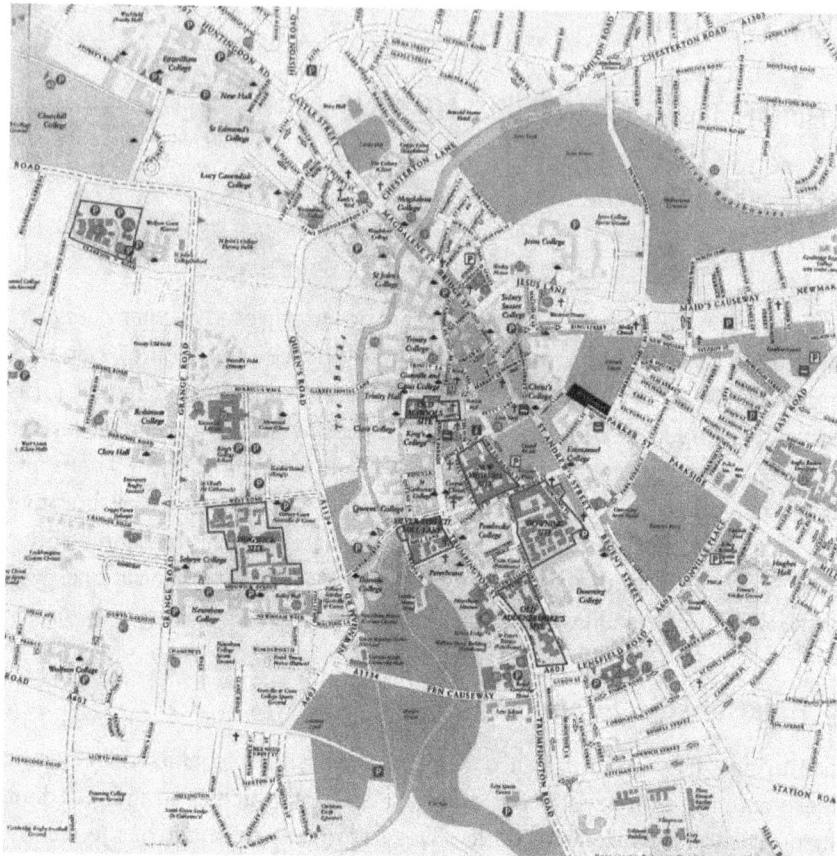

Fig. 4.1 Cambridge has no campus. The University and its colleges are scattered throughout the city. *University of Cambridge Official Map* 4th ed. © Cambridge University Press and the University of Cambridge Computing Service. Adapted and reproduced with permission.

Oxford, too).[1] This would have sited the principal buildings of both institutions around a forum of positively Roman grandeur and ordered the city with gateways, axes, monuments and vistas of a totally un-English character. Sadly, no one had commissioned Hawksmoor (one of England's greatest architects) and nothing came of his proposal. So the new city quarter currently under construction, North West Cambridge, will be the first example of deliberately planned university/city integration — initiated, developed and managed by the University.[2]

Thus, instead of an easily identifiable campus, the University and colleges of Cambridge are scattered all over the western half of the city (Fig. 4.1).

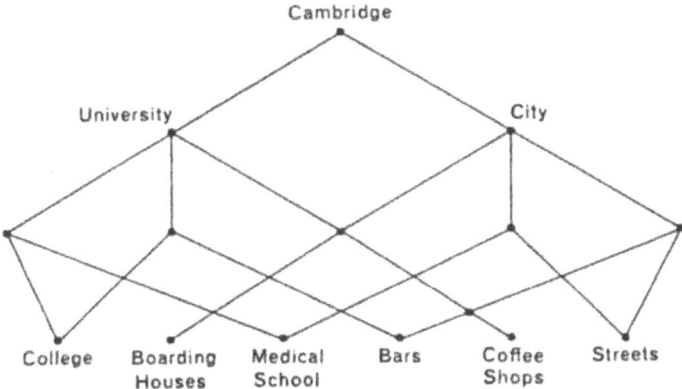

Fig. 4.2 Christopher Alexander's semi-lattice diagram, based on Cambridge, demonstrates the interconnectedness of university and city. Courtesy *Design*

Just how this combines to form a single entity was elegantly encapsulated almost 50 years ago by the Berkeley academic Christopher Alexander. In a diagram for his ground-breaking essay, "A city is not a tree",[3] he drew on his undergraduate experience in Cambridge, to show how, in contrast to a campus university, the University of Cambridge is physically embedded into its host city (Fig. 4.2). The bottom line of his diagram was based on his daily walk (or cycle ride) from his College, Trinity, past the student lodging houses, the city hospital, bars and coffee-shops along his route to the architecture school. The lattice above the bottom line showed the many links between these places and how they combine into the university city of Cambridge. Alexander's diagram was, of course, highly simplified — and Cambridge has changed since. The boarding houses have been amalgamated into large college-run courts or hostels, there are far more bars and coffee-shops and the old city hospital (relocated to the outskirts alongside a large bio-medical campus) is now occupied by the University management school. There are also new campuses for the arts and the sciences but there is still no university campus in the traditional, North American, sense.

Disagreements and Dialogue

The physical proximity of university and city might suggest good relations and a high degree of collaboration. But, until recently, this has not been the case. Cambridge, which was only granted city status in 1951, is quite small (its current population is less than 100,000 if you discount the 25,000 students) and, although a significant trading centre in mediaeval times, it was, for many of the successive centuries, no more than a market town heavily dependent on agriculture. With no nearby coal or iron ore, the industrial revolution which might have made the city wealthy passed Cambridge by. The only local concentration of wealth was in the University and its constituent colleges — it was they and not the city who dominated the scene. They even had their own Parliamentary representative and, in the form of Cambridge University Press (founded in 1584), the university sponsored the largest and oldest manufacturing business in the city — publishing the fruits of scholarship.

Over the centuries, there were plenty of squabbles between the University and civic authorities but these did not generally relate to issues affecting the physical development of the University. The 1948 Town and Country Planning Act changed all that. For the first time, local government development plans had to be approved by central government and land owners' building proposals had to be approved by the local authority. No longer could the University build where it wanted. Nor could the colleges — many of which were major landowners in their own right. So profound were the disagreements that in 1962 the University proposed its own plan for Cambridge[4] (Fig. 4.3). It was rejected, although the suggestion that a regional shopping centre should be constructed away from the historic centre was accepted. A while later, IBM, wishing to develop close links with university research, applied to build its European research centre in Cambridge. The proposal did not comply with the development plan and was rejected. By then small start-up companies were being spun-out from University science departments — the start of the "Cambridge Phenomenon".[5] IBM's rejection stirred the University into action and, following an extensive review, it, together with one of the colleges, persuaded the local authority to allow the establishment, in 1973, of the UK's first science park. Over the years, as the Phenomenon developed, more such parks have followed, often located beyond the city boundary.

Another significant disagreement on planning policy occurred in 1994 when the University sought to develop a new science campus on

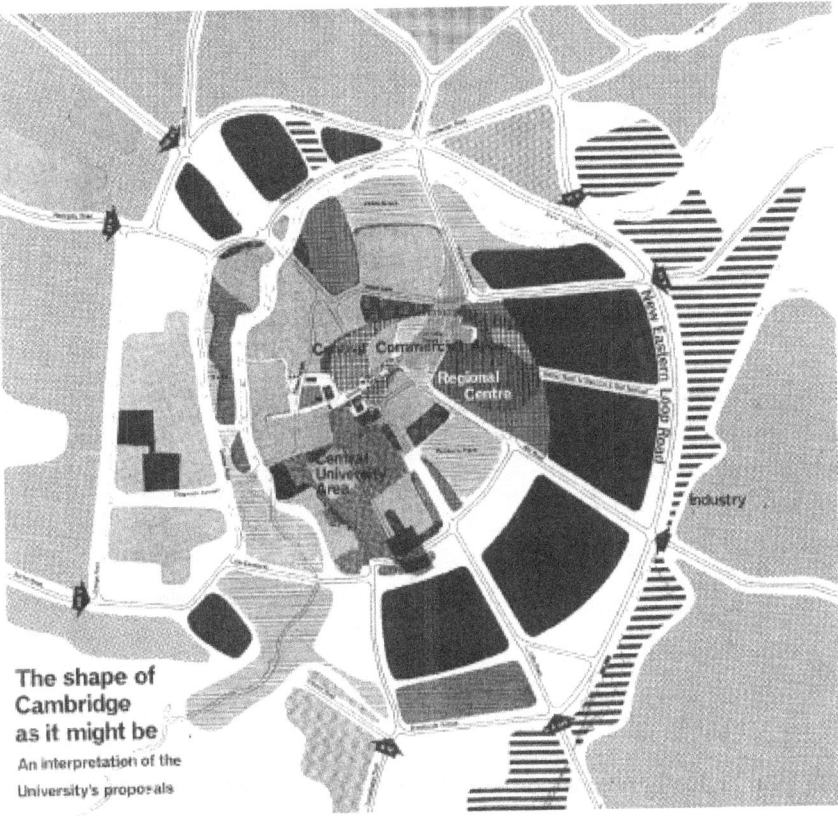

Fig. 4.3 The University's 1962 plan for Cambridge proposed creating a new regional shopping centre and a new eastern loop road. The former was implemented, the latter was never completed.

what is now the West Cambridge site. The city was initially against the proposal and only approved it on condition that the density was very low — a requirement now widely agreed to have been a mistake. It was the unsatisfactory confrontational nature of the University/city negotiations surrounding this project that provided the spur for the initiation of Cambridge Futures in 1996 (Fig. 4.4). The Futures project was fully described in the first volume in this series, *Univer-Cities: Strategic Implications for Asia: Readings from Cambridge and Berkeley to Singapore*.[6] Suffice it to say here that this was the first time that the

Fig. 4.4 Cambridge Futures logo. This town/gown collaboration heavily influenced the current expansion of the city.

local academic, business and government communities had combined to consider — in a non-confrontational context and with the aid of a University research project — possible forms for the area's future land use and transport systems. Initiated at a time of growing public and political antagonism to the "growth agenda", it transformed opinion and led to the development of the growth-led structure (development) plan in 2003.[7]

A Gradual Loss of Focus

Implementation of development plans in the UK is a complex, time-consuming business involving many authorities and stakeholders. But by the time the worldwide economic crisis broke in 2008, much had been accomplished on the planning side and there was enough evidence on the ground to generate concern among city residents about the impact on their neighbourhoods. In one sense this had been foreseen in an important component of the Cambridge Futures project — a survey of local residents' reactions to the seven options studied.[8] Overall, the survey revealed strong support for the growth agenda but close inspection of the results indicated that respondents tended to support those options which were unlikely to affect their own neighbourhood. The NIMBY — or not-in-my-back-yard — factor was present. By 2008 this had resulted in the revival of existing residents' associations, the creation of new ones and their combination under the umbrella of the Federation of Cambridge

Residents' Associations (FeCRA). Even more significantly, the long dormant Cambridge Preservation Society found a new lease of life and was steadily moving towards its rebranding as Cambridge Past Present and Future (CPPF).[9]

By 2009 there were two contradictory tendencies in evidence. On the one hand there were those who rejected the growth agenda while, on the other, there were those who felt that not enough was being done to explain planning policies and monitor their implementation. Among the latter were academics, businessmen and even environmental campaigners who felt that there was no clear vision of the kind of area to which the community aspired in, say, twenty to thirty years time. This was a view rejected by the planners and politicians who had drawn up and approved the 2003 structure plan and the related local plan and were now implementing it. Unfortunately, the documentation describing such plans typically consist of endless words and, once approved, tends to get lost to public view.

A feature in a local professional journal reported on this situation and asked:

> Is it not time that we combined as a community to consider the context in which we shall be living in two or three decades, decide how we should address this and what we should start doing now to achieve these objectives? This task could be undertaken in the same non-confrontational, inclusive manner as Cambridge Futures [...] Central to any study would be firmly establishing the idea of the city-region [...].

On publication, the feature, rather unwisely titled *"Time to wise up"* and rather provocatively presented,[10] attracted headlines in the local paper and fury from some planners and politicians.[11] But it attracted the interest of CPPF, an organization whose aim "is to champion the protection and enjoyment of green open spaces and the sustainable development of the city and its surroundings [and wants] to see Cambridge continue to prosper and grow both economically and socially". After the briefest of discussions CPPF agreed to support the study which became known as the 2030 Vision for the Cambridge sub-region.

The Sub-Region

At this point, we must, once more, look back at the history, albeit recent, of Cambridge.

The city of Cambridge changed remarkably little during the last half of the 20th century. This was because the 1952 Development Plan established a policy of constraint rather than growth. Unlike London or Liverpool, Plymouth or Coventry, Cambridge suffered almost no bomb damage during World War II — reconstruction was not needed. Indeed, the very reverse was proposed: Cambridge was not to suffer the fate of Oxford, where, before and during the war, large factories had been built. Instead, the Development Plan proposed that it should be preserved as a mainly university town, free from polluting industry and unrestricted expansion. The city's population was to be limited to 100,000 and a Green Belt, an area of open country where new development was forbidden, was to be drawn around the city, preserving its rural setting (Fig. 4.5).

In one way, this policy worked. By the mid-1990s, the city's population had only increased by some 9,500. But, beyond the Green Belt, the population of the villages and small market towns dispersed around the region had considerably expanded. The numbers of those working in the city but living outside it had almost quadrupled, creating serious rush-hour and parking problems. The Development Plan constraints affected not only housing but workplaces as well. New research and light industrial activity, much with close links to university research, clustered in science parks beyond the Green Belt.[12]

Recognizing the fact that the city and surrounding area had developed into a single economic entity, the Cambridge Futures study had focused its research on the area within, roughly, a 25-mile radius of the city. This approach was incorporated into the subsequent Structure Plan and the area is now known as the Cambridge Sub-region. However, old structures and habits continue — the sub-region is still administered by several local authorities and city and country folk tend to consider themselves different to each other. City folk fight against any erosion of the Green Belt, country folk against village

Cambridge: Beyond the Univer-City

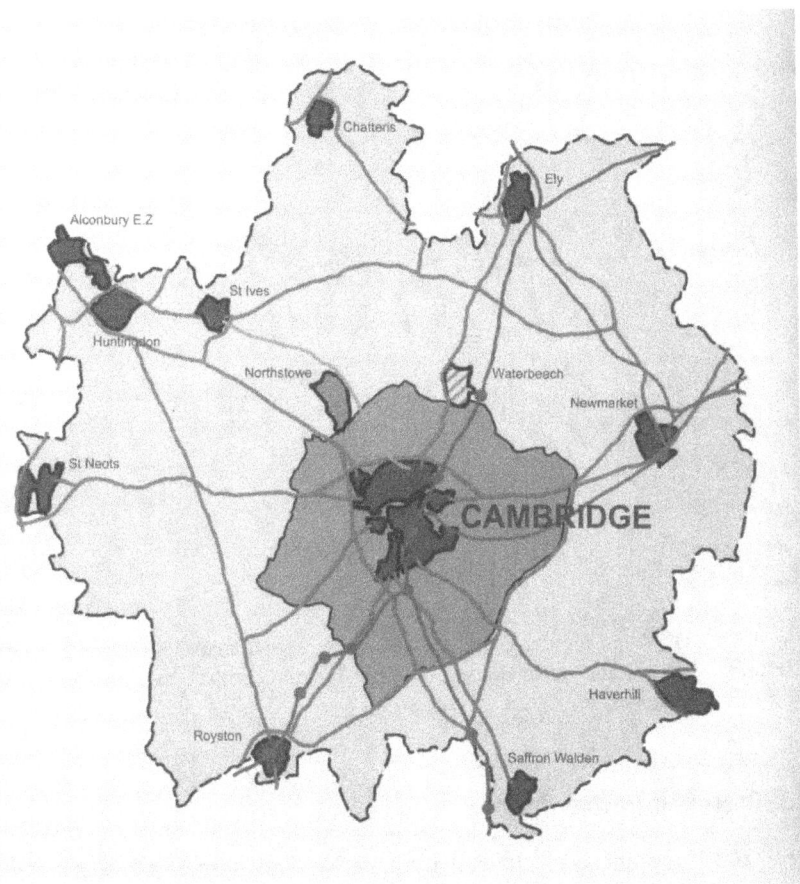

Fig 4.5 The Cambridge sub-region. The darker area around the city of Cambridge is the Green Belt in which development has been very heavily restricted for over 50 years.

expansion — both acknowledging but resisting the pressure for additional housing. The idea that a better future might lie in accepting the interdependence of the two and working to exploit the economic, social and scenic potential of the city-region is not common, let alone popular. When people talk of Cambridge, they almost always mean the city. We hoped that the 2030 project might go some way to changing this mind-set (Fig. 4.6).

Fig. 4.6 2030 Vision for the Cambridge Sub-region report cover. Less ambitious than Cambridge Futures and minimally resourced, this recent project has provoked further town/gown initiatives.

2030: Reviving the debate

The 2030 project was chaired by a retired academic, a historian (and former Deputy Vice Chancellor of the University)[13] and co-directed by two other retirees — a particle physicist (chairman of CPPF's planning committee)[14] and an architect (myself). A small steering committee acted as a sounding board. Our aims were simple:

- To bring together local people with a desire to influence the future shape of the sub-region
- To reach conclusions that could inform policy, enhance the local quality of life and help increase the area's contribution to the national economy
- To create connections that would act as drivers for change

Central to the project was the idea that rational decisions about the future of the sub-region can only be made by looking at the area as a whole.

We selected ten topics :

- economics and technology
- housing
- education and skills
- business and retail
- agriculture and green spaces
- land use
- social cohesion
- culture, leisure and sport
- transport
- energy, water and waste

and agreed to cover five topics a year over two years. Health was not included because a similar group[15] was covering it and housing was focused almost entirely on matters of energy use (although housing location was considered in the land-use workshops). A chance encounter with an airport executive resulted in the promise of £20,000 over two years to fund the project (the money coming from a proportion of public car park operating profits allocated to social uses). This funding, together with a small private donation, covered all our expenses, ranging from venue hire and catering to report and video production. All our events were held in the University's Centre for Mathematical Sciences and promotion and organizational support was provided by CPPF.

Each of the ten topics was explored in two "workshop" sessions. The first was an afternoon event at which three or four experts would talk to an invited group of about twenty-five "informed" persons from the academic, business and local government communities. A one-page summary of the outcome would be posted on the website within a week. The second workshop would take place in the evening a few weeks later and was open to all comers. Besides the general public, local politicians and local government officers frequently attended and FeCRA assisted in promoting events and facilitating syndicates. Following this second session, the one-page summary was modified and re-posted on the web. It was the intention, on completion of the workshops, to synthesize the ten summaries into a single vision. Over 600 persons attended our workshops[16] and, in addition, we organized three extra and highly productive workshops for sixth form students. Our one regret was that, for logistical reasons, we were unable to attract more out-of-Cambridge participants to the second workshops.

Looking Ahead

This is not the place for a detailed account of the findings of the 2030 project. These can be found at <www.2030vision.org> together with a link to a short You Tube video compiled in order to make the findings available to a wider (and younger) audience.[17] Although it is too early to ascertain the long-term impact of the study it is possible to report on some of the benefits so far identified. First, the "expert" workshops brought together people who would not otherwise have met: the forging of new links between business and secondary education has been one outcome. Second, at a time when local authorities are under extreme financial pressure, the project helped fill a gap in the "visioning" process. Third, one workshop in particular — on business and retail — brought together an exceptionally high-powered group of participants and has led to the formation of Cambridge Ahead (CA) — "a business and academic member group dedicated to the successful growth of Cambridge and its region in the long term" with the vision for it to be "the pre-eminent, small city in the world". The organization was launched in November 2013 and details may be found at <www.cambridgeahead.co.uk>.

To an outsider it must seem strange that Cambridge should need an organisation like CA. Should it not have one already? The answer is that there have been business/local authority groups in the past. Indeed, some still exist but these were responses to a different economic and political climate. There were three key drivers for setting up CA. First, Cambridge's economic base has spread beyond the city boundary into the surrounding area which is administered by no less than three local authorities, whose interests and politics do not always coincide. A single organization is needed to present the case for local business. Second, the changing way in which the nation is administered makes it essential that the wealth-creators in any region speak swiftly and with one voice to central government. Third, these same highly-motivated wealth-creators need to combine and explore alternative "what if" scenarios free of the political and funding constraints imposed on such exercises when undertaken by local (or national) government. Intriguingly, one of CA's first tasks is to explore and evaluate possible new physical planning scenarios, using University research resources and Cambridge Futures' software.

The initiative behind the setting up of CA came from the business community but senior members of both universities in the city — the older, University of Cambridge, and the newer, Anglia Ruskin University — are also heavily involved. This is a remarkable turnaround in a city where the "town/gown" divide used to be famous. It still exists, but much less so. One of the benefits of a small city is that it's easy for people to meet and talk. And one of the benefits of the older University is the extra-ordinary freedom allowed to senior (and even retired) members to set up projects like Cambridge Futures and 2030 Vision, invoking the name of the University and bringing together citizens to discuss, in a non-confrontational context, matters of common concern.

The Univer-City-Region

History, as this survey makes clear, weighs heavy on Cambridge — its form the result of its mediaeval origins, its scale a relic of its non-industrial past and the planning constraints (intended to retain its historic character, rural setting and small size) imposed in the 1950s. At the same time, the impact of the Cambridge Phenomenon has been profound — with many new "Cambridge" firms locating in the surrounding, largely agricultural, sub-region. Just as the University and colleges are hidden in the city, so are the premises of the high-tech clusters of the Phenomenon dispersed, half-hidden, in the surrounding countryside — the so-called Silicon Fen (Fig. 4.7). Just as tourists find it impossible to find the "university campus" — so do

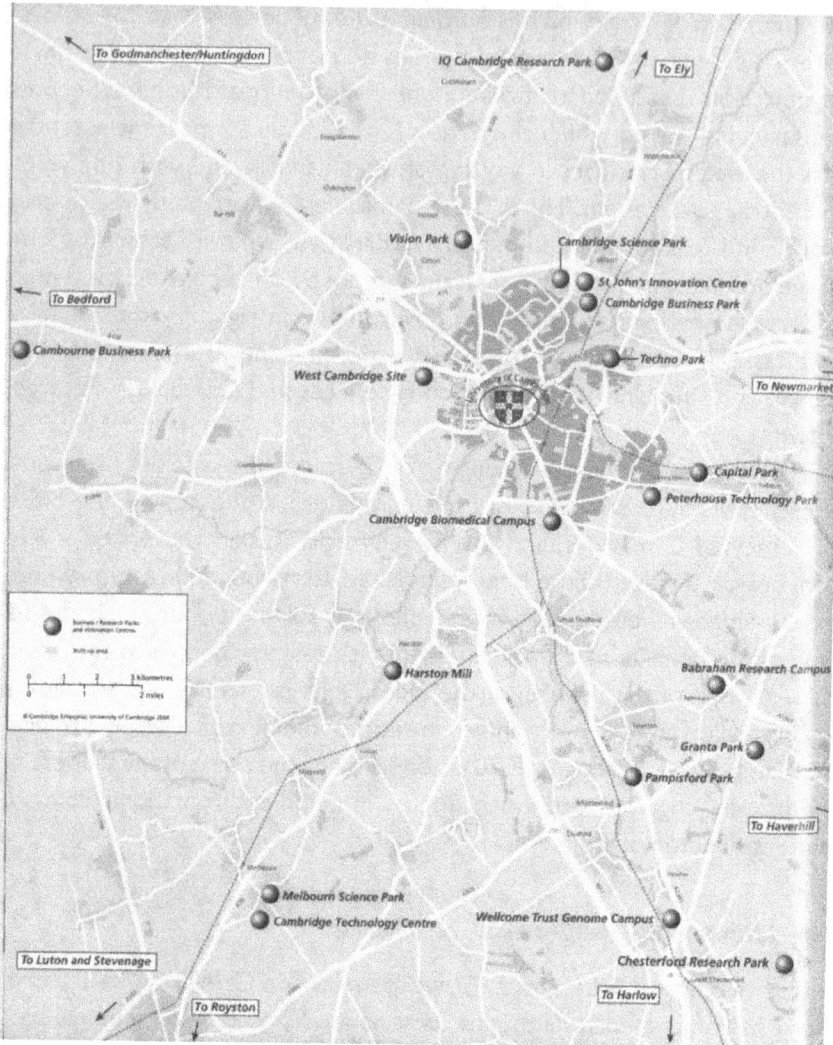

Fig. 4.7 Silicon Fen. Many research parks and innovation centres are located on the city periphery but even more are hidden in the surrounding countryside. *Courtesy Cambridge Enterprise*

visiting businessmen find it difficult to locate one of the largest clusters of high-tech research and industry in Europe. The two are totally interdependent. It is time to think and speak of "Cambridge" in a different way and to plan, promote and manage it accordingly — as a univer-city-region.

Notes

1. D. Roberts (1955), *The town of Cambridge as it ought to be reformed: The Plan of Nicholas Hawksmoor interpreted in an essay by David Roberts, and a set of eight drawings by Gordon Cullen* (Cambridge: Cambridge University Press).
2. <www.nwcambridge.co.uk>
3. C. Alexander (1966), "A city is not a tree" in Design 206, February, pp. 46–55.
4. This plan was never published in full but see *Cambridge Opinion 30: The Planning of an Old Town*, 1962 and P. Carolin (2013), "Shaping Modern Cambridge" in *Scroope: Cambridge Architectural Journal* 22, pp. 110–119.
5. K. Kirk and C. Cotton (2012), *The Cambridge Phenomenon: 50 Years of Innovation and Enterprise* (London: Third Millennium Publishing).
6. P. Carolin (2013), "Cambridge Futures: Enabling Consensus on Growth and Change" in A.S.C. Teo, ed., *Univer-Cities: Strategic Implications for Asia: Readings from Cambridge and Berkeley to Singapore* (Singapore, World Scientific Publishing), pp. 23–50.
7. Cambridgeshire County Council (2003), *Cambridgeshire and Peterborough Structure Plan*.
8. Cambridge Architectural Research Ltd. and Cambridge Media Lab 1999, *Cambridge Futures Survey Report*.
9. See <www.cambridgeppf.org>
10. P. Carolin (2009), "Time to wise up" in *Cambridge Architecture Gazette* 59, Autumn/Winter, pp. 3–5.
11. P. Carolin (2010), Time to move on in *Cambridge Architecture Gazette* 60, Spring/summer, p. 3.
12. Such dispersal runs right against the 3-D formula of urban density, shortened distances and removed divisions promoted in the World Bank's 2009 World Development Report Reshaping Economic Geography.
13. Dr Gordon Johnson, Chapter 11 in this volume.
14. Professor Peter Landshoff.
15. <www.cambridgenetwork.co.uk/events/cambridge-network-events/policy-fen-group>
16. A list of the 170 organizations associated with individual participants is given in the 2030 report.

17. One of the primary objectives of the video was to demonstrate — for the first time in media available to the public — the location of the Green Belt and the extent of the Cambridge Sub-Region.

About the Author

Peter Carolin is Emeritus Professor of Architecture at the University of Cambridge where he was Head of the Department of Architecture 1989–2000.

CHAPTER FIVE

UNIVERSITI KEBANGSAAN MALAYSIA (UKM): EAST-WEST VIEWS OF UNIVER-CITIES — UKM WITH BANGI, KUALA LUMPUR AND TIGER MALAYSIA

SHARIFAH HAPSAH SYED HASAN SHAHABUDIN

Introduction

This chapter aims to provide an interpretation of the title "East-West Views of Univer-Cities — UKM with Bangi, Kuala Lumpur and Tiger Malaysia". I begin with a brief description of the context in which UKM is situated as a univer-city, followed by UKM's responses to national aspirations, and some examples of its contributions.

Physical Context: Campus within a Mega Region

UKM is located in the Bernam-Linggi Mega Region where it has three campuses, the main one in Bangi in the south and the other two are in Kuala Lumpur, the capital city. UKM's total land bank is 1,219.35 hectares or 3,013 acres. When UKM was constructed in Bangi in the mid-1970s, its surroundings were agricultural land, villages, settlements of indigenous people and secondary jungle. With industrialization which started about the time UKM was established in 1970, the population grew very rapidly with massive rural-urban migration to industrial centres and new towns. By 2009, housing projects initially built for staff of UKM, schools and other educational institutions, health facilities, transportation, recreation and other supporting social infrastructures, and amenities took shape and grew to merge with those expanding from Kuala Lumpur. Soon Kuala Lumpur was extended to Port Klang on the coast, Seremban to the south, encompassing Bangi, the Putrajaya Administrative capital,

Cyber City and the Kuala Lumpur International Airport. To the north is the Bernam basin where the national car industry, Proton and Kancil are situated.

The Bangi campus is 2,689 acres with the Langat River as its northern boundary, the North-South Highway on its western border and housing estates and other educational institutions all around it. Today, it has a commuter station named after it on the northeastern corner. Along the Langat River are situated the green technology park and business incubators, which are accessible to industry and investors. UKM has dedicated 100 acres of permanent forest as the green lung, 25 acres for a herbarium and fernarium and 120 acres for golf and other sports facilities. The built-up area consists of administration buildings, 13 faculties and 12 research institutes. The Permata School for the Gifted and Talented is also situated on the main campus. Still under development is the research and innovation cluster.

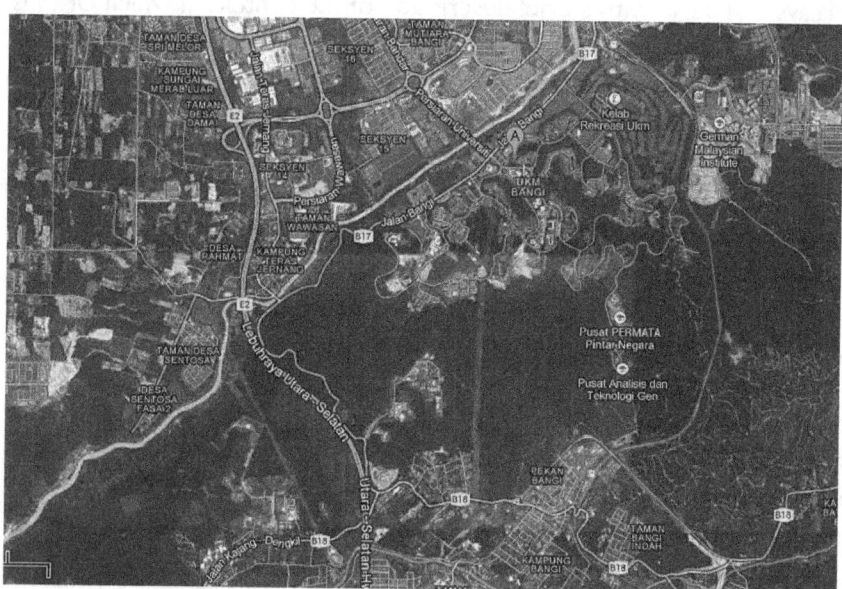

UKM Main Campus, Bangi. Reproduced with permission.

The Cheras medical centre campus in Kuala Lumpur is also ringed by the city. Nearing completion are the Institute for Research in Medical

Molecular Biology and the 21-storey complex for the integrated medical curriculum and multi-disciplinary research. Work has started on the first Specialist Children's Hospital in the country. Recently, the government granted more land to the Cheras campus. Being in the capital city, there is great opportunity to plan for a univer-city.

The Kuala Lumpur campus houses the Faculties of Dentistry, Pharmacy and Health Sciences.

Socio-Economic Context: Towards Vision 2020 as Tiger Malaysia

In 1990, after 20 years of industrialization, the government articulated Vision 2020, an ambitious journey to steer middle-income Malaysia to becoming a developed nation by 2020. Towards this end, access to higher education was expanded through private transnational education and the expansion of public universities. By 2006, the government recognized the "significant relationship between economic growth and R&D activities in higher education institutions". Research universities were created and UKM was one of the universities selected.

In 2010, a frank appraisal revealed that Malaysia was caught in the middle income trap and Vision 2020 may remain a dream. The New Economic Model or NEM was unveiled and an ambitious National Transformation Programme was initiated to bridge income gaps and accelerate Malaysia's progress towards Vision 2020.

New Economic Model (NEM)

The New Economic Model (NEM) is designed to raise per capita income to US$15,000 per capita by boosting growth, creating high paying jobs and attracting investments. It is an inclusive economy, where no one should be left out and all communities should benefit from the wealth of the country. It is a sustainable economy where development activities will not compromise future generations. The ultimate outcome is a better quality of life for the people. In this NEM, universities play a major role in strengthening the innovation culture that contributes to the nation's economic growth.

National Transformation Programme (NTP)

Accompanying the NEM is the National Transformation Programme (NTP), with the overarching goal of achieving economic progress while preserving unity. The four transformation initiatives are:

(a) Government Transformation Programme or GTP
(b) Economic Transformation Programme or ETP
(c) Social Transformation Programme or STP to ensure that all communities benefit from the NTP and
(d) Political Transformation Programme or PTP to pave the way for a modern and progressive Malaysia with a mature and respected democracy. Education, research and innovation are fundamental processes in the transformation

UKM's Responses to National Aspirations

What is UKM's response? How does it change from being a teaching university founded on 18 May 1970 to a research university that is supposed to fulfill the national aspiration of becoming a developed nation?

Historically, UKM is a bottom-up or people's university, born out of the aspirations of the nationalists, the Malay Rulers and the ordinary people to promote the national language, Malay or Bahasa Melayu, as an academic language. *Kebangsaan* in the university's name, Universiti Kebangsaan Malaysia, means national. Until today, UKM is the only national university in the country. Even when it was elevated to research university status in 2006, UKM did not lose sight of its national mission and moral obligation to produce, protect and inculcate the idea of national self-knowledge or culture and values, with a common national language as the unifying force for the nation. Engaging with society and environmental protection are approaches for sustainability that complement the research and teaching functions.

UKM is a comprehensive research university. In the main campus, disciplines range from engineering and technology to the natural sciences, social sciences and humanities. Medicine and health sciences are offered in the campuses in Kuala Lumpur.

Its academic staff total 2,247, of whom 60 per cent are young faculty and researchers working alongside 10 per cent professors and 16 per cent associate professors. As of October 2013, the total full-time student enrolment was 19,909 out of which 10,165 or 51.2 per cent were post-graduates. Of the postgraduates, 35.7 per cent were enrolled at doctoral level. About one quarter or 19.6 per cent of postgraduates are international students, 64.5 per cent of whom are in doctoral programmes.

In fulfilling the national aspiration, building a Knowledge Eco-system is quintessential. Lessons are gleaned from approaches used by successful companies in emerging markets. Focus, interdisciplinary approach and effective delivery were three approaches that were adopted. The practice of working in disciplinary silos was revamped by focusing on twelve interdisciplinary research areas that support the National Transformation Initiatives. These areas include challenges in building a nation state with its expanded areas in education and civilization; rural transformation; politics and security; economics, business and finance; climate change, sustainable development and renewable energy; biodiversity and biotechnology; nanotechnology and advanced materials; health and medical technology and visual informatics. Driver projects that propel the national and international missions in a balanced way were selected to raise the research profile at the global level while promoting national agenda issues such as the Malay language, national identity and culture. Procedures were revamped to develop an efficient delivery system which enhances quality for its three core missions of education, research and service. A machinery to monitor the transformation process was also established.

A crucial strategy was to adopt the fundamental concept that UKM is an integral part of an innovation system, working together with other partners to fuel Malaysia's socio-economic development. UKM's significant role is in generating innovations that can bring sustainable financial and social returns for the institution, the region and the nation. This is done by unlocking the potential of its assets to produce a new talent pool, create innovative technology from its intellectual property and bringing them to the marketplace as well as to transfer knowledge to benefit communities. In the process, UKM also creates jobs.

UKM's Contributions

In producing a new talent pool, building an innovation and entrepreneurship culture in the university is crucial. This is done by integrating education with research and commercialization at both the undergraduate and postgraduate levels. The model used is called technogenesis, developed by UKM's collaborating partner, Stevens Institute of Technology, New Jersey. In this model, faculty and students are incentivized in an enriched learning environment as they bring research inventions and services to the marketplace, define solutions to technical challenges, develop marketable solutions for Small and Medium Enterprises (SMEs), and develop rewarding research partnerships with business and industry. A two-credit module is compulsory for first-year students to make them aware from the very beginning that creating their own jobs through entrepreneurship is a good alternative to seeking employment in a world of job scarcity. To date, students have graduated with the confidence and ability to grow and launch more than 100 companies. UKM becomes a source of innovative and entrepreneurial graduates for the new economy.

Another outcome of the technogenesis model is the development of start-up companies, which are crucial to vitalize the economy and create jobs. UKM has established 33 start-up technology-based companies using intellectual property arising from its research. An accelerator programme has been initiated to upscale the companies faster and to take them global.

An important contribution of UKM is the education for the gifted and talented called the Permata Pintar programme. Through this programme, conducted in collaboration with Johns Hopkins University Centre for Talented Youth, gifted students who would otherwise be neglected by the school system are identified early and given special education to nurture their intellectual abilities in a holistic manner. Gifted children aged eight to 15 years attend annual camps that challenge their intellectual abilities with modules such as space science, renewable energy, biotechnology, robotics, cryptology and creative writing. Students aged 13 to 15 who pass a special intelligence test called *UKM 3* are admitted into the Permata Pintar school. The special programme includes mentoring by UKM professors in research projects and scientific publications. Many have been admitted into prestigious American and British universities as well as into UKM at 16 years of age. In 2013, the Nobelist Mindset programme was initiated at Permata Pintar, in collaboration with the New York Academy of Sciences. The aim of the programme is to motivate a community of students, teachers and young scientists to develop the mindset necessary to become a Nobel Laureate. Some students are selected to attend the Summer Academy in New York where they meet Nobel Laureates and visit state-of-the art laboratories.

Ensuing from its mission, UKM has a moral obligation to inculcate the idea of national self-knowledge, values and culture. Preservation of national heritage is promoted by the Institute of Malay World and Civilisation. An example is the Pantun garden by the banks of the Langat River, complete with an old palace built in the traditional architecture of the Malays. *Pantun* is Malay poetry which draws rhyming words from the physical and biological environment.

Societal Engagement

In line with the aspirations of inclusivity and sustainability in the NEM, social sensitivity to responsibly address community problems remains a high priority in UKM. The university exercises its academic freedom to think and give opinions on societal issues independently. It is able to fulfill its role as an active agent and partner in social change by promoting sustainable regional development and inculcating ethics, values, traditions and responsibility through real world lessons from the community as the classroom.

To engage with communities, UKM invests in facilities for conducting research and for sharing knowledge with communities. To date, UKM has five sub-campuses or living laboratories dedicated to scientific and sociological research on the sustainability of different ecological systems in the country. These are the Langkawi UNESCO (United Nations Educational, Scientific and Cultural Organization) Geopark station, renamed Tuanku Abdul Halim Muadzam Shah Campus, after His Majesty the King, Mersing tropical marine station, Fraser's Hill montane system, Pahang Lake Chini and fresh water system, and Teluk Intan Community Health campus.

Dayang Bunting Geoforest Park, Langkawi Island. Reproduced with permission.

As a living laboratory, the more than 20 years of research from the Langkawi Research Station, has contributed to the declaration of Langkawi as the first UNESCO Global Geopark in Southeast Asia on 1 June 2007. The research station collaborates with the Langkawi Development Authority in preserving the culture and traditions of the people and in providing training for sustainable ecotourism activities. Awareness programmes on keeping the geopark sustainable are conducted for the island community.

The impact of UKM in regional growth can be measured in several ways. Its graduates are more innovative and entrepreneurial. Economic opportunities are enhanced through entrepreneurship and start-up companies, social business, ecotourism and other industries. Environmental sustainability, including community activities to mitigate climate change is promoted. Although more difficult to measure, there is community value in terms of social well-being, intercultural understanding and national unity. Community engagement also develops "good neighbour" relationships. All in all, societal engagement brings a better quality of life to the community and university.

In serving cities or regions, it is important to be an integral part of the innovation system. As Goethe said, "Knowing is not enough, we must apply; willing is not enough, we must do."

About the Author

Sharifah Hapsah Syed Hasan Shahabudin is Vice-Chancellor, Universiti Kebangsaan Malaysia (UKM); President of National Council of Women's Organisations of Malaysia; President of ASEAN Confederation of Women's Organisations (ACWO); President of Association of Universities in Asia-Pacific (AUAP); and Member of the Steering Committee of the Talloires Network of Community-Engaged Universities.

CHAPTER SIX

UNIVERSITY OF NEWCASTLE: RECASTING THE CITY OF NEWCASTLE AS A UNIVER-CITY — THE JOURNEY FROM "OLDE" NEWCASTLE-UPON-TYNE TO THE NEW SILK ROAD

NANCY CUSHING, KATRINA QUINN AND CAROLINE MCMILLEN

> *"He who knows himself and other will also recognize that East and West cannot be separated"*   *Goethe*

The economy of Newcastle in New South Wales, one of Australia's earliest European settlements, was founded on coal, steel, manufacturing and the role of Newcastle Harbour as a major port. During the past decade, this economic base has been recast with an increased focus on education, research and innovation. The city is emerging as a univer-city and a global knowledge hub positioned to engage with the next Asian Century and aligned with the reimagined New Silk Road.

Introduction

The global flow of capital and ideas is not, as is sometimes implied, a phenomenon which has emerged predominantly in modern times. The Silk Road between Asia and Europe not only assisted the exchange of goods in the ancient world, but also resulted in a diffusion of religious and cultural traditions, and ideas and innovation through cross-cultural interactions, that represented one of the first manifestations of "globalization".

    These cross-cultural interactions can be traced back to as early as 3500–2000 B.C.E, a time which saw the development and spread of a range of technologies including horse transportation, spoke-wheeled chariots and metallurgy along the precursor trade routes of the Silk

Road (Bentley, 1996). The routes along the Silk Road continued to play a central role during the classical era uniting previously self-contained regions of the East and West, and by 1492 as shipping routes opened up new interactions, "the regions of the world came into permanent and sustained contact with each other" to shape *"the world's common history"* (Bentley, 1996: 751, 770). As early as the 11th century, the possession of industrial techniques such as coal production, iron smelting, and various innovations such as the wheelbarrow, the compass, paper, printing, gunpowder and porcelain made China one of the economic powerhouses in world trade. China was using coal for smelting iron and producing "as many as 125,000 tons of pig iron by the late 11th century — a figure not achieved by Britain until 700 years later with the emergence of the Industrial Revolution" (Landes, 2006: 5).

More recently, the new Chinese Government has articulated an intent to embed a "Silk Road" as a centrepiece of its economic policy, including the building of a new rail link that will connect central China's logistics and manufacturing hub of Chengdu to Germany and the establishment of the Shanghai Cooperation Organisation as a broker of regional currency convertibility and transport agreements to bolster regional trade (Pearcey, 2013). With the emergence of a New Silk Road as a powerful enabler of knowledge exchange, industrial innovation and world trade, it has concurrently been reimagined as a global route well-travelled by students, researchers and academics to and from Asia (Dang, 2013). The European Union (EU) and the Association of Southeast Asian Nations (ASEAN) have been making significant attempts to shape new modes of knowledge exchange through the creation of an interregional forum, the Asia-Europe Meeting (ASEM), with higher education and lifelong learning emerging as main topics for the exchange of ideas between these two regions. The White Paper on "Australia in the Asian Century" by the Australian Government, also recognized that as the global economic centre of gravity moves back towards Asia, there is a need for Australia to create deeper connections with the people of that continent to broaden the flow of ideas and exchange new knowledge and capabilities.

This chapter focuses on the city of Newcastle in New South Wales (NSW), Australia, as a case study which illustrates the journey of a city built by convict labour and dependent on coal and steel to one recast as a univer-city that is well-placed to engage with the Asian Century as Australia contributes to the education, research and innovation agenda of the reimagined New Silk Road.

The Origins of the City of Newcastle, NSW

Convicts and coal

Newcastle, like all of colonial Australia, was born modern. The new colonies of Australia were disconnected from the hunter-gatherer societies they disrupted and neither did they grow organically from a subsistence agricultural society. The landmark innovations of the Industrial Revolution, Watt's steam engine and Hargreaves' spinning jenny, were both patented in the decade prior to the departure of the First Fleet in 1787. Newcastle emerged fully formed as part of a bold venture in which the world's most technologically advanced nation, Great Britain (GB), used its convicts to claim a continent.

With Sydney established as the port and administrative centre in 1788 and the fertile land around Parramatta ensuring food security, the search began for ways to recoup the costs of colonization. Whaling and sealing provided some income but the discovery of coal at the Hunter River in 1797 was warmly welcomed as providing a potential staple export. As plans were made for a settlement at the site in 1801, Governor Philip Gidley King wrote that coal would be the "first natural produce of the colony that has tended to any advantage" (King, 1801). Within two years, intercultural trade commenced with the sale of coal to India and the Cape of Good Hope (King, 1803). The settlement was made permanent in 1804 when a workforce for the coalmines was provided in the form of reconvicted convicts, including Irish transportees who had staged a rebellion that year. Governor King gave the settlement its permanent name at that time, stating that no other name "appears to me so applicable" (King, 1804). He was referencing prosperous Newcastle upon Tyne in England, by then a city of over 28,000 people with a heritage of several centuries of coal mining and export (King, 1804). By 1820, the Newcastle secondary penal settlement in Australia was a bustling village of almost 1,200 people producing not only coal but also the lime and timber needed by Sydney's building industry.

While Newcastle's coal mining and industrial heritage are well known, what was less noted until recently was that it was also a centre of high culture. Commandants Thomas Skottowe (1811–14) and James Wallis (1816–18) gathered about them skilled convict artists who created sketches, watercolours and oil paintings of the Indigenous Awabakal people, the local landscapes, plants and animals.[1] The colonial government sought through hard work, minimal amenities and a lack of personal freedom to make Newcastle a place which would deter convicts elsewhere from committing further crimes but even at its worst, the settlement also had a rich cultural life.

In 1822, it was decided that the penal colony should be removed further north to Port Macquarie and Newcastle was opened as a free town and gateway to the fertile Hunter Valley. When Henry Dangar surveyed the town in 1823, he expanded the association with Newcastle upon Tyne by naming the principal cross streets after the engineers and inventors whose work had enabled Britain to become the workshop of the world.[2] The prosperity of Newcastle upon Tyne and its shift from being a provincial port to an international centre, was something many hoped this new Newcastle would be able to replicate (Macleod, 1989).

Coal mining by the government continued in a small way through the 1820s while negotiations to take over the mines were conducted with the Australian Agricultural Company (AACo). Although formed with the intention of employing convicts in large-scale agriculture, the AACo was interested in other profit-making enterprises and judged that good quality coal on the east coast of Australia could be used in the trade with the countries of southern Asia (Turner, 1972). When they took charge in 1831, the company supplemented their convict workforce with free labourers, creating new centres of population around pit heads which were later to become the suburbs of Newcastle. Newcastle began a long tradition of innovation through pioneering the use of new technologies such as the gravity powered tramways with imported iron rails used to carry coal to the harbour where it was loaded onto ships. Australia's first steamship, the *Sophia Jane*, started on the Sydney to the Hunter River route in 1831 (*Sydney Gazette*, 1831).

Paddle Steamer, *"Sophia Jane"*
(*Source*: Cultural Collections, the University of Newcastle, Australia)

Building an industrial city

The availability of coal led to a series of industrial undertakings over the following decades including salt making, a chemical works, a meat preserving works and a woollen mill (Turner, 1980). Many of these enterprises were located on the north shore of Newcastle Harbour at a place named Stockton after Stockton-on-Tees where Newcastle upon Tyne's coal was first used to make iron. Local lobbying led to Newcastle being made a Free Warehousing Port, which could conduct direct trade with the rest of the world, in 1846 (Linge, 1979). The city responded to the demand for coal from gold rush California in 1849 and from 1851 to the clamour for coal from gold rush Victoria. Conveniently, the AACo's mining monopoly had been challenged and withdrawn by the colonial government in 1847 so both the older mines and those of newly established mining companies could respond (NSW Legislative Council, 1847). By the late 1860s, the three largest export markets for Newcastle coal were Victoria, New Zealand and China (Newcastle Chronicle, 1869).[3]

The rise of the coal mining industry gave Newcastle a more secure economic base and encouraged a new round of coal consuming enterprises. Rodgers Brothers engineering works opened in 1854 as the Newcastle Iron and Brass Foundry making agricultural machinery, flour milling gears, ships' pumps and boilers (Newcastle Chronicle, 1859). Heavy engineering was a key industry in itself and as the provider of inputs and services to other enterprises. Smelting and manufacturing works including one that went on to become Australia's favourite biscuit brand, William Arnott's bakery, provided employment and profit for residents of Newcastle. The degree of industrialization in the 19th century should not be overstated, however. Manufacturing was kept to a small breadth and scale by a lack of capital, the absence of protective tariffs and a transportation system which emanated out of Sydney (Burnley, 1980; Alpin, 1982). The centre of manufacturing in NSW was always Sydney although this was played down in public discourse. (Fitzgerald, 1987)[4]

It was coal that gave Newcastle its importance in the 19th century. Many of Newcastle's industries had been established to serve the port function: foundries, shipyards, warehouses, meat processing works, financial agencies, branches of insurance companies and rail yards. The port also served the ever lengthening Great Northern Railway built out from Newcastle from 1857. Unlike towns serving only a limited adjacent hinterland, Newcastle was actively involved in the world economy. In 1870, the tonnage of exports clearing Newcastle was higher than that of Sydney; double Melbourne's and three times that of Adelaide (Gallagher, 1979). Newcastle was not a mere mining village, but a commercial centre in which coal comprised the principal medium of exchange and the elite was made up of mine owners, agents, financiers and ship owners. Newcastle was well connected to the outside world and well known as a coaling depot by ships of all nations which frequented the south Pacific.

From coal to steel

This focus on coal created concern in the early 20th century as new coal measures were discovered further up the Hunter Valley and, one by one, the less profitable Newcastle coal mines closed. While coal export continued, the city needed a new source of local employment. Fortuitously, mining company Broken Hill Proprietary Ltd (BHP) had plans for Newcastle. BHP was formed in 1885 to exploit the riches of the Broken Hill silver, zinc and lead reserves and purchased land on Newcastle Harbour in 1896 with the intention of building a smelter. A decade and a half later, their ambitions had grown and they brought out an American expert to investigate the site for Australia's first integrated steelworks. Although he favoured establishing a steelworks south of Sydney at Port Kembla, David Baker found everything BHP needed in Newcastle: well-priced coal, available land, established international trade, a harbour improved by the state government and a disciplined workforce (NSW Legislative Assembly, 1912; Cushing, 2005). The decision to build the steelworks at Newcastle using the latest American technology was made in 1912 and three years later, the first steel rail was rolled. The date was 24 April 1915, the day before the landing at Gallipoli which for many Australians marked the birth of the nation. The two events share an enduring national significance.[5]

British and Australian consumers of steel established works in Newcastle to take advantage of new economies of scale. These included Lysaghts (galvanized iron), Commonwealth Steel (axles and wheels for railway rolling stock), the Austral Nail Company which merged with Rylands Bros (wire netting and steel rods), Stewarts and Lloyds (tubes) and the Titan Manufacturing Company (nails and barbed wire) (Jay, 1999). Most of these firms were subsequently taken over by BHP as subsidiaries. Existing industries such as Goninans Engineering expanded, new ones including Australian General Electric and Peter's Ice Cream (both 1927) arrived and BHP opened its own coal mines to the south and west of Newcastle (Docherty, 1983). The presence of the steelworks gave Newcastle a new identity and a new importance as a key player in the national economy. Working people flocked to Newcastle looking for employment in the large industries, the middle classes bought shares in the companies and everyone used their products. BHP's guide to the works for 1939 asserted its national importance by pointing to its provision of steel for the Sydney Harbour Bridge, rails sent overseas during World War I, rails to link Port Augusta with the mining centre of Kalgoorlie in Western Australia and plates for steamships (BHP, 1939). Iron and steel made in Australia were seen as a sign of maturity, because they were "metals that irrigate the fields of industry, metals that are symbolic of strength, of permanence and of security" (Souvenir of Civic Week, 1929).

BHP made Newcastle the centre of industry its promoters had long hoped it would become and no longer did they clamour for the associations with coal and Newcastle upon Tyne.

BHP Steelworks, Newcastle, NSW [n.d.]
(*Source*: Cultural Collections, the University of Newcastle, Australia)

New Cultural and Intellectual Horizons: The Emergence of the University of Newcastle (UON)

The benefits and costs of being a steel city

As well as benefits, being a steel city had its costs for Newcastle. As the major employer, the city's fortunes rose and fell with those of the steelworks, booming when profits were high and suffering from unemployment when they faltered, as in 1922–23 when the steelworks was closed for nine months as BHP sought ways to reduce its costs of production.

Those lucky enough to be taken on at the steelworks laboured seven days a week, with no weekends or holidays (Jay, 1999). The 24 hour a day operation of the massive blast furnaces required the burning of huge amounts of coal which covered the city in smoke and dust unless the winds were favourable. The rapid growth in population as aspiring workers flocked to the city caused overcrowding and soaring costs for housing. The employment of large numbers of unskilled and semi-skilled workers continued the perception of Newcastle, which had been established in the 19th century, as a place of hard physical labour, frequent strikes and the simple relaxations of the pub and the playing field. A steel city had associations, real and imagined, some which Newcastle embraced and others which it contested. The wealth generated in Newcastle was rarely spent there and when governments did invest, they focused on productive measures such as port improvements.[6] When Sydney-based book collector David Scott Mitchell was deciding on a home for his unrivalled collection of 60,000 volumes related to Australasia in the late 19th century, he did not choose to find a library in Newcastle, his mother's home and the location of much of his father's business activity which had allowed him to build the collection, but added his volumes to the Public Library in Sydney (Richardson, 1974).

Building education opportunities

This absence of large, well-funded institutions meant that Novocastrians relied on smaller-scale facilities for self-improvement. The miners from the north of England and Wales who had peopled the Newcastle district brought with them a strong tradition of self-help. They educated themselves on both technical and cultural matters through lectures and libraries associated with the Mechanics Institutes and Schools of Arts which were established in most mining villages from 1835 onward (Goold, 1937). Trade unions, consumer cooperatives and commercial lending libraries provided further opportunities for learning. From the 1880s, Newcastle Technical College offered evening courses in carpentry and other forms of manual work (Evening News, 1895).

The establishment of the steelworks brought a new group of well-educated people to Newcastle and an increased demand for structured learning. As well as adopting and adapting innovations in steel making, leading minds in technology and business sought more efficient ways of running the large enterprise. BHP general manager Essington Lewis' concept of the shadow-board, invented to manage the storage of tens of thousands of tools at the steelworks, was taken up by industries around the world (Jay, 1999).

This educated elite of managers and technicians developed a staff training system for cadets and apprentices from 1927 which relied on having a quality technical education available near the works. The heavy industries helped to fund the building of a new campus for the Technical College at Tighes Hill in the late 1930s with BHP providing the 22 acre site. The new facility opened in 1942 with some 4,000 students. These well trained technicians helped BHP to respond to war-time demands with a series of innovations in processes and materials, including a new form of bullet-proof steel using titanium and a new process for manufacturing more durable machine tools with tungsten carbide (Morris, 1947).

Other educational opportunities initiated in the interwar period were the classes offered jointly by Sydney University's extension programme and the Workers Educational Association through their Newcastle Regional Office (May and Bunn, 2013). In 1949, Newcastle Teachers' College was opened. Scholarships allowed students to complete the two-year course in exchange for working as a teacher for three years after graduation. The importance of these local opportunities was captured by one early Teacher's College student who recalled his relief at being able to study locally: "to an unsophisticated Newcastle boy, Sydney was a big place and you could easily get lost both physically and socially" (Pryde, n.d.).

World War II was the major turning point of the 20th century and Newcastle was carried along with this momentum. The extraordinary contribution provided by the city through its heavy industry led to a surge in self-confidence and a raising of expectations. After the war, the City Council lobbied for and was granted the right to use the term Lord Mayor, the only non-capital city in the Commonwealth to have this distinction (Sesquicentenary of Local Government in Newcastle, n.d.). Novocastrians wanted continued growth and prosperity but finally began to challenge the negative aspects of being an industrial city. A key goal was the establishment of a university. Parents and Citizens' Associations along with unions, heavy industry, local professionals and churches began this call in 1942 (Wright, 1992). The project received a boost in 1949 when the state government exchanged BHP land at Shortland in the city's west for the right to extend the steelworks site across a shallow channel of the Hunter River. It was agreed that the land should be used for educational purposes but the form they would take was debated for many years.

The establishment of UON

Rejecting a proposal for an Institute of Technology, the Newcastle University Establishment Group was formed in 1950 under president Reg Ellis, an industrial officer in a BHP subsidiary.[7] The Group argued for the establishment of an academic university in Newcastle to ease the strain on families seeking to provide a university education for their children, to break down the class distinction in tertiary education by encouraging a broader range of young people to participate and to enrich the region's cultural life. Sydney University was very reluctant to go beyond their extension classes they offered in Newcastle but the new NSW University of Technology under Acting Director Philip Baxter was more willing to expand. Along with campuses at Wollongong and Broken Hill, they opened Newcastle University College at the Newcastle Technical College late in 1951 offering degrees in maths, engineering and applied science as well as some individual humanities courses. The University of Technology could not grant Arts degrees so the University of New England was brought in to allow studies in this area under the local direction of Associate Professor James J. Auchmuty (Wright, 1992).

The staff of Newcastle University College were eager to contribute to the local community and mutual cooperation was high. Experienced academics who taught at the University College were very pleased with the quality and enthusiasm of the students, many of whom were first in their families of tradesmen or clerks to attend university. As the historian of the University wrote, "there was a two-way traffic between the city and the University which brought: new cultural and intellectual horizons to a provincial city which had hitherto been essentially parochial in outlook and whose tiny middle class had been eager to escape to the music, theatre and excitement of Sydney either temporarily or permanently" (Wright, 1992).

Newcastle Technical College, Tighes Hill, Australia — 1960s
(*Source*: Cultural Collections, the University of Newcastle, Australia)

With the university's presence secured and the demand from students established, the next push was for autonomy from what became in 1958 the University of NSW. Supported by the Lord Mayor's Committee for the Establishment of an Autonomous University of Newcastle, Auchmuty built up senior staff and facilities to demonstrate readiness for autonomy. The former BHP land was selected as the preferred site, with its proximity to BHP's Central Research Labs seen as an asset. Autonomy was finally granted by an Act of State Parliament taking effect in 1965 with Professor J.J. Auchmuty as founding Vice-Chancellor. This made Newcastle the second of the so called "gum tree universities" established in Australia in the 1960s and 1970s to educate the suburban and regional children of the baby boom (May & Bunn, 2013). Constructing the new campus, for the University and the Newcastle Teacher's College,[8] proceeded incrementally with the last elements of the University leaving the Tighes' Hill site in 1970. While government grants covered teaching, administrative spaces and a progressive library, a Great Hall for concerts, exams and graduations had to be funded through community donations, including Aus$ 200,000 from BHP and associated industries.

Emergence of the UON identity: equity, excellence and innovation

In the late 1960s, Newcastle's largest employers were BHP with 11,200 workers, Stewarts and Lloyds (3,000), Commonwealth Steel (1,900) and the State Dockyard (1,900). Newcastle contained the nation's largest concentration of heavy industry and its harbour was the second busiest port (The Hunter Valley Region, 1968). It might have seemed to some a place that did not need a university but this period, just a few years before the OPEC Oil crisis and the slow decline which led to the halving of the steelworks workforce in the early 1980s, can be seen as the peak of Newcastle's industrial might.

As their financial and in kind support of the development of the University demonstrated, the industries themselves saw a local university as an asset. This close relationship persisted. Newcastle students had a distinctive profile, in some ways more like busy contemporary undergraduates than those at other universities at the time. In 1964, 62 per cent were enrolled part time and of them, 60 per cent were apprentices or trainees in heavy industry or in the public service (Wright, 1992). Science and Engineering, in particular, relied on these trainees and met regularly with the industry training officers who ran these programmes. BHP invested in the latest technology and shared its resources with academics. One example was an *IBM 1620* computer installed at the works in 1962 which was made available to staff of the Mathematics Department and later relocated to the University. A commercial arm of the university, The UON Research Associates Ltd (TUNRA) was set up to manage research and consultancies conducted with private funding.

Having been established through the unceasing efforts of local people, UON put academic programmes in place to cater to its particular local constituency. Cooperation with industry and public service training programmes had already been discussed. Equity was another issue which guided practice at UON. One legacy of its coal mining and heavy industrial past was a lack of opportunities for women in the public sphere. UON demonstrated its equal opportunity credentials in 1969, when Professor Beryl Nashar of the Geology Department became the country's first female Dean of Science. Women were underrepresented in other academic positions and in the student body, with only 20 per cent in 1964 being female and very few married women attending classes (Wright, 1992).

One means of addressing this was the Open Foundation Program. Inspired by Britain's Open University and other European schemes, this programme was set up by Brian Smith, Director of Community

Programmes in 1974. It offered a programme of two introductory evening courses over one year which qualified adults over the age of 25 (later reduced to 20) who had not matriculated, to enter the University (Wright, 1992). Enabling Programs have now supported over 37,000 people otherwise barred from tertiary study to gain a degree, the majority of them women. Community Programmes also undertook other forms of outreach, including continuing professional education, short courses and media work, and its own radio station which began broadcasting in 1978.

In 1975, a Medical School was added to the University. Serious claims for this medical school had emerged in the late 1950s, based on the reputation of the Royal Newcastle Hospital for postgraduate medical training and the need in the state as a whole for more doctors, but it was a national enquiry into medical education in 1972 which led to its creation under the Vice-Chancellorship of Don George and with David Maddison, previously Dean of Sydney's Medical School, as Foundation Dean.

Once again, as a "disruptive innovator", UON decided not to do things in quite the same way as in older more traditional institutions, but to place the emphasis on preparing doctors who would be actively involved in their communities. For half of each year's intake, admission to Medicine at Newcastle was by personality tests and interviews with a panel of academics, practitioners and community members. Teaching was interdisciplinary, in small groups and problem based. The result was a Medical School which developed an international reputation for high quality graduates. This practical approach was more recently turned to attracting Indigenous students and Newcastle now graduates more Indigenous Australian doctors than any other university, many of whom return home to work in their communities.

The crowning achievement was first to weave the Medical School's innovation into a practical and coherent whole, and then to share its experience with other medical schools at home and abroad to enable them to reform medical education to fit their own circumstance. The UON Medical School has led national innovations such as the Australian Medical Council Accreditation; medical education for rural and remote communities; the *Quality of Australian Health Care* study; and the training of International Medical Graduates. Its partnerships or consultations have extended internationally with South Africa, Nigeria, Botswana, Bahrain,

Oman, Saudi Arabia, Papua New Guinea, Fiji, Pacific Islands, Malaysia, India, Nepal, and Bangladesh.

The Seismic Shift of a City from Heavy Industry to Education, Research and Innovation

On 28 December 1989, the city of Newcastle was hit by an earthquake with a Richter magnitude of 5.6 which was felt over an area of 200,000 square kilometers. The earthquake claimed 13 lives and hospitalized 160 Novocastrians. More than 50,000 buildings were damaged and 300,000 were affected, including 1,000 left homeless. The total damage bill was estimated to be Aus$4 billion (Newcastle City Council, 2013).

The earthquake hit at a time when the Newcastle's BHP steelworks was gradually closing down the operations of what was once the "linchpin of the Hunter Valley economy and the engine room of Australian heavy industry" (Jay, 1999: 220). BHP suffered considerable damage, particularly to its already outdated blast furnaces. The steelworks had been in decline, wrestling with labour productivity, an inefficient plant, competition arising from global innovations, and Korean and Japanese expansions into the steel industry which offered low cost imports (Jay, 1999). In 1989, BHP management and the unions engaged in revolutionary negotiations for a new workplace agreement that allowed a significant company restructure. The group general manager of the Rod and Bar Division, who would lead BHP into its new era of steel manufacturing, was Mr Paul Jeans who is currently the Chancellor of UON. Mr Jean's heritage, like that of many Novocastrians, was closely linked to Newcastle's early history and the British diaspora. His great grandfather journeyed to Newcastle from Wales to work in the coal industry, sinking shafts in nearby Lake Macquarie (Jay, 1999).

Mr Jeans took the reins during a critical point in BHP's and Newcastle's history when the cost of producing steel was rising, while demand was declining. However, the scaling back of the steelworks did not have the dire consequences for the city and region that many predicted. Many steel workers found employment in emerging industries as the economy began to diversify, with commentators equating the eventual closure of the BHP steelworks in 1999 to Newcastle being *"Reborn"* (*Newcastle Herald*, 2009).

The closure of BHP forced the Hunter Region to move rapidly from a concentration of activities in traditional industries towards new opportunities in areas such as sustainable energy, health and services, and the creative industries. UON with its partners from industry, business, government and the community has and will continue to play a major role in the transition of Newcastle from a "steel city" to a global innovation hub.

UON building participation in higher education and a univer-city

UON continues to build access and participation in higher education for the people in each of its regions. In 2011, the proportion of the adult population in Newcastle, the Hunter and the Central Coast who had attained a Bachelors degree or higher was 13 per cent and 8 per cent respectively, below the participation rates in NSW (16 per cent) and Australia (15 per cent). UON has approximately 38,000 students enrolled and importantly equity remains part of its DNA with a higher proportion of students from disadvantaged backgrounds and double the proportion of Indigenous students compared to the Australian average. The contribution of UON to the development of a tertiary educated workforce is critical to the participation of Newcastle and the Hunter Region in Australia's changing economy. The Australian Government's *2013 National Workforce Development Strategy* reports that to meet the increasingly complex and rapidly changing needs of future industry, maintaining Australia's position as a high-skilled country is largely about increasing participation in higher education. In a little over a decade, Australia's workforce will need to expand by three and a half million people to meet industry demands, with the total number of tertiary qualifications needing to grow annually by a minimum of three per cent to 2025 if we are to position ourselves as a knowledge economy and add value via cutting-edge innovation (Australian Workforce and Productivity Agency Report, 2013).

In 2013, UON received funding from the Federal and NSW State governments to contribute to the building of a Aus$ 95 million NeW

Space Education Precinct in the heart of the Newcastle CBD (Central Business District) alongside the City Hall, new law courts and the UON Conservatorium of Music. The NeW Space facility will be a technology-enabled learning and teaching hub which will offer university-supported activities across all faculties including: business and law programmes; digital library services and information commons collaborative learning and research spaces; work integrated learning, facilities for industry, professional and community engagement and interactive social spaces. The announcement of the funding for the Precinct was shortly followed by key announcements by the NSW State government of plans to reopen the city to its harbour by replacing a heavy rail corridor with light rail and building more residential accommodation and boutique retail outlets to "activate" the city. With the building of a stronger university presence in the city with some 3,000 students travelling to and from and living and working in the heart of Newcastle, the city will take on the characteristics of a univer-city and is also well positioned to continue to attract international students to enhance its vibrancy and diversity.

UON also has a thriving presence in Singapore where it delivers a strong suite of educational programmes through UON Singapore. This relationship has resulted in the development of strong educational partnerships in Asia. In 2013, UON Singapore and the Building and Construction Authority (BCA) Academy launched a new Bachelor of Construction Management (Building) degree programme jointly offered by the BCA and UON. With the bilateral movement of talented staff and students between UON and our partner institutions across Asia, new routes of knowledge exchange and work-integrated learning are opened up in a reimagined New Silk Road which will enhance cross cultural literacy, engagement and productive collaborations between individuals and institutions for a long-term impact.

UON Building a Global Knowledge and Innovation Hub

During its first 50 years, UON has established itself in the Top three per cent of the world's universities and is also ranked in the

Top 50 universities under 50 in the world and as the best of Australia's universities under 50 years old (as determined by the 2014 Times Higher Education 100 Under 50 Rankings). In the most recent Excellence in Research for Australia assessment exercise, UON was ranked in the Top seven in Australia for research rated as "well above world standard" with particular strengths highlighted across the engineering, science and health research disciplines. The University's two flagship research institutes — the Newcastle Institute for Energy and Resources (NIER) and the Hunter Medical Research Institute (HMRI) — have been built with a multidisciplinary focus and an emphasis on engagement with partners to deliver innovation and impact.

Global leadership in engineering research and translation to world-class innovation

The current UON "NeW Directions Strategic Plan" expresses a clear vision that by 2025, the University will be a global leader in each of its spheres of achievement — such as engineering and health — and that through engagement with partners, UON will deliver world-class innovation to support the social, economic and environmental development of strong regional communities. With NIER and the CSIRO (Commonwealth Scientific and Industrial Research Organisation) Energy Transformed Flagship and the National Solar Centre all located in Newcastle, as well as the role of the Hunter Region in the production of 60 per cent of the state's energy supply, there is a demonstrable capacity to build on global leadership with partners to drive first-class innovation and creative collaboration to deliver international and national energy solutions.

One example of global innovation, the acclaimed Jameson Cell, a flotation technology for the coal industry, has created almost Aus$ 25 billion of export income for Australia. It was created by a UON researcher, Laureate Professor Graham Jameson. His colleague, Professor Kevin Galvin, also developed the Reflux Classifier in collaboration with commercial partner Ludowici, a revolutionary innovation which separates fine particles on the basis of density and has been a game-changer for the energy industry. It is this calibre of research and innovation which allows

UON to tackle global challenges through international collaboration and gain access to world-class facilities to develop innovative solutions and enabling technologies. Working in conjunction with business innovators such as Liddell Power Station, where a world first integration of solar thermal technology with coal-fired power generation was pioneered, UON and industry partners across Newcastle and the Hunter region have a unique competitive advantage, which the Hunter Innovation Scorecard will help to leverage in emerging areas of strength such as sustainable energy. As summarized by Lord Sainsbury in the UK's *"Race to the Top"* Review of the Government's Science and Innovation, "the paradox is that while innovation is a global phenomenon, the role of regions as the critical nexus for innovation based economic growth has increased" (Sainsbury, 2007).

NIER acts as a multidisiplinary research and innovation hub with strong partnerships across Asia. This is built through the recruitment of talented staff and research trainees from across the Asian region. Such engagement with Asia and beyond also supports the development of introductions and collaborations between the industry partners of universities, which will in turn, support the economic development of the region and connect to the changing global landscape of research. As the recent European Commission Communication on enhancing international cooperation in research and innovation emphasized:

> Global research and innovation were, until recently dominated by the European Union, the USA and Japan. As the emerging economies continue to strengthen their research and innovation systems, a multipolar system is developing in which countries such as Brazil, India, China and South Korea (BRICS) exert increasing influence. The share of the BRICS in global expenditure on R&D doubled between 2000 and 2009 (European Commission, 2012).

In a nice piece of symmetry, the new buildings housing NIER have been built on the original BHP's research and development (R&D) site adjacent to the University campus, demonstrating the transition from a focus on national industry R&D to one on international university-industry research and innovation.

The NIER is located in the former BHP Billiton Newcastle Technology Centre, Shortland.
(*Source*: Cultural Collections, the University of Newcastle, Australia)

Global leadership in health and medical research and translation to world-class innovation

The HMRI, a collaboration between UON and Hunter New England Health District is housed in an Aus$ 90 million building on the John Hunter Hospital campus, and has attracted world leading researchers with outstanding track records of translating world-class research into clinical and population interventions. Conjoint Professor Chris Levi, an internationally recognized stroke neurologist, researcher and co-director of the University's Centre for Translational Neuroscience and Mental Health Research at HMRI, conducted a groundbreaking study in partnership with Harbin Medical University, China, into methods of cooling the brain after a stroke. Researchers at Harbin developed a helmet that works to cool the brain, while the team at Newcastle looked into methods of whole body cooling. This world-class treatment "buys time" for patients by allowing the clot to begin to breakdown on its own, resulting in lives being saved and the reduction in the damaging effects of a stroke.

Professor John Forbes, another of HMRI's leading medical researchers, led the study of treatments for a particular type of breast cancer that resulted in the adoption of an alternative treatment, anastrozole, which saw cancer recurrence drop by 24 per cent in clinical trials. This medical breakthrough is estimated to have benefited over one million women worldwide. Similarly, the Centre for Magnetic Resonance in Health at HMRI has a unique research and commercial partnership with global technology giant Siemens, with Newcastle, one of only a few worldwide development sites for magnetic resonance spectroscopy and the first in the Southern hemisphere to receive a next-generation MRI (magnetic resonance imaging) scanner. These established linkages with health systems and international industry partners, made possible by the integrated HMRI model and its unique facilities, not only act as drivers for economic development in the region (in which Health Care and Social Assistance is the largest employment sector) but also position Newcastle as a leader on the world stage with existing education and research partnerships with health researchers across the US, Europe and Asia.

The HMRI, located at John Hunter Hospital, Newcastle.
(*Source*: Cultural Collections, the University of Newcastle, Australia)

Plans to launch three new Research and Innovation Clusters are another important part of the UON *NeW Directions Strategic Plan* which will act as "one-stop-shops" to bring industry partners together with researchers across different discipline areas that are important to generate solutions to complex problems.

Conclusion

The city of Newcastle and the Hunter region have a remarkable history with their early origins shaped by colonial ambitions and an Industrial Revolution half a world away. The city of Newcastle emerged during the last century with a strong economic base founded on coal, steel and manufacturing, and a world-class port which shaped its international identity as a trade hub in resources. Due to the vision and commitment of the Newcastle community, a new university was formed in Newcastle in 1965 with a strong mission and focus on equity, excellence and engagement. As the economic base of Newcastle has transitioned, UON has played a key role through education, research and innovation, by positioning the city as a destination of choice for talented international staff and students, and as a partner of choice in driving world-class innovation in each of its areas of strength. The next transition will see Newcastle emerge as a knowledge hub and univer-city no longer dependent on its colonial origins or its English namesake for identity, but realigned with a future captured by the New Silk Road.

Notes

1. Much of this work was brought together for an exhibition at the Newcastle Region Art Gallery from March to May 2013. See *Treasures of Newcastle from the Macquarie Era* (catalogue), Elizabeth Ellis curator. (Sydney: State Library of NSW, 2013.)
2. From east to west these were: James Watt, Matthew Bo(u)lton, Thomas Newcomen, Arthur Woolf or Wolfe, Jacob Perkins and Samuel Brown.
3. In 1868, 165,715 tons of coal were sold to Victoria, 86,207 tons to New Zealand and 69,995 to China.
4. Sydney was the home of 64 per cent of factory workers in 1901 when it held 36 per cent of the state's population and 79 per cent of factory workers in 1933 when it accounted for 48 per cent of the population (Berry, 1984).
5. Date of first steel rail from Delprat Diary entry for 24 April 1915: "First steel rail rolled in soft steel 10:30 a.m". (National Library of Australia, MS 1630/15) The official opening was on 2 June 1915.
6. The first regional art gallery in the British Empire opened in Ballarat in 1890. The Ballarat School of Mines began in 1870, making it the third oldest

post-secondary institution in Australia, and a Technical Art School was added to it in 1915.
7. Much of this history of the formation and early years of UON is drawn from Don Wright (1992), *Looking Back, A History of the University of Newcastle*.
8. The Teacher's College became the Newcastle College of Advanced Education in 1974. It was renamed the Hunter Institute of Higher Education in 1988 and was made part of the University in 1989.

References

Aplin, Graeme (1982). "Models of Urban Change: Sydney, 1820–1870". *Australian Geographical Studies* 20, no. 2, pp. 144–58.

Australian Government (2012). *Australia in the Asian Century: White Paper*. Canberra: Commonwealth of Australia.

Australian Workforce and Productivity Agency (2013). *Future Focus: 2013 National Workforce Development Strategy*. Canberra: Commonwealth of Australia.

Beckwith, Christopher (2009). *Empires of the Silk Road: A History of Central Eurasia from the Bronze Age to the Present*. New Jersey: Princeton University Press.

Bentley, Jerry (1996). "Cross-Cultural Interaction and Periodization in World History", *American Historical Review*, June.

Berry, Michael (1984). "Urbanization and Social Change: Australia in the Twentieth Century" in S. Encel and L. Bryson, eds, *Australian Society, Introductory Essays*, 4th edn. Melbourne: Longman Cheshire.

Broken Hill Proprietary Company (1939). *Progress, Guide to Works, 1939*, August.

Burnley, I.H. (1980). *The Australian Urban System, Growth, Change and Differentiation*. Melbourne: Longman Cheshire.

Clarke, John (1997). *Oriental Enlightenment: The Encounter Between Asian and Western Thought*. New York: Taylor & Francis.

Convict Lumber Yard or Stockade site listing, available online at <http://www.environment.nsw.gov.au/heritageapp/ViewHeritageItemDetails.aspx?ID=5044978 > [accessed 12 September 2013].

Cushing, Nancy (2005). "David Baker (1861–1942)". *Australian Dictionary of Biography*, Australian National University, <http://adb.anu.edu.au/biography/baker-david12781/text23059> [accessed 23 September 2013].

Dang Q.A (2013). "ASEM — The Modern Silk Road: Travelling ideas for education reforms and partnerships between Asia and Europe". *Comparative Education* 49, no. 1, pp. 107–19.

Docherty J.C. (1983). *Newcastle, The Making of an Australian City*. Sydney: Hale & Iremonger.

European Commission (2012), *Communication on Enhancing International Cooperation in Research and Innovation*, available online at <http://eur-lex.europa.eu/Notice.do?mode=dbl&lang=en&ihmlang=en&lng1=en,en&lng2=bg,cs,da,de,el,en,es,et,fi,fr,hu,it,lt,lv,mt,nl,pl,pt,ro,sk,sl,sv,&val=688582:cs> [date accessed 23 September 2013]

Evening News, 20 November 1895, p. 8.

Fitzgerald, Shirley (1987). *Rising Damp, Sydney 1870–90*. Melbourne: OUP Australia and New Zealand.

Ford, Lisa and Roberts, David Andrew (forthcoming 2014). "New South Wales penal settlements and the transformation of secondary punishment in the nineteenth-century British Empire". *Journal of Colonialism and Colonial History* 15, no. 3.

Gallagher, James (1979). "The Outports of New South Wales, A Paradigm of Regionalism", PhD Thesis, University of Newcastle.

Goold, W.J. (1937). "The Pioneers — The Reverend Wilton of Christ Church". *Newcastle School of Arts Journal* 1, no. 3.

Governor King to the Duke of Portland, 21 August 1801, *Historical Records of New South Wales (HRNSW)*, IV, 477.

Governor King to Lord Hobart, 9 May 1803, *Historical Records of New South Wales (HRNSW)*, IV, 117.

———. 16 April 1804, *Historical Records of New South Wales (HRNSW)*, I, IV, 612.

Jay, Christopher (1999). *A Future More Prosperous: The History of Newcastle Steelworks 1912–1999*. Newcastle: Broken Hill Proprietary Company Limited.

Landes, David S. (2006). "Why Europe and the West? Why Not China?" *Journal of Economic Perspectives* 20, no. 2.

Linge (1979). *Industrial Awakening, A Geography of Manufacturing in Australia, 1788–1900*. Canberra: Australian National University Press.

Macleod, Dianne Sachlco (1989). "Private and Public Patronage in Victorian Newcastle". *Journal of the Warburg and Courtauld Institutes* 52, pp. 1–280.

May and Bunn (2013). "1974–1976: The seeds of flexibility in the pathway to tertiary participation at University of Newcastle, NSW". The National Association of Enabling Educators of Australia Conference. Melbourne, Victoria: The Australian Catholic University.

Menzies to King (19 April 1804). HRNSW, V, 368. King's Town was used in the *Sydney Gazette* occasionally until 1809.

Morris D.O (1947), "A Review of the War-Time activities of the Newcastle Steel Plant of the Broken Hill Pty. Co. Ltd and its Associated and Subsidiary Industries". Proceedings (Australasian Institute of Mining and Metallurgy), Series: 146. Newcastle: Australasian Institute of Mining and Metallurgy.

Newcastle City Council (n.d). "History of Newcastle upon Tyne". *Local Studies Factsheet No.6*, Available online at <http://www.newcastle.gov.uk/wwwfileroot/legacy/libraries/HistoryofNewcastlemainbody.pdf> [accessed 18 September 2013]

New South Wales Legislative Council (1847). "Votes and Proceedings. II, 1847". Report from the Select Committee on the Coal Inquiry.

NSW Legislative Assembly (1912). Select Committee of Inquiry into the Newcastle Iron and Steel Works Bill. Appendix D: Letter from G. Delprat to Premier J.S. McGowen, 1 August 1912.

Newcastle Chronicle, 31 December 1859.

Newcastle City Council (2013). "Earthquake". *Newcastle City Council*, available at <http://www.newcastle.nsw.gov.au/about_newcastle/history_and_heritage/earthquake> [accessed 18 September 2013].

Newcastle Herald (2009). "Ten years after BHP". Newcastle Herald online, available at <http://www.theherald.com.au/story/446711/ten-years-after-bhp/> [accessed 19 September 2013]

Pearcey, L (2013). "Xi Jinping's New Silk Road: Chinese foreign policy, energy security and ideology". The Conversation, 16 September available online at <http://theconversation.com/xi-jinpings-new-silk-road-chinese-foreign-policy-energy-security-and-ideology-17994> [accessed 22 September 2013)

Pryde, Noel (n.d). "From a Pioneer Student". Speaking of Union Street: Reminiscences of Newcastle Teacher's College, 1949–1973, typescript held by University of Newcastle Archives, <http://www.newcastle.edu.au/Resources/Divisions/Academic/Library/Cultural%20Collections/pdf/union-street.pdf>

Richardson, G. D. (1974). "Mitchell, David Scott (1836–1907)". *Australian Dictionary of Biography*. National Centre of Biography, Australian National University, available at <http://adb.anu.edu.au/biography/mitchell-david-scott-4210/text6781> [accessed 15 September 2013]

Shaffer Lynda. "China, Technology and Change". *World History Bulletin*, Fall/Winter 1986/87.

Sainsbury, Lord of Turville (2007). "The Race to the Top: A Review of Government's Science and Innovation Policies". HM Treasury, London. Available online at

<http://webarchive.nationalarchives.gov.uk/+/http:/www.hm-treasury.gov.uk/d/sainsbury_review051007.pdf> [accessed 19 September 2013].

Sequicentenary of Local Government in Newcastle, UoN Cultural Collection, <http://uoncc.wordpress.com/2009/08/13/sequicentenary-of-local-government-in-newcastle/> (accessed 27 October 2011).

Souvenir of Civic Week (1929), n.p. (section on Industrial Development), Newcastle.

Sydney Gazette (1831). "Sophia Jane" (advertisement), 14 June, p. 1.

The Hunter Valley Region (1968). Newcastle: Hunter Valley Regional Authority; Submissions by VA Moore, Chief Health Inspector, Newcastle City Council to Senate Select Committee on Air Pollution, 26 July.

Turner, John (1972). "The Entry of the Australian Agricultural Company into the New South Wales Coal Industry". *Royal Australian Historical Society Journal and Proceedings* 58, no. 4, p. 234.

Turner, J. W. & Newcastle Public Library (NSW) (1980). *Manufacturing in Newcastle, 1801–1900*. Newcastle: Newcastle Public Library.

Wright, Don (1992). *Looking Back, A History of the University of Newcastle*. Newcastle: University of Newcastle.

About the Authors

Nancy Cushing, B.A. (Hons) (Dalhousie), M.MusStud (Toronto), PhD (Newcastle); is Senior Lecturer, School of Humanities and Social Science; University of Newcastle.

Katrina Quinn, B.SocSci (UON), M.HRM (UON) is Innovation and Business Development Manager in the Faculty of Education and Arts, University of Newcastle.

Caroline McMillen, MA, Dphil (Oxon), MB, BChir (Cantab) is Vice-Chancellor and President, University of Newcastle.

CHAPTER SEVEN

FROM BURNABY'S MOUNTAIN TOP TO VANCOUVER AND SURREY: THE MAKING OF AN ENGAGED UNIVERSITY

ANDREW PETTER, RICHARD LITTLEMORE AND JOANNE CURRY

Introduction

The lessons of history are clear: the educative, innovative and transformative influences of universities cannot be contained. Even in the days when universities were designed as cloisters, as places where knowledge could be concentrated, protected and perhaps even hidden away, townsfolk inevitably beat a path to the institutional door; the academics so often had a better way of doing things. Of course, there was dynamic tension between town and gown, arising sometimes because the universities advocated too aggressively for "progress" — for change beyond what the entrenched interests of the day were prepared to accept. But over time, the combined advantages of old knowledge and new research always prevailed. There was too much to be gained, from educated students who would fill future jobs or from researchers who could answer current questions or animate the economy with new discoveries. Ultimately, individual academies and nearby communities always made the effort to engage.

Rarely, however, have these acts of engagement been part of a broad and deliberate strategy. Universities have engaged tactically when they needed financial or other support from the local community or where their interests were at risk; for example, they engaged with local planning authorities to resolve concerns about conflicting land uses in close proximity. Academics have engaged altruistically when they felt their ideas or discoveries would enhance social well-being or enrich the economy. Similarly, communities have initiated engagement when they wanted or needed something from nearby universities; for example, communities supported post-secondary institutions because they wanted artists and authors or they needed doctors, lawyers or scientists. Businesses supported the academy because they could see direct benefit from applied research.

These acts of engagement have, therefore, occurred separately and irregularly, driven by the particular need or momentary desire of one party or the other. The relationships are either transactional, in which one party is a supplicant or client to the other, or altruistic, in which one party is acting out of a sense of benevolence or generosity towards the other.

We will argue in this chapter that universities miss an important opportunity if they adhere to this pattern of discrete and disconnected acts of engagement. Rather, an organic and comprehensive approach to university-community engagement offers so much potential for mutual benefit that it is worth considering for any institution and community. Physical engagement — which in some places is the point of friction between a traditional academic cloister and an unruly urban neighbour — has the potential to transform both the academy and the community to mutual advantage. However, this potential can be made much greater if physical engagement is accompanied by an overarching commitment to engagement in all aspects of the university's mission. Interaction and cooperation between universities and communities can improve the quality of education even as they expand the opportunities for those being educated. Engagement can provoke and inspire creative and innovative research even as it improves the chances that discoveries and inventions will find wide support and ready application. It can also give rise to all manner of collaborations with respect to programmes and initiatives that add purpose to the university while contributing value to the community.

To illustrate this, we will consider as a case study, the experience of Simon Fraser University (SFU) in the Metro Vancouver region of British Columbia (BC), Canada. Through the unique approach that SFU has taken in developing its three separate campuses, the university has leveraged its physical infrastructure to: revitalize a declining urban area; transform a suburban neighbourhood in transition; and create a model sustainable community in a relative greenfield. In each case, the university gained as much as the communities it acted to assist. And far from having to fight with planning authorities or mollify displaced or discomfited neighbours, the university has enjoyed a warm welcome — and gained a further impetus for engagement. We will then review with examples how, in tandem with these physical developments, SFU's faculty, administration and staff have utilized community engagement to enrich the university's educational programmes, enhance its research endeavours, and extend its other activities, to the point that a commitment to engagement has recently been incorporated as a core component of the University's strategic vision.

The Traditional Academy: Welcome to the Neighbourhood

It has been typical in academic history that universities have been at pains to keep themselves in out of the way places. This often took the form of a retreat to the ivory tower; universities established themselves at some remove from large population centres to ensure that they could function independently of social and political influences that might challenge their longstanding practices or disrupt the process of learning. On other occasions, universities were separated physically from population centres by reasons of economic necessity; universities were dispatched to distant or suburban locations because the land was more affordable, and there was insufficient recognition of the value, even the necessity, of convenient access between the academy and the community.

Whatever the reasons for their original distance from each other, universities and communities have subsequently come together physically. In some instances, traditional cloisters such as Oxford and Cambridge universities in England or Harvard and Stanford universities in the United States became magnets for creative populations and engines for local innovation economies. People pushed their homes and businesses ever closer to the universities, and new communities emerged and integrated with the campuses. In other cases, such as McGill University and the University of Toronto in Canada, the founders chose locations that seemed to be a sensible distance from economic centres, only to be quickly surrounded by urban expansion. The cities were then forced to contend with universities because they became suddenly, if unintentionally, close to the urban core.

There were immediate, though often overlooked, advantages to such physical proximity. The universities were more accessible, not only to young students committed to full-time study, but also to those who wished to drop in periodically to pursue intellectual interests or seek continuing education. The social and business environments around the universities also benefited from immediate access to the universities' experts, as well as from the presence and custom of students, staff and faculty. And the institutions emerged as cultural centres, whether by virtue of their excellent libraries, theatres, galleries or sports arenas.

A First Act of Engagement: Moving from the Mountaintop

Simon Fraser University opened its first campus in 1965 in a spectacular setting atop Burnaby Mountain. (Courtesy of David Ashcroft)

These advantages were difficult to replicate for an institution such as SFU, which was founded in 1965 on top of an undeveloped mountain in the Vancouver suburb of Burnaby. Blessed with an institutional infrastructure designed by the iconic Canadian architect Arthur Erickson and his partner Geoff Massey, the campus was an exquisite example of an ivory tower, albeit in the modernist form of a concrete citadel. But as an instant university, established in the restive and unruly 1960s, SFU was not about to accept its isolation.

From the outset, it was clear that SFU would be a cauldron for rebellious students and radical faculty members bent upon social reform. Still, the university population faced significant physical barriers when it came to connecting with the larger community. And on a commuter campus with no residences other than dormitories, and few commercial or service components, it was even more awkward and time-consuming for the community to come to the mountain.

While the radicalism that characterized SFU's culture in the 1960s mellowed into a less ideological form of social activism in the ensuing decades, the urge to engage with the community remained strong. So, in the 1980s, SFU decided to transport some of the best parts of the university into the centre of Vancouver. It began tentatively in the early part of the decade, but in 1989, SFU negotiated to assume space recently vacated by a department store that had fallen victim to an economic shift in the city's commercial core.

The location, SFU Harbour Centre, had once been at the very heart of the regional shopping, banking and office district, but it was also near a neighbourhood that is known to be Canada's poorest — Vancouver's Downtown Eastside. As high-end boutiques migrated to a more fashionable area, this particular part of the downtown had become hollowed out, deserted, dilapidated and increasingly dangerous. Yet, as the late urban theorist Jane Jacobs has pointed out, crowds are the greatest protection against crime.

As SFU populated the new campus, the introduction of students, faculty and staff had an immediate benefit, bringing life back into a neglected district. Business people and downtown residents eager for continuing education opportunities also followed the crowd of younger students. The location quickly became a centre for lectures and conferences, to the benefit of the university and the community alike. SFU faculty gained important community connections, and the university as a whole expanded markedly its relevance to the community at large.

The latest addition to SFU's Vancouver campus is the Goldcorp Centre of the Arts, home to its School for the Contemporary Arts and its Vancity Office of Community Engagement. (Courtesy of SFU Creative Services)

In the years that followed, the university continued to develop this educational precinct. In 2001, it opened the Morris J. Wosk Centre for Dialogue in a heritage building that had once been the largest western Canadian branch of the Toronto Dominion Bank (across the street from Harbour Centre). Four years later, it added the Segal Graduate School of Business in another former bank building two blocks to the southwest. In 2010, it opened the Goldcorp Centre of the Arts as home for its School for the Contemporary Arts in an area that had been abandoned by another of Vancouver's oldest and best known department stores. This location, inside the boundaries of the Downtown Eastside and two-and-a-half blocks east of Harbour Centre, was deliberately chosen with the goal that a cultural facility, its student population and programming would help to enrich and revitalize a struggling community. In 2011, SFU was given ownership of the Bill Reid Foundation's collection of Northwest Coast Art at the Foundation's downtown gallery, rounding out SFU's downtown presence to-date.

Thanks to these initiatives, SFU's Vancouver campus now comprises 380,000 square feet, making it by far the largest post-secondary presence in the city centre. This downtown campus currently offers undergraduate courses through 28 different departments, as well as 18 graduate-level programmes, to a total of nearly 4,000 students. Including non-credit offerings, the total number of courses available in its downtown facilities rises to 571, satisfying the needs of 7,500 students of all ages. In addition, the university hosts some 9,000 different events (such as meetings, conferences, dialogues, public lectures and performances) in an average year.

In large part due to SFU's presence, the neighbourhood is now secure, vibrant and economically stable. Indeed, so significant has been the university's contribution that the province's largest newspaper, the *Vancouver Sun,* has acknowledged SFU as "the intellectual heart of Vancouver".

Suburban Transformation: *Vancouverism* Spreads to Surrey

SFU's Surrey campus is part of a mixed-used complex that includes a shopping centre and office tower set in an emerging city centre. Reproduced with permission from Blackwood Partners.

A second opportunity for SFU's external physical engagement emerged in the late 1990s, when one of Canada's leading architects, Bing Thom, persuaded the provincial government of the day to situate a new university campus in a troubled part of the suburban municipality of Surrey. As with its Vancouver location before SFU arrived, others might have viewed this setting as anything but perfect. It was marked by a shopping centre where people seldom shopped and a rapid-transit station where people were reluctant to stop. It was, like the downtown location, increasingly desolate, derelict and dangerous. But Thom, a former student of Arthur Erickson, saw a suburban brownfield ready for transformation. He argued that a new university campus would have tremendous potential as a catalyst for urban renewal.

It is relevant here to address an innovation in urban planning that, in reference to its place of inception, is known as "Vancouverism". The style is characterized by dense, walkable and highly liveable mixed-use urban developments — neighbourhoods where the services and amenities are sufficient to answer the desires and demands of local residents. The campus that SFU developed in Surrey, and that was ultimately designed by Thom, has been hailed as a prime example of Vancouverism. In terms of mixed use, the building retains the fully redeveloped shopping centre at its base, with the university campus occupying a new, multi-story galleria overhead, plus the podium floors of a contiguous office tower. After touring the stunning facility in 2011, American architect, author and professor, Witold Rybczynski (2011), praised its marriage of commerce and education as a model for meeting "the challenge of the coming decade". This he identified as "making the suburbs more urban; that is, making them denser and creating active, concentrated, walkable town centers".

As Thom had predicted, the campus also catalyzed new development, helping trigger a transformation that municipal officials in the City of Surrey welcomed and abetted. They chose the adjacent square at the location for their Surrey Central Library — in which SFU now occupies space for community programming and continuing education classes — and for a new City Hall. And they up-zoned the surrounding area to accommodate a series of high-density residential and office developments. One project announced recently will include a 50-story hotel and residential tower.

Given that the City of Vancouver is centred on a peninsula, the fastest-growing jurisdiction in the metropolitan area is the once-sprawling, suburb of Surrey, which is expected to overtake Vancouver during the next 20 years as the largest municipality in the region. And the increasingly dense section Surrey surrounding SFU's facility has now — by official municipal policy — been designated as Surrey's new City Centre. For SFU's part, what started as a campus of 500 in 2002 now welcomes 8,000 students a year.

This again illustrates the mutuality of advantage that has flowed from SFU's engagement. In addition to the opportunity to help transform a deteriorating suburb into a thriving urban centre, SFU has also been able to quickly expand its own capacities while meeting the most pressing educational needs of the region's fastest-growing community. For example, SFU established Western Canada's first school of Mechatronics Systems Engineering and has partnered with the City of Surrey, with the provincial Crown corporation, BC Hydro, and with the private sector to position Surrey as a hub for clean-energy research and development. At the same time, the new campus has begun to address the dramatic shortage of post-secondary seats in a region that is graduating more high school students than any other district in the province.

Univer-City: A Model Sustainable Development

Adjacent to its original campus, SFU is building a model sustainable community called Univer-City. (Courtesy of SFU Creative Services)

The third example of SFU's physical and infrastructural engagement is, by a happy coincidence, called "Univer-City". It is a new community emerging next to the original Burnaby Mountain campus. It is also a functional repudiation of the earlier calculation that SFU could not "bring the community to the mountaintop" — for it has done just that.

As was typical for many universities founded in the 20th century, SFU was endowed at the outset with land surplus to its needs, on the assumption that it would develop the surrounding property and use the proceeds to build its financial endowment, thereby making an ongoing contribution to the university's mission of teaching and research. In this instance, SFU determined that it had a significant amount of property — mostly in the form of undeveloped mountainside forests — that were surplus to its long-term requirements for campus development.

By the mid-1990s, however, the university dismissed the original plans to cover this land with suburban tract housing over the entire property as being socially, economically and environmentally inappropriate. Instead, SFU announced its intention to build a *"model of sustainability"*, something that would meet the university's own need for a supportive community immediately adjacent to the campus while also demonstrating the best in sustainable urban development practices. Accordingly, SFU and the City of Burnaby concluded negotiations for SFU to surrender 313 hectares to the Burnaby Mountain Conservation Area, doubling the size of a natural preserve that is now protected in perpetuity. In return, the university received approval from the zoning authority, the City of Burnaby, to transfer the anticipated development potential of 4,500 residential units onto the remaining 65 hectares, all of which is within convenient walking distance of the SFU campus.

In the years since, the university's development agency, the SFU Community Trust, has indeed created a univer-city. Given its physical isolation, the original campus had been bereft of lodgings or services that could support a local population. Aside from students who lived in residence, everyone else — including every staff and faculty member — was required to commute long distances each day. Even students in dorms wound up having to commute in reverse every time they wanted to shop for necessities. The Trust therefore began by building condominiums and townhouses — some particularly targeted to SFU faculty and staff. But it quickly added a High Street commercial development, including the shops and services that residents, students, faculty and staff might want or need — everything from a grocery store and pharmacy to a bank and a selection of eateries. The Trust then added an elementary school and childcare centre, enabling faculty and staff who live in Univer-City to drop their children off on the short walk to work.

As a project demonstrating the potential of sustainable development, Univer-City has been an unquestioned success. Working with the City of Burnaby, the Trust developed one of the most ambitious green zoning bylaws in North America. All structures built within Univer-City must be 30 per cent more energy efficient and 40 per cent more water efficient than the standards required by Canada's Model National Energy Code for Buildings. The Trust can also offer a density bonus to developers who improve upon the energy standard by another 50 per cent or who add beneficial water management features.

In that regard, Univer-City's storm water management system includes a series of rain gardens, infiltration galleries and ponds that capture and restore rainwater to pre-development quality. Unlike conventional stormwater drains that lead to underground pipe systems, these features also preserve traditional flows — a particularly important consideration in BC, where protection of the much-revered salmon is a measure of environmental performance. This is so much the case that Trust has stated publicly that its goal is to build a development on the top of the mountain that will create no inconvenience whatsoever for salmon swimming and spawning in the fresh-flowing creeks at the bottom.

The building standards at Univer-City are also among the most environmentally sustainable in North America. LEED Gold has been the typical target for residential and commercial buildings and for the University Highlands Elementary School. The Univer-City Childcare Centre is expected to be certified as the first building in Canada to achieve the International Living Future Institute standard for a Living Building. To do so, it must generate more energy and harvest or recycle more water than its inhabitants consume. The Trust also must demonstrate that the building was constructed from, and will be operated with, non-toxic materials sourced from within 500 kilometres. Any carbon dioxide generated in the construction or operations must be offset, in perpetuity.

On its opening day in April 2012, Jason McLennan, CEO of the International Living Future Institute and author of the *Living Building standard* called it, "the greenest childcare on the planet". Perhaps as impressive is the fact that it was built at a cost 18 per cent below that estimated for an equivalent conventional childcare facility, demonstrating that environmental sustainability need not come at the expense of economic sustainability, and that every aspect is replicable and affordable in another community.

The advantages of this exercise in community building are social, practical and economic. In the last category, SFU Community Trust has already contributed C$30 million to the SFU endowment and has provided another C$15 million in infrastructure that benefits the university's ongoing operations. Nearly half the 3,600 residents of Univer-City work or study at SFU — a ratio that will likely stay constant as the community expands to a population of more than 8,000. And the students, faculty and staff on the mountaintop campus now have daily access to a whole set of services that were previously unavailable.

SFU is also engaged academically in Univer-City. The Education Faculty, for example, leads and participates in early learning research at the school and childcare centre, and SFU has signed a Memorandum of Understanding to work with the Prince's Foundation for Building Community using Univer-City as a template for excellence in sustainable development.

From Serendipity to Strategy: A Vision of Engagement

All of these developments unfolded in a manner contrary to what might have been expected based on anecdotal accounts and academic surveys of university/community engagement. Chris Huxham (2003, pp. 420–21), for example, has written that "making collaboration work effectively is highly resource-consuming and often painful ... don't do it unless you have to". Yet, SFU's experience has been marked by a sharp lack of what Huxham characterizes as "pain". There certainly were instances in which the university presented challenges to the community and, especially, to municipal regulators. For example, the City of Burnaby was nonplussed when the SFU Community Trust, acting as a developer, demanded that its property be subjected to more stringent zoning requirements for energy and water efficiency.

But the three cities (Burnaby, Vancouver and Surrey), and the residents and businesses whose affairs were most directly affected, generally welcomed and often celebrated SFU's place-making initiatives. Even as the university was exploring efficient and affordable methods to create or expand new campuses in the midst of high-demand areas, most neighbours applauded the advance of an institution that they believed would have a positive influence — rehabilitating underutilized properties, creating public amenities, and supporting local commerce. This expansion also occurred during a period in which residents in the metropolitan area were beginning to understand and embrace elements of Vancouverism, and especially the benefits of mixed-use, higher-density developments. It created a noticeable pattern of mutual gain at the physical and infrastructural level.

Over the same time, and driven by the same impulse to engage society, SFU was developing community connections in other ways. For example, the university systematically extended its co-op education programmes to cover a broad range of disciplines, while adding and expanding other experiential learning opportunities locally and abroad. These programmes and opportunities enabled SFU students to acquire civic literacy, workplace skills, global connections and other learning dividends while providing concurrent benefits to the communities and organizations with which students engaged.

Meanwhile, SFU faculty, also motivated by a desire to be socially engaged, started getting more involved in community-based and community-focused research, again creating reciprocal benefits for themselves and communities. By seeking answers to urgent and challenging community issues, researchers discovered new research collaborators and champions. They also became more sought after as media commentators and community educators, and enjoyed the gratification of being able to experience first-hand the impacts of and appreciation for their research efforts.

Accordingly, in 2011, when SFU initiated a process to develop a new strategic vision for the university, people inside and outside the institution identified community engagement as a defining strength that should be nurtured and developed. At the same time, they made clear that physical engagement was just one part of a much larger picture. Their implicit message was that, if SFU wished to realize its full transformative potential, it would have to go beyond the physical to embrace a comprehensive form of engagement. As a consequence, SFU launched a new Strategic Vision early in 2012 calling for engagement in all aspects of the university's mission.

Released under the heading "The Engaged University" (and accompanied by the tagline "Engaging the World"), the Vision calls on SFU to be "the leading engaged university defined by its dynamic integration of innovative education, cutting-edge research, and far-reaching community engagement". It goes on to set goals for "engaging students", "engaging research" and "engaging communities". These goals are explicated within the Vision and can be illustrated by reference to specific examples. With regard to "engaging students", the goal is "to equip SFU students with the knowledge, skills, and experiences that prepare them for life in an ever-changing and challenging world". The aim here is to provide students with innovative and diverse educational opportunities that enable them to gain the research skills, workplace knowledge and social understanding needed to become effective and engaged citizens.

A prime example of this goal in action is provided by SFU's Semester in Dialogue. This full-time, interdisciplinary cohort programme brings together students from diverse disciplines for an entire semester to study a theme or topic that they help to develop. Recent themes have involved issues such as energy utilization, healthcare ethics and environmental sustainability. Students then work collaboratively amongst themselves — and with community thought leaders — not only to enhance their own understanding, but to promote discussion and policy advancement in the community. In the process, they learn how to work within civil society to influence decision-making in both the public and private spheres. Students who have taken this programme say that the approach and experience have had an extraordinary impact on their learning and their lives. Typical is the reaction of a young man who recently told one of the authors that the programme had transformed his outlook on life. He said that he began his studies with the assumption that there was little he could do to influence social, economic or environmental issues. The Semester in Dialogue opened his eyes to a multitude of avenues and means by which he, as a citizen, could make important and positive differences in his community. The Semester in Dialogue, he said, had enabled him to discover his voice.

With regard to "engaging research", the Vision's goal is "to be a world leader in research mobilization building on a strong foundation of fundamental research". The objective here is for SFU to encourage researchers to use their knowledge and expertise to support communities to develop the capacities and policies they require to address the social, economic and environmental issues they face.

A project that illustrates this goal is the Hakai Network for Coastal People, Ecosystems and Management. This inter-disciplinary research network seeks to advance environmental and economic sustainability on

BC's central coast — home of the Great Bear Rainforest and an area of unparalleled beauty and environmental richness. Launched in 2010 through a partnership involving SFU, the Tula Foundation and coastal First Nations, the Network enables SFU faculty, students and post-doctoral researchers in diverse science and social science disciplines to collaborate with First Nations partners and others on projects aimed at enhancing the sustainability, resilience and well-being of the people and ecosystems of this remarkable area. The Network is founded on the principle that community-based research should be collaborative — that it should be done *with* rather *for* communities — with First Nations peoples engaged as full partners in, rather than subjects of, such enquiry. This intermingling of university research with Indigenous and local knowledge is producing greater benefits for everyone. The people of the Central Coast are acquiring information and advice that will assist them to develop more sustainable communities. And SFU researchers are gaining a fuller and deeper understanding of the complex issues they are exploring in this unique area.

Participants in SFU's Hakai Network for Coastal People, Ecosystems and Management work with First Nations to advance environmental and economic sustainability on BC's central coast. (Courtesy of SFU Creative Services)

When it comes to "engaging communities", the goal is "to be Canada's most community-engaged research university". The ambition here is for SFU, in the Vision's words, to "develop partnerships and maximize the capacities of its three campuses to enhance the social, economic, environmental and cultural well-being of communities both locally and globally". This is to be done by building "respectful and mutually beneficial community relationships". One particular objective is for SFU to "be BC's public square for enlightenment and dialogue on key public issues, and [to] be known as the institution to which the community looks for education, discussion and solutions".

To this end, the University last year launched "SFU Public Square", an initiative that seeks to foster community education, dialogue and deliberation on key issues of the day. SFU has the facilities to host public gatherings, the technology for virtual communications, and the expertise to inform, facilitate and mediate productive conversations — which grow increasingly critical at a time when public discourse about domestic and international issues so often seems to generate more heat than light. In an effort to promote true community engagement, SFU Public Square convenes an annual, week-long Community Summit on a topic of pressing concern, while working the rest of the year to convene, accommodate and facilitate events that provide enlightenment and encourage dialogue on key public issues.

This year's Summit, focusing on the challenges associated with "Charting British Columbia's Economic Future", included a youth summit, 100 community conversations in 27 locales across the province, forums on issues of taxation and immigration, a public event with economist Robert Reich, a deliberate dialogue involving over 150 representatives from diverse interest groups and constituencies, and a wrap-up comedy cabaret. Over 1,000 people contributed to its research and over 4,000 people attended Summit events. An additional 22,000 visited the Summit webpage (where they lingered on average for almost 5 minutes) and, during the Reich event, SFU Public Square trended nationally on twitter. The results of all this engagement will become the subject of a report summarizing the ideas and strategies generated by the Summit and proposing further actions.

Participants at the launch of SFU Public Square, one of the university's signature community engagement initiatives. (Courtesy of SFU Creative Services)

SFU's Morris J. Wosk Centre for Dialogue is one of many university facilities that support community dialogue and engagement. (Courtesy of SFU Creative Services)

Conclusion

Notwithstanding a history of mutual suspicion that has served to separate the academy from the larger community, most universities today accept that acts of engagement are frequently unavoidable and often beneficial. However, the SFU experience suggests that the benefits for both sides can be more meaningful and enduring when university-community engagement is not undertaken as an altruistic or episodic activity, but rather as a deliberate and systemic pursuit. This requires universities and communities to move beyond transactional relationships (in which the parties' engagement is limited to discrete transactions of the kind that occur when a university seeks a development permit from a city) to transformational relationships (in which the parties regard each other as valued partners in an evolving, mutually beneficial affiliation).

This progression, from the transactional to the transformative, tends to emerge only when both partners recognize and welcome the possibility that their collaborative work is not only intrinsically worthwhile, but that it also has the potential to transform them for the better (Enos and Morton, 2003). This sense of mutual benefit is not something that can be negotiated or contracted; it must be developed in concert as the parties build trust and confidence in one another. It is a dividend of engagement that can only be earned through shared vision and a commitment to the relationship.

By embracing university-community engagement in all of its forms, SFU has reaped rewards even as it has contributed to community betterment and built increasingly rewarding relationships. The university's efforts have been characterized by a remarkable reciprocity. Students who participate in co-op and other experiential learning programmes gain skills and insights — about themselves and about the communities in which they are working — while the organizations with which they engage reap the benefits of student input, often establishing relationships with individual students that lead to employment or longer-term connections, while building broader connections with the university as a whole. Faculty who participate in community-based research find immediate application and growing demand for their expertise. They are liable to encounter new and interesting challenges, and their solutions and recommendations are more likely to be applied, immediately and broadly. Members of the community, meanwhile, increasingly regard these researchers' work as valuable and worthy of support, which may be philosophical (as when community groups rally behind evidence-based solutions) or financial (as when leaders in the private or public sector recognize that a short-term investment in the university constitutes a long-term investment in the community itself).

SFU's unique commitments to physical and programmatic engagement further demonstrate that a university that exhibits a systemic and consistent commitment to community betterment is likely to be rewarded by equal enthusiasm and support from the community for its presence and success. Rather than being regarded as a separate service provider to which the community must periodically look for seeking assistance, the university becomes seen as an integrated civic institution upon whom the well-being of the community depends on.

This relationship does not guarantee an end to the friction that can sometimes arise between what has been characterized by as "town and gown". A university that never produced unsettling ideas or disruptive technologies would be failing its community in a fundamental way. But a deep, mutually beneficial integration of university and community interests — and the kind of reciprocal commitment that broad-based engagement fosters — can go a long way towards safeguarding the univer-city relationship on occasions when troublesome issues arise. For a relationship founded upon a shared assumption that the benefits are, indeed, mutual and potentially transformative for both parties, is a relationship that not only is more likely to be worthwhile and productive, but also is better able to withstand the pressures that are placed upon it from time to time.

References

Bender, R., Marthinsen, E., Parman, J. (2013). "Berkeley Campus and Community". *Univer-Cities: Strategic Implications for Asia,* pp. 51–84.

Editorial, *The Vancouver Sun* (5 May 2009). "For 20 years, SFU has provided downtown's intellectual heart."

Enos, S. & Morton, K. (2003). "Developing a theory and practice of campus-community partnerships". In B. Jacoby & Associates, eds., *Building partnerships for service-learning*, pp. 20–41. San Francisco: John Wiley & Sons, Inc.

Huxham, C. (2003). "Theorizing Collaboration Practice". *Public Management Review*, 5, no, 3, pp. 410–423.

Leslie, T. *Burnaby News Leader* (12 April 2012). "Greenest facility 'on the planet' opens doors at UniverCity".

Rybczynksi, W. (2011). "The University in the Shopping Mall". *Slate* online. Available from <http://www.slate.com/articles/arts/architecture/2011/12/surrey_central_city_how_they_put_a_university_in_a_shopping_mall_.html> [accessed October 2013].

Simon Fraser University Strategic Vision, 2012. *The Engaged University*. Available from. <http://www.sfu.ca/content/dam/sfu/engage/StrategicVision.pdf> [accessed October 2013].

Simon Fraser University Video Animation (2012). *SFU: The Engaged University*. Available from <http://www.youtube.com/watch?v=2H_GvkWomuo#t=14> [accessed October 2013].

About the Authors

Andrew Petter is President and Vice-Chancellor of Simon Fraser University and Professor in the School of Public Policy.

Richard Littlemore is writer/consultant who works extensively in the academic sector.

Joanne Curry is Associate Vice-President External Relations at Simon Fraser University.

CHAPTER EIGHT

MODELLING GOOD URBAN (DESIGN) BEHAVIOUR: UNIVERSITY-LED NEIGHBOURHOOD DEVELOPMENT, UNIVERSITY OF MANITOBA

RICHARD MILGROM, DAVID T. BARNARD AND MICHELLE RICHARD

Background

In 2009, the University of Manitoba (UofM) purchased land previously used as a golf course at its Fort Garry Campus. The land separates the campus from adjacent neighbourhoods, and its acquisition presents opportunities for the University to make better connections on a range of levels with Winnipeg's communities, and to act as a role model for development of excellent urban environments. Although the outcomes of the University's endeavours are yet to be realized, the process has the potential to be an example for other institutions to follow, even those within very different contexts.

Over the last 50 years, development in Winnipeg has been predominately low-density and automobile-oriented. This, combined with slow population growth, hollowed out the core and reduced the walkability of older neighbourhoods. In addition to ecological concerns about sprawl, the City currently has an infrastructure deficit (the money needed to maintain the existing roads and sewers) of eight billion dollars. The University's vision for integrating the former golf course land into the Fort Garry Campus is to provide a 24-hour social environment, moving beyond its current status as a daytime destination with few amenities for the small population in student residences. There will be housing for about 8,000 new residents in a neighbourhood incorporating new transit initiatives and providing a mix of uses in a walkable urban environment. Improving its connections with the surroundings will add to the sustainability of the campus and complement the adjacent areas that also lack services.

This development can serve the University's research and pedagogical objectives. The new neighbourhood can be a laboratory, welcoming researchers to monitor the social and ecological impacts of the designed environments, and to test prototypes. The development can contribute to conventional teaching projects in faculties but can also play a role in public education, providing models for the broader community to experience, and for developers to study for application elsewhere.

The University initiated this project by choosing the campus planning and design team through an anonymous open international competition that attracted 45 entries. This approach opens up the space of possibilities for design beyond conventional thinking. The exhibition of entries itself acts as a catalyst for public discussion about urban development (not just on the University campus).

Competitions — mostly architecture competitions — are often criticized for their lack of opportunity for stakeholders to participate in the design process. Planning and urban design competitions are more open, and in this case, the University endeavoured to include communities extensively. More than 80 meetings were held with stakeholders during the development of instructions to the competitors, and a broad range of interests were represented on the competition jury and on the panel of technical advisors. Perhaps most importantly, the objective of the competition was not to select a plan or design but to select the *planning team*. Although entries presented design proposals, these were not understood as literal, implementable schemes, but as indications of intent and illustrative of the concerns that the teams would bring to the process. Now that the winner has been declared, the real work of developing the campus design will begin with the participation of a broad range of communities.

There will be many challenges. The University anticipates that the development models used may not meet the conventional expectations of the developers or the City authorities. In addition, the University will face its own internal hurdles as it develops lands that will accommodate more uses and users, as well as dedicated academic facilities.

Introduction

UofM is a medical/doctoral university with a mission to serve the 1,200,000 people in the Province of Manitoba through learning, discovery and engagement in the community. It is a member of the U15 group of research-intensive universities in Canada. There are approximately 30,000 students enrolled in the current academic year. While there is an important health sciences campus in the core of the city of Winnipeg, and other smaller locations in the city and elsewhere, during most of its 137-year history, the University has had a main campus (the Fort Garry campus) that is located several kilometres to the south of the city centre, set back a kilometre from the major arterial route that serves it. The University is frequently perceived by the larger community to be remote and inward looking in its physical form.

The *Strategic Planning Framework* for the University (endorsed by Senate and the Board of Governors in 2009, to be reviewed in 2013–14) identifies four pillars: academic enhancement in selected areas, Indigenous achievement (recognizing the importance of the Indigenous population of the Province), providing an outstanding student experience and being an employer of choice.

As has been the case at most universities, in recent decades, growth in numbers of students coupled with growth in the research enterprise have resulted in expansion of facilities. Some aspects of this physical growth have not kept pace with the rapid expansion of activity: residential space for students, recreational facilities, performance and exhibition spaces for the arts, research and incubation space in the research park located adjacent to the core academic precinct of the campus.

The decision by the Southwood Golf Club adjacent to the Fort Garry campus to relocate, and to offer the golf course lands to the University for purchase, resulted in a decision to acquire 40 hectares of additional land. The University took possession of this land two years ago and is involved in a process that will develop a large area *master plan* incorporating the new land into an overall concept for the enlarged campus. Many aspects of the physical expression of the University and its aspirations are thus open for consideration as the new plan is developed: how to treat the boundaries of the campus (residential neighbourhoods to the north and south, a major artery to the west and a river to the east), how to increase residential density, how to improve access and transit, provision of a spatial focus for the existing research park, how to draw the larger community to the campus, among others.

Since the ideas expressed in the plan will steer the development of the entire campus for decades, the formation of the plan, and the process for forming it, are critically important to the University, its near neighbours and the entire city. The University wants to produce a great plan for itself, and wants to use the opportunity to think about how its development can help shape development in the larger community.

This chapter documents the intentions of the University in undertaking this master planning development project. While the planning project incorporates consideration of the entire Fort Garry campus (academic buildings, agricultural research lands, a research and development park, a recreational and athletics area and the new Southwood lands), this chapter focuses principally on the new lands and their new uses. We provide an overview of Winnipeg's urban history and the resulting urban fabric in which the Fort Garry Campus is located. This necessarily touches on past planning that has created the city's largely car-dependent form. This is followed by a discussion of the opportunities the Southwood lands present for both UofM and the broader city and regional context. The University decided to use an *International Urban Design Competition*, and the paper discusses some of the reasons for this decision. It then recounts some of the more important aspects of the process, including efforts to engage a broad range of stakeholders and communities in the process. Because the results of this competition were announced in November 2013, it is too early to discuss its ramifications. However, this chapter concludes with thoughts about next steps and challenges that the University will face.

Winnipeg Context

Before discussing how the University should develop and how it might connect better with the adjacent neighbourhoods, the city and the region, we will first discuss the urban context and Winnipeg's trajectory. The physical form of the city, particularly the patterns of development over the last half century has not been particularly supportive of strategies of sustainability, in ecological, social and economic terms.

When the City of Winnipeg was founded in 1874, its population was only 3,700. By the turn of the century, that number had grown to 42,000; but over the next 13 years, the population grew dramatically to more than 150,000 (an average of more than 10 per cent per year). Geographical circumstances forced national rail lines through the limited space between Lake Winnipeg to the north and the border with the United States (US) 120 km to the south, creating a "gateway to the west" that, combined with expanding agricultural activity, formed the basis of the city's early economy.

With the opening of the Panama Canal in 1914, reliance on rail transport for shipment of goods across the continent was dramatically reduced, and Winnipeg's growth slowed. Another period of more rapid growth followed at the end of World War II as the global population redistributed itself. However, between 1960 and 2010, growth was best described as slow. In some years it was negligible. Between 1960 and 2000, the total population grew by only 34 per cent, an average of less than 1 per cent annually. In contrast, the urbanized area more than doubled.

Through much of this period, plans and policies anticipated growth that did not occur (Leo & Brown, 2000; Leo & Anderson, 2005). More to the point, the implementation of the plans that favoured suburban car-oriented development, *required* the growth for success (Milgrom, 2011) — there was not enough population growth to satisfy the building supply on the periphery while still maintaining a well-populated downtown and inner city. Following the planning trends that dominated most North American cities, Winnipeg employed strategies that supported Logan and Molotch's (2007 {1987}) thesis that cities are "growth machines". These machines are driven by "growth coalitions", urban actors whose economic interests are best served by new land development. These coalitions can include landowners, homebuilders, and the construction industry, but also other supporting players including politicians and the media that act as boosters and promoters.

This combination of rapid expansion and slow population growth resulted in a loss of overall density (by 2000, it was 50 per cent of its peak overall density in the 1950s). Loss of density has made the operation of public transit inefficient and unpopular, and further increased reliance on private automobiles. In turn, this has required driveways, garages and parking, the increase in traffic has fuelled demand for wider roads and "collector streets" (considerations for cars and drivers) have further spread out development, reducing walkability of neighbourhoods. City regulations about street design are typically written from the perspective of drivers; required street widths and turning radii designed to maintain traffic flow would hinder the best intention of a developer who wanted to increase density beyond the conventional (see Ben-Joseph, 2005).

Retail centres and jobs followed the populations to the periphery and the downtown was hollowed out. Robert Beauregard (2006) has referred to this type of development as "parasitic urbanism" — the growth of new urban areas at the expense of others. While homebuilders have favoured the easily developed greenfield sites on the fringe of the city, the downtown and inner city have declined in population, and lost amenities and services. Although the core still accommodates approximately 25 per cent of the employment in the city (Altus Clayton and Urban Strategies, 2009), most workers return to their suburban homes in the evenings, leaving a landscape of underused shop fronts and surface parking lots.

The ecological implications of this urbanism are becoming apparent in Winnipeg and elsewhere, as the carbon footprint of car dependence has grown. Socially, segregation by income is increasing as the communities that remain in the inner city include those who cannot afford the choice to move and serious health concerns are being raised in cities across the continent related to inactive lifestyles (see, for example, Frank et al., 2006). Economically, the infrastructure of the city has grown faster than the tax base; low-density urban areas require more roads and sewers per capita than compact areas. In Winnipeg's case, this has resulted in an eight billion Canadian dollars infrastructure deficit — the amount needed to bring existing infrastructure up to acceptable standards. Social infrastructure is also stressed as, for example, growing suburban communities demand new schools while inner city schools are closed when the populations they serve dwindle.

Planners within the City have recognized these shortcomings and challenges, and official plans for the city have recognized the need to embrace more compact development, and sustainability. *Plan Winnipeg 2020* (2000) called for a "downtown first" policy that would focus development in the core. The plan suggested ways in which the City's progress would be seen. For example, "more people working and living in the downtown; fewer vacant properties and less underdeveloped land in the downtown; rising value of inner city homes and commercial properties" (p. 12) were expected as results of renewal of the urban core. However, the goals of the plan were largely ignored because the city council put its faith in developers and their understandings of the market to determine how the city grew (see Leo, 2013).

A particular example was the planning and approval of Waverley West in the southwest corner of the city. The area was intended to house more than 50,000 people and was justified by an analysis that suggested land for new housing was running out, and that has been criticized for its lack of rigour (see, for example, Sjoberg, 2005). Approval of this plan required an amendment to the *Plan Winnipeg 2020* since it clearly ran contrary to the ideas of the compact city, and to the "downtown first" policy. This and other similar developments alleviated pressure to push housing development back into the centre of the city.

UofM engaged in the dialogue about Waverley West. In 2004, the Faculty of Architecture participated in the organization and running of charrette — an intense time-limited design exercise intended to stimulate new ideas. The results, published as the *Southwest For Garry Design Charrette* (2004), suggested ways that this area could avoid some of the problems associated with urban sprawl and emphasized respect for the prairie landscape in which the neighbourhood would be built. However, few of these suggestions were incorporated into the final plans. Although there are nods to sustainability such as walking trails and some geothermal heating, the casual observer would be hard pressed to find significant difference between Waverley West and other car-dependent suburbs.

Near the end of the millennium's first decade, Winnipeg was showing more rapid growth. In 2009, the City embarked on a public process to produce a new plan, *OurWinnipeg* (accepted by council in 2011). The City's website notes that more than 80,000 Winnipegers had opportunities to express their desires and concerns, in venues that ranges from questionnaires to forums and charrettes, online and in person. The documents that emerged showed more consideration for urban design — for the configuration of the public realm and the social spaces of the city. In particular, the supporting *Complete Communities: Directions Strategy* (City of Winnipeg, 2009) argues for development that embraces diversity and choice in housing and land uses, and the development of neighbourhoods that support everyday life and all of its functions, rather than just subdivisions of houses.

Although full of good intentions, that plan lacks strong measures of progress, or any indication of which areas of the city should receive development priority. Rather than placing sole emphasis on the downtown area, the latest iteration suggests more centres throughout the urbanized area, and shows greenfield sites within city limits as locations for new neighbourhoods. Nevertheless, the City has continued to approve proposals for areas of the sort already described. One of the proposals received preliminary approval from the Council's Executive Policy Committee even though the developer refused to build streets wide enough to accommodate transit (one of the primary tenets of *Complete Communities*) (Santin, 2013). Such actions undermine serious progress towards a more sustainable city, but also fail to address social justice, further exacerbating social segregation by making little provision for affordable or rental housing.

Southwood Opportunity

The development of the former Southwood Golf Course can serve the growth needs of the University, but also presents a unique opportunity to align with the City's stated planning intentions. In *OurWinnipeg* (City of Winnipeg, 2009), Southwood is one of several "major redevelopment sites" that "will provide transformative opportunities for the development of complete communities with significant residential and employment densities and attractive urban design ... within the existing urban fabric" (p. 37). The University can control planning and design efforts, and lead by example while setting its own agenda. This does not imply the imposition of a vision — it is also the University's intention to model good planning *process*, providing for consultation and engagement of local communities and stakeholders, from the university, adjacent communities, and interests throughout the region.

The University's mission states that it intends "to create, preserve and communicate knowledge, and thereby, contribute to the cultural, social and economic well-being of the people of Manitoba, Canada and the world" (University of Manitoba, 2009). The approach to the development of Southwood takes this statement seriously, and goes beyond the usually assumed limits of universities' roles of conventional teaching and research. It also provides opportunities to address the areas of academic enhancement that were defined in 2009:

- Healthy, safe, secure and sustainable food and bioproducts;
- Sustainable prairie and northern communities;
- Human rights;
- Innovations in public and population health;
- New materials and technologies; and
- Culture and creativity (University of Manitoba, 2009).

Southwood and the entire Fort Garry Campus present many possibilities for research addressing all of these themes. For example, urban agriculture could play a role in the redeveloped site (and connect to the University's agricultural roots); strategies for improving ecological sustainability could be implemented and monitored; human rights issues for the Indigenous peoples can be addressed in the design of the new neighbourhood, and in making the existing campus more accessible; issues of age-friendly cities (WHO, 2007) can be accommodated in the design of environments and the provision of services; materials and technologies can be tested in new construction and the provision of infrastructure; and the design itself can engage with the creative culture present at the University and make it more available to the city and the region.

While economic sustainability will be important, the University is not limited by business cases with immediate or short-term returns. The University is able and willing to address issues of social mix, to address emerging issues of climate change, and to design a neighbourhood around public transit improvements that are yet to be implemented. It can make stronger connections with broader communities in the city and the region by increasing population adjacent to campus, and by increasing the attractiveness of the campus as a destination for events beyond the usual daytime uses (and occasional stadium events). At the same time, the

University's profile can be raised by leading development, and its visibility can literally be increased by augmenting its presence on the closest arterial road, Pembina Highway, the main road connection between downtown and the US border to the south.

Redesign of the campus and development of the adjacent lands also presents opportunities to enhance teaching possibilities. Some of these are obvious, such as: the involvement of the Faculty of Architecture in planning of the sites and the design of buildings, landscapes and public spaces; roles for Engineering students in the development of infrastructure and provision of energy from alternative sources; study of alternative water management systems in the Faculty of Environment, Earth and Resources; or urban food production projects for the Faculty of Agriculture and Food Sciences. Others, particularly those that address social impacts, are less obvious, such as: opportunities for the Faculty of Education to develop a public school curriculum about the built environment or the ability of students in gerontology to work with and learn from seniors who live locally.

But the pedagogical possibilities of the project go well beyond the teaching of university students and the research of faculty members. The University has a public education role to play here — showing how current and emerging research should help shape development to promote more socially just and ecologically sustainable urban environments. The processes used in determining plans and designs for the area should be as open and engaging as possible to include the public in informed debate about the future of Winnipeg.

In this regard, we might distinguish between teaching and pedagogy. Roger Simon (1992) distinguishes between *teaching*, as the methods and processes of "classroom practice", from the broader understanding of *pedagogy*, as a social and political project, addressing not only how material is taught, but also what is taught and why.

> It must not be forgotten that education is implicated in the production, accessibility and legitimization of the languages and images that give our relations with our social and material world a particular intelligibility. ... This means that educational practice is always implicated in the construction of a horizon of possibility for ourselves, our students, and our communities (p. 56).

For Simon, pedagogy, like planning and design, is intended to help students (and here we might include the general public) to "envisage versions of the world that is 'not yet' — in order to be able to alter the ground on which life is lived" (p. 57). Simon argues, therefore, that pedagogical projects involve more than just those conventionally categorized as teachers. He calls for the involvement of all "cultural workers", those involved in the production of meaning. Designers and planners have roles to play and although Simon is not specific, his language is suggestive and parallels the possible processes that are emerging at UofM. He notes:

> If we assume people always come to an engagement with symbolic productions already knowing and with concerns and questions important to their lives, the task of the progressive cultural worker it to engage such people so as to provoke their inquiry into and challenge their exiting views of "the way things are and should be" (p. 47).

Public discussion about the future of the Fort Garry Campus and its connections to the city presents an opportunity to challenge conventional development patterns, and to promote public debate about visions of the world that is "not yet", and what the city "should be".

Competitions

To begin the current discussion about the future of the campus, the University decided to hold an open international urban design competition to find the team that would lead the development of the master plan. This approach was seen as addressing a number of important strategic objectives: it would open up the range of possibilities — or broaden the "search/solution space" (Banerjee & Loukaitou-Sideris, 1990) — bringing new ideas and different experiences to the task from around the world; the exploration of many options would promote debate about the direction that the plan should take; and it would garner international attention to the University's efforts.

Competitions have a long history — although most high profile competitions have been architectural projects (see for example, Mattie & de Jong, 2000). Architectural competitions have typically focused on the built object (e.g., Tribune Tower in Chicago, Sydney Opera House, Jewish Museum in Berlin) and have produced mixed results in terms of users' responses.

Perhaps due to their broader scope, planning and urban design competitions are less familiar, however, they also have a long history. Not as narrowly focused on individual projects, Alexander and Witzling (1990) note that they have been "a tool to generate new concepts and ways of viewing cities and their parts" (p. 92). They may be divided into two broad categories: those intended for implementation and that generate immediate commissions for the winners, and those intended primarily to generate new, often critical, concepts or ideas (when the sponsor does not have immediate plans to implement the designs). Sagalyn (2006) notes that urban design competitions are more likely than their architectural cousins to draw on multiple disciplines, will always focus on "relationships among architectural and non-architectural elements", and must address "a complex combination of public and private interests and domains" (p. 29). Most importantly, and as reflected in UofM's attempt to model good development practices, she argues that they are always political:

> The reasons for holding these competitions are different, but always political. Urban design and planning competitions are about political issues as much as about new design possibilities. Innovative solutions or design visions. Political considerations drive the decision to mount a competition, and though less transparent, shape the details of how a competition is structured and implemented (p. 29).

In terms of format, competitions also generally fall into two categories. One-stage competitions, especially for those that are intended to produce an implementable plan, are more likely to be limited to invited participants, in which case the participants may be known to the jury that is deciding the outcome. In two-stage competitions, the preliminary submission is almost always anonymous and the entrants receive no remuneration. The jury chooses a short list of finalists who then prepare a second more detailed submission and will often provide some sort of stipend for the extra work.

The jury for architectural competitions is tightly regulated in many jurisdictions, often with a requirement that the majority of the jurors be registered practitioners from the profession. Because the issues addressed in planning and urban design competitions are frequently more complex and cross-disciplinary concerns, juries are also more varied and may even include "lay people" (those not drawn from design professions). Ollswang (1990) argues strongly for the inclusion of non-designers on urban design and juries for the practical and experiential perspectives that they bring to the deliberations, and suggests that their inclusion increases the possibility of the plan being implemented and reduces the possibility of "design professionals selecting a 'good-looking' design which in its usefulness or implement ability, is defective and/or flawed" (p. 110).

Visionary (re)Generation Competition

First, the University started designing the competition knowing that one of the shortcomings of many similar processes was their lack of community engagement — the typical architectural competition produces a design without any significant engagement with those who have the most at stake in the project, the communities of users (see Nasar, 1999). With this in mind, the University, through the Campus Planning Office (CPO) developed a strategy to engage communities that had interests in the campus. This was undertaken with an aim to produce a neighbourhood on the Southwood site, and make the campus as a whole more accessible to and connected with the wider city — and all of this will require collaboration and partnerships over the coming decades. The outcome of this first phase of the engagement process was the competition brief, a 192-page document that outlined in detail the University's requirements, values and desires that guided those preparing competition entries.

Second, the University was clear that, although the competition would produce designs for the Fort Garry Campus, the objective was to *hire a planning and design team* rather than to determine the specifics of the *plan*. The plans and the schemes that were submitted for the completion were viewed as visions of the designers that illustrated the concerns and intentions that they would bring to the process. They were *not* intended to illustrate a plan that would be implemented. In this way, the competition focused on ideas rather than specific directions. The implementable plans would be developed by the winning team, working with the diverse range of stakeholders on and off campus, over the following years.

Third, the University's approach recognizes that a successful plan, one that reflects its intentions and that will act as a model for other developments in the city and region, cannot be implemented without meaningful engagement, partnership and collaboration, throughout the entire process. Although the Visionary (re)Generation competition, like most, was anonymous and allowed only limited contact between the competitors and the sponsor (and none with other stakeholders), extensive participation of stakeholders framed the brief, and will continue with the planning team. The University hopes that this level of participation will enable it not only to advance its desires to develop its assets but also, and perhaps most importantly, in doing so, to be and to be seen as welcoming to and engaged with the larger community.

Engagement to Date

Far too often in Winnipeg (and other municipalities), the proponents of projects underestimate the value of meaningful engagement and working *with* stakeholders to determine visions for planning and development, instead seeking "buy-in", or at least acceptance for proposals that serve limited interests. Unfortunately, this attitude to city building usually misses opportunities to realize good urban form at a range of scales from individual buildings to entire precincts and neighbourhoods. In the case of the Southwood lands and indeed the entire UofM Fort Garry Campus, the University hopes to practise what it preaches, taking advantage of its pedagogical and research agendas and employing good planning practices to redevelop this site and to support the functions of the institution, to complement adjacent communities and to provide amenities for the city and the region.

Early in the process, CPO identified stakeholders with whom the University should engage. These included the University communities of students, faculty and staff; neighbouring residents; elected officials whose support for proposals would be needed; public servants from various levels of government who would need to understand the approvals processes and could provide valuable technical assistance; private interests including developers who may be interested in building on the site; and participants in community-based activities representing a range of interests. The plan was, and remains, to engage with these constituencies with the hope that they can be inspired to see Southwood redeveloped as a model sustainable community and be motivated to participate in realizing the vision. In seeking new, or at least different, development patterns for Winnipeg, the University acknowledges that forms stand a better chance of acceptance if the stakeholders are included in the process from the outset. Further, it can see no good reason to exclude anyone from the process, one that will involve opportunities for public education and debate about the urban future.

Initial engagement process

The first phase of the engagement process was intended to define the issues that the plan would address. This phase included:

- Conceptualizing possibilities through a design charrette, to identify priorities of stakeholder groups in the community;
- Crafting principles and objectives that would guide the writing of the competition brief and the subsequent planning process for a new *Campus Master Plan*, Southwood Precinct Plan and an initial demonstration project;
- Providing opportunities for individuals, groups, organizations, advocates and decision-makers to inform the drafting of the Competition Brief;
- Encouraging collaboration with key stakeholders including the City of Winnipeg (the planning authority for the site) and the Province of Manitoba (the University's primary funder);
- Developing a venue for on-going discussions with local residents about new buildings and landscapes that may occupy lands adjacent to or in close proximity to their homes;
- Identifying potential partners for the development and nurture those relationships; and
- Raising the profile of the project and building excitement about its possibilities and for the Visionary (re)Generation Open Urban Design Competition.

Over 18 months, CPO organized 80 meetings providing opportunities to present information and engage with communities about the process, building a foundation for the Competition and starting the planning processes that will be needed to transform the former golf course and the existing campus into a sustainable neighbourhood.

Local Residents

While all stakeholders have indicated some level of appreciation for the engagement effort, the community members who have demonstrated the most significant evolution in their perspective are those who live in the neighbourhoods adjacent to the university. They are now champions of the process.

Initial discussions with local residents were not positive and there was significant distrust of the process — distrust that can be explained by the recent construction of a new stadium on the university campus, one that many residents opposed. Their initial response to the University's proposals for new development, in some cases very much in their backyards, was resistance to anything other than a park that would maintain the open space of the golf course.

The process of community engagement with the local residents was extensive and will continue as the project develops. It took time and many meetings to establish that the University intended to take residents' concerns seriously, but also to argue that a new neighbourhood, if designed well, can bring positive change to the lives of the community members. This relationship will require on-going attention and the University's actions will have to demonstrate its sincerity over time.

To-date, though, a neighbourhood network has been established, and participation is growing. The University has opened the now unused golf course temporarily as publicly accessible open space but only did this after seeking concurrence from the neighbourhood network regarding the operations of the space, and discussing how it would be used during special events (it forms a "buffer" now between the neighbourhood and the stadium). Members of the network have also participated in drafting and reviewing the competition brief. CPO is confident that there is genuine excitement from residents about the redevelopment possibilities — especially related to sustainability, open spaces and access to amenities within walking distance to their homes. A level of trust has been established, but maintaining that trust, and meeting the expectations of the residents, during a complex development process will be a challenge.

University Constituencies

Diverse views exist inside the University community as well as outside even after the initial stage of the consultation process has run its course. Philosophical differences between constituencies will not be easily resolved, and certainly conventional methods of consultations (occasional information sessions and open houses) will not be sufficient. There are differing views on the overall process, its vision and principles, including the expectation that the site will be redeveloped as a sustainable mixed-use community. While there are strong supporters on campus, some have been critical of the process to-date, suggesting concerns that start with the decision to purchase the Southwood Lands, and the lack of faculty and student representation on the competition jury.

Some members of the University feel strongly that the University should not have acquired the lands and should not endeavour to redevelop them, and that the lands should remain open space. Even though efforts have been made to demonstrate a commitment to not "over develop" the site, including a competition requirement that 50 per cent of the land remain as public open spaces and parklands, there remains considerable concern. Others cite concerns that the redevelopment of the lands will "chip away" at the integrity and mandate of the University, ultimately leading to the commercialization of the institution.

Of key importance will be the continued involvement of members of the internal community as the process moves from vision and concept to a more practical exercise of master planning. Finally, the true test to the collaborative effort will only be realized as the University seeks partners to develop its plan, including its current critics.

Regulating Authorities

While the University hopes to lead by example by building a walkable, sustainable neighbourhood, there are regulatory and political hurdles to be overcome. It is entirely possible that the urban design intentions for the expanded campus will not match cleanly with existing zoning by-laws or regulations that govern the design of streets. Therefore, the University has forged relationships with the regulating authorities from the start of the process, involving them in all aspects of the discussion.

The City of Winnipeg, through its official plan, *OurWinnipeg*, has deemed the development of Southwood Lands an important component in its efforts to meet its objectives. It is identified as one of 11 "redevelopment" sites within city limits, all of which are considered appropriate for mixed land uses. In contrast to the low density development so typical in recent decades, these should be at higher residential densities, more walkable, and support the everyday lives of residents — in other words, they should be "complete communities" as supporting documents for the official plan outline.

The City of Winnipeg has been a major contributor and participant in the process to-date, and representatives from the Planning, Policy and Development Department, the transit authority and the local councillor have all played active roles in defining the vision and goals for Southwood, drafting the competition brief, and participating as technical experts for the competition jury. At some point, the City's role will change from that of a collaborator in the development of neighbourhood and campus concepts, to that of a regulator — as the lands will all be subject to local planning and zoning by-laws and regulations. Much of the site will be subject to re-zoning processes, and may challenge existing regulations and standards as it is used to suggest more sustainable urban forms and infrastructure. A key to navigating through a land use planning regulatory approval process will be the continued alignment and sharing of ideas with the City of Winnipeg.

Maintaining the Visionary Momentum?

With the announcement of the winner, the Visionary (re)Generation competitions has come to a close, and the real work of planning has begun. The University plans to have three plans completed in the 18 months following the award of the contract to the master planning team — a new *campus master plan*; a more detailed precinct plan for the Southwood Lands, and specific site plan for a phase one demonstration project intended to set the tone for the developments to follow. To successfully achieve the goals that the University has set for itself, planning will have to continue with the robust process of engagement that was used in the production of the competition programme and brief.

Although the immediate goal of this work is to produce a plan, if the plan is to be realized, this engagement will have to be sustained into the future. The process will also have to raise expectations of shared responsibilities, and different roles will need to be assumed by the University community, the City, the business community, local residents, investors, and other special interest groups.

The University will face challenges — a plan that does not fit neatly with current conventions is bound to meet resistance. Some of this may come from the local development community who will be asked to build unfamiliar building types, the City that may be asked to approve non-conventional drainage systems, or some neighbours who are opposed to increased residential densities. But some may come from within the University itself as a period of budgetary restraint looms on the horizon.

If any institution has the capacity to rise to these challenges, it should be a university. By undertaking a high-profile planning process and engaging a broad range of participants, UofM has the opportunity to increase the visibility of planning issues in the Winnipeg region. By studying the results of its efforts, it has the opportunity to make significant contributions to more far-reaching debates about urban development processes and their outcomes, efforts that may have both local and international implications.

References

Alexander, E. and Witzling, L. (1990). "Planning and Urban Design Competitions: Introduction and Overview". *Journal of Architectural and Planning Research* 7, no. 2, pp. 91–104.

Altus Clayton and Urban Strategies Inc. (2009). *Downtown Winnipeg Employment Study*. Winnipeg, City of Winnipeg, Planning, Property and Development Department, p. 89.

Artibise, A. (1977). *Winnipeg: An Illustrated History*. Toronto, James Lorimer & Company Publishers, National Museum of Man, National Museums of Canada.

Banerjee, T. and Loukoitou-Sider, A. (1990). "Competition as a Design Method: An Inquiry". *Journal of Architectural and Planning Research* 7, no. 2, pp. 114–31.

Beauregard, R. A. (2006). *When America Became Suburban*. Minneapolis: University of Minnesota Press.

Ben-Joseph, Eran (2005). *The Code of the City: Standard and the Hidden Language of Place Making*. Cambridge, MA: MIT Press.

City of Winnipeg (2001). *Plan Winnipeg 2020 Vision — A Long Range Policy Plan for City Council*. Winnipeg: City of Winnipeg, p. 67.

——— (2004a). *City of Winnipeg Residential Land Supply Study*. Winnipeg: Planning, Property and Development, Planning and Land Use Division, City of Winnipeg, p. 24.

——— (2004b). *Waverley West Proposed Plan Winnipeg Amendment City of Winnipeg Financial Impact Analysis*. Winnipeg: City of Winnipeg, p. 15.

——— (2010). *Call to Action for OurWinnipeg: Visions and Directions for the OurWinnipeg Plan*. Winnipeg: City of Winnipeg, p. 65.

Frank, L. D, Sallis, J. F., Conway, T. L., Chapman, J. E., Saelens, B. E. and Bachman, W. (2006). "Many Pathways from Land Use to Health: Associations between Neighborhood Walkability and Active Transportation, Body Mass Index, and Air Quality". *Journal of the American Planning Association* 7, no.1, pp. 75–87.

Gillham, O. (2002). *The Limitless City: A Primer on, the Urban Sprawl Debate*. Washington: Island Press.

Jonas, A. E. G. and Wilson, D. (1999). "The City as a Growth Machine: Critical Reflection Two Decades Later". In A. E. G. Jonas and D. Wilson, Albany, eds, *The Urban Growth Machine: Critical Reflection Two Decades Later*. NY: The State University of New York Press.

Leo, C. and Anderson, K. (2005). "Being Realistic about Urban Growth". Winnipeg: Canadian Centre for Policy Alternatives MB, p. 26.

Leo, C. and Brown, W. (2000). "Slow Growth and Urban Development Policy". *Journal of Urban Affairs* 22, no. 2, pp. 193–213.

Leo, C. (2013). "Winnipeg: Aspirational Planning, Chaotic Development". Paper presented at the Canadian Political Science Association Conference, Victoria, BC, 5 June 2013. Retrieved from <www.cpsa-acsp.ca/papers-2013/Leo.pdf > 11 October 2013.

Logan, J. R. and Molotch, H. L. (2007 [1987]). *Urban Fortunes: The Political Economy of Space*. Berkeley, CA: University of California Press.

Mattie, E. and de Jong, C., eds. (2000). *Architectural Competitions: 1792–1949 and 1950-Today*. New York: Taschen.

Milgrom, R. (2011). "Slow Growth versus the Sprawl Machine: Winnipeg, Manitoba". In D. Young, P. B. Wood and R. Keil, eds, *In Between Infrastructure: Urban Connectivity in an Age of Vulnerability*, pp. 87–100. Kelowna, B.C.: Praxis (e)Press.

MMM Group (2007). "Waverley West Innovative New Suburb or 'same old, same old'".Powerpoint presentation by Paul McNeil and Richard Tebinka 13 March 2007. <http://www.apegm.mb.ca/pdnet/papers /wwest.pdf> 20 October 2013.

Molotch, H. (1976). "The City as a Growth Machine". *American Journal of Sociology* 82 (September): 309–32.

Nasar, J. L. (1999). *Design by Competition: Making Design Competition Work*. New York: Cambridge University Press.

ND Lea (2004). *Waverley West Plan Winnipeg Amendment Housing and Population Report*. Winnipeg: Planning, Property and Development Department, City of Winnipeg.

———— (2005). *Area Structure Plan — Waverley West: Draft Plan*. Winnipeg: City of Winnipeg, p. 65.

Ollswang, J.E. (1990). "Successful Competitions: Planning for Quality, Equity and Useful Results". *Journal of Architectural and Planning Research* 7, no. 2, pp. 105–13.

Pendall, R. (2003). *Sprawl without Growth: The Upstate Paradox*. Washington, DC: The Brookings Institution, Center on Urban and Metropolitan Policy.

Province of Manitoba (2006a). "Legislation Would Direct MHRC Land-Sale Profits to Housing in Areas of Need". Press release, Minister of Family Services and Housing, 13 April 2006.

———— (2006b). "Waverley West — A New Development for a Growing City". Press release, Minister of Family Services and Housing.

Sagalyn, Lynne B. (2006). "The Political Fabric of Design Competitions". In Catherine Malmberg, ed., *Politics of Design: Competitions for Public Projects*. Section 1, pp. 29–52.

Santin, Aldo (2013, October 3). "Planners lose on subdivision: City panel OK's big new project on Jefferson". *Winnipeg Free Press*. Retrieved from <http:www.winnipegfreepress.com>

Seidel, A. (1990). "Design Competitions Receive Mixed Reviews". *Journal of Architectural and Planning Research* 7, no. 2, pp. 172–80.

Simon, R. I. (1992). *Teaching against the Grain: Texts for a Pedagogy of Possibility*. Toronto: OISE Press.

Sjoberg, K. (2005). "3000 Acres of Phony Demand: Consideration on Waverley West". Winnipeg: Canadian Centre for Policy Alternatives, p 25.

University of Manitoba, Faculty of Architecture (2004). *Southwest Fort Garry Design Charrette*. Report. Winnipeg, MB: Faculty of Architecture, University of Manitoba.

University of Manitoba (2009). *Strategic Planning Framework*. Retrieved from <http://umanitoba.ca/admin/president/strategic_plan/2311.html>

World Health Organization (2007). *Global Age-friendly Cities: A Guide*. Geneva: World Health Organization.

About the Authors

Richard Milgrom is Associate Dean, Faculty of Architecture, University of Manitoba.

David T. Barnard is President and Vice-Chancellor, University of Manitoba.

Michelle Richard is a Partner at Richard Wiintrup & Associates.

CHAPTER NINE

CARLETON UNIVERSITY: THE ARCHITECTURE OF KNOWLEDGE AND THE KNOWLEDGE OF ARCHITECTURE

ROSEANN O'REILLY RUNTE

Introduction

Cities and universities enjoy a symbiotic relationship and can successfully build a sustainable future by working together. In a time when information and information technology are highly accessible, the organization of knowledge, is the next challenge to resolve and in its resolution resides the new key to power. Universities need to provide flexible spaces to accommodate new technologies and ways of teaching. Campuses will more than ever embrace their surroundings. As community engagement and social responsibility become part of the teaching, learning and research agendas, the city will become part of the campus, a living laboratory. The city which supports the integration of post-secondary institutions in its design and fabric will be a creative leader. Cities, like Ottawa, Canada, with two universities have the potential of becoming models for the future. With communications technology, leading universities and cities around the world will form constellations of expertise and networks of strong economic and social development.

The Architecture of Knowledge and the Knowledge of Architecture

Knowledge is power. access to knowledge equates access to power. Cities endowed with universities, or, even better, clusters of universities are naturally home to strong and sustainable populations. One need only look at the Boston area or Silicon Valley in the United States to observe the link between an educated population and development in the sectors of science, technology and the arts. Richard Florida has written about centres of creativity and innovation where the arts flourish alongside technology. The common ingredient to all creative spaces is at least one strong university, and most likely several such institutions, filled with lively, innovative minds.

As information technology becomes less expensive and ever more ubiquitous, access to knowledge is not limited geographically. Yet, despite the ever-increasing availability of information, people still require places of learning. They need to come together to learn through discussion and debate. Information only becomes knowledge when it is organized, mentally processed and understood. Before knowledge is applied, one must think and test ideas and concepts. This can, of course, be done through experience, a lengthy process of often painful trial and costly error. It can also be accomplished in a shorter period with the advice and counsel of mentors, the inspiration of brilliant lecturers and professors who engage students by tracing a path of suggested readings, experiments and experiences.

The organization of information is the key to creating leadership for the future. When so much information is widely available, we need to deal not only with data but massive data, not only with the books in the local library but with the literatures of the world, not only with the politics and economies, of our nation but also those of our globe. Resolving scientific problems will require the work of teams of researchers in networks around the world. Together, we will reach further into space and deeper into the understanding of our universe, past and present.

When Gutenberg developed the printing press, it is unlikely that he thought entire populations would be reading books and public education would be so widespread that international agencies would publish universal literacy as a goal. Today, with nearly instantaneous access to enormous amounts of information, we have the possibility to make wiser policies and better regulations than ever. However, our brains cannot keep up with the speed and quantity of information. We have information architectures: classifying things alphabetically, sequentially, by group, by geographic origin, by number of "hits", by key words. If information technology has been revolutionary in democratizing access, the program which manages to classify the information accessibly in the most coherent and useful fashion will be the next building block, the reformation. The architecture of information technology is the means to classify and make sense of incredible amounts of data. Today, we can begin to imagine the structure which will make information not only accessible but useful and then make not only information but knowledge accessible.

Universities have long denied any relationship to *ivory* towers, strongly affirming their footing in reality, in service to their communities. Yet, ivy-covered towers still capture our imagination and even today, we fondly picture Pope's lonely "towers lit through the midnight hour". Despite our romantic musings, libraries have become home to technology, welcoming more people and relegating hard copies of the classics to storage. Laboratories have become hives of international activity as students are connected via video-teleconference or Skype to others in labs around the world. When the Higgs-Boson particle physics experiment occurred at Cerne, in Switzerland last year, students at Carleton, in Canada were participating in real time. When faculty were researching economic development in Spain, they were joined by their colleagues in Canada directly on-line. The architecture of the university must encourage imagination, communication with local and global communities, access to evolving technology. At the same time, it must, as Yi-Fu Tuan noted, serve as "the primary text for handing down a tradition...". This means the university must represent past and inspire future while serving an immediate present. The university must be both "space and place." We know that people react to their environments and this experience shapes their thinking and habits. It can expand or limit their horizons. What is the architecture of the university which opens our minds and eliminates boundaries created by the limitations of our budgets, our experiences, our abilities to imagine and encourage the imagination of the as-yet unimagined possibilities of humankind?

A Tale of Two Universities

It is always the "best of times and the worst of times" in universities. Never are revenues sufficient to permit the realization of the multitude of dreams spun by the academic community. But then, should funding be sufficient, one might infer a paucity of ideas, a situation far worse! Within the academy, Faculties compete for attention and funding. Communities clamour for greater measures of civic engagement, socially responsible volunteering, and massive commitments to economic development with investments largely in short-term, applied and practically-oriented research. Faculty members remind us of the importance of longer-term thinking and theoretical inquiry. Governments push for greater transparency, the creation of specific targets with measurable results, differentiation among institutions and easy transferability of credits. University administrations and boards worry about deferred maintenance while investing in teaching and research programmes requiring new facilities.

Nearly every great city is home to at least one university. The greatest boast more than one. Montreal attributes its strength to the number of strong institutions it has attracted and supported. Communities surrounding universities like Waterloo, Ontario, have come together to provide funding, land and services for the burgeoning institution which has, in turn, offered economic growth, employment and cultural vitality to their regions.

Whenever the possibility that a government or foundation is considering the development of a university, college or research institute arises, local communities vie for the opportunity to host the institution. When people select a new location, the first question they ask is about the presence of educational institutions that open the doors to the future for their children and provide them intellectual and cultural activities, athletic events and facilities. When companies, in particular, those requiring an educated workforce, choose new sites, they look to locations with clusters of universities.

The City of Ottawa is fortunate to boast of two community colleges and two major universities: the University of Ottawa and Carleton University. Situated at a distance of approximately seven kilometers one from the other, at either end of the Rideau Canal, one of UNESCO's heritage sites, the two universities enjoy a unique relationship. The University of Ottawa was founded in 1848 by the Catholic Church and is a bilingual (French and English) institution while Carleton was founded in 1943 by the community and is a unilingual, English-speaking university. Divided by nearly a century, diverse cultures and linguistic differences, the two institutions have developed an impressive list of collaborative activities. Undergraduate students may take courses at either university without paying additional fees. The universities simply do a joint accounting at the end of each academic year. When undergraduate programmes have small enrolments, faculty members share teaching. For example, in Latin or Greek courses where enrolments are not very large at the present time, rather than duplicating efforts, each university offers half the programme, effectively sharing enrolments. There are 28 joint Graduate Institutes, particularly in science and engineering where faculty co-supervise and teach Masters and PhD students. Some departments have developed carefully over the years, making efforts not to duplicate areas of specialization within fields. This means that together, the universities offer the City of Ottawa the best possible range of courses, fields of inquiry and research. It would not be healthy without a bit of competition in the midst of this symbiosis. Just as the two university communities relish the friendly rivalry of sporting events, faculty sometimes compete for grants and prizes, thereby, raising the standards of excellence in both institutions. The result of this extraordinary relationship is the largely unrecognized fact that the two universities together bring to the City of Ottawa and the Province of Ontario, the second highest number and amount of research grants and awards in Ontario. Together, they serve over 70,000 students and provide a strong spark to the regional economy.

When students can don skates and move from one university to the other in less than 15 minutes, it is rather understandable that the two institutions have not invested precious funds in distance-learning technologies to foster communication between them. The movement of non-skaters is facilitated by the transit system and parking facilities on both campuses.

To date, no joint facilities or facilities in support of the many shared academic and research initiatives have been developed. Both campuses lack sufficient teaching, study and research infrastructure. The fact that the institutions are located in the nation's Capital, might make it appear that they would enjoy access to additional space at the many museums and government facilities in the city. While this is indeed the case, these facilities are not primarily dedicated to the universities' use or specific needs, are not free of charge, and are not necessarily available at appropriate times. This provides the opportunity to imagine new architectural designs which would promote the extraordinary collaboration which currently exists. Could we design buildings which would enhance and offer a visual demonstration of the unique concept which has been intellectually established? People need to belong to a place and to have a place that belongs to them. They must have a safe and secure environment but also one in which they will encounter new concepts and ways of thinking. We need to redesign space to challenge us to reinvent our thought processes. In Gothic architecture, the pillars focussed one's gaze upwards to raise perceptions and inspire thoughts of greatness. What building today would make us raise our sights and dare to dream?

It has been suggested that the two institutions are like anchor stores at either end of a mall. Should one espouse that concept, one might imagine the development of Bank Street as a kind of link between the two institutions. The City might encourage the further development of the kind of shops favoured by students, a mix of condos for faculty and apartments for students. There might be incubators for nascent businesses and the siting of some shared research units. It would be a superb location for galleries and a drawing card for the private schools in the region which could seek to share some facilities as well. The entire area could offer high speed, wireless computing and provide a hub of attraction for the city. As the City has undertaken the reconstruction of a stadium, condominiums, and a shopping area just off this street, one might imagine a theatre which would be shared by the universities and the community as well as a small concert hall for the many itinerant musical groups in the city. The private ballet school could be located there as well. The corridor between the two institutions could become the municipal centre for the arts. Access to these facilities would buttress the academic arts programmes at both universities.

It has also been suggested that the two institutions be considered as the hub to high tech activity not only for the City of Ottawa, but for the region. Carleton University faculty and students have worked with the community to create 400 new companies in recent years. The university has created a minor in entrepreneurship and for the last two years, Carleton students have taken the top awards in the Idea contest among Canadian universities. In addition, the Canadian student entrepreneur of the year is a Carleton chemistry major. The University of Ottawa is equally proud of its business development initiatives and, in particular, of its contest which has been endowed by its alumni and which offers as prizes, funds to develop businesses. The University of Ottawa has invited Carleton students to participate officially. Faculty and students at both universities work in close collaboration to serve not only the City of Ottawa but all of Eastern Ontario. Not satisfied to limit such activities to the nation's capital, Carleton graduate, Wes Nicol, created a competition to spark entrepreneurial activities across the country. One might extend the shopping mall metaphor to a high tech crescent which would run from the Waterloo region to Toronto to Ottawa with a number of universities tracing the outline like so many stars in a constellation. If this were the goal, spaces for new businesses and the activities young entrepreneurs would enjoy should be featured along with incubators for technology, design, and digital media companies.

As scientific research becomes more complex and data management more difficult, universities need to work as networks. Then the crescent in Ontario should be but part of the Milky Way of universities around the world. Each represents a point of data collection and analysis. Each is host to brilliant minds. Each contributes to the advancement of knowledge and humankind.

What shape will knowledge take? What will be the form of the ideal campus? How do we create the conditions necessary to promote the connections between and among institutions, locally, regionally and globally?

If as Yi-Fu Tuan (1977) writes, "place is security and space is freedom, how do we create adequate structures for the first and sufficient room for the second (pp. 3-5)? If we are attached to home and the edifices in which we have comfortably dwelt, why do we long for the other? Can that desire, when combined with the potential created by amassing the energies of more than one institution, be what sparks successful cities and nations?"

Utopia and the Campus Master Plan

The origins of the word, *utopia*, indicate either a place away from all places or a place which does not exist. Nonetheless, nearly every written description of utopia begins with a map describing its location, naming sites and identifying specific places, thereby, documenting its existence. Every utopian narrative is recounted by someone who claims to have seen the land, met someone who did or uncovered a manuscript which is either appended or provides the basis for the text presented. The map of utopia, like a campus master plan, reflects the aspirations of the inhabitants. Yet, unlike universities which actually work, utopias are irrevocably destined to failure. At the same time, utopias are perfect while universities are imperfect works in progress. One might well ask the reason. Utopias cannot succeed because they do not permit change. Utopias are formulaic constructs in which there can neither be passions nor the passage of time. These two characteristics of the human race are universal. We all share the notion of the passage of time. Humankind has always measured time by the stars and moon, the seasons, by the change in light between day and night, and by the reflection of our own changing image in the glass or tidal pool. The awareness of time confirms our mortality and our vulnerability. It motivates us to achieve goals within the space of our existence. A utopia represents perfection: the population never ages, never becomes ill, never suffers hunger, discomfort or fear. A utopian population is without want or need and thus has no desires. There is no reason for discord, no hatred and no love. The residents of utopia have nothing to which they can aspire. On the other hand, the university is an evolving place where a principal goal is to encourage every inhabitant to question, to think, to change him or herself and to seek change in society. Campus master plans are constantly updated with the arrival of new technologies, new theories of learning, new concepts of space and identity, and the passionate desires of the campus community. Libraries, always the refuge of scholars, were once the temple of books. The fewer windows, the better — to preserve the pages from damaging light rays. Small, uncomfortable nooks for scholars were inserted discretely among the stacks. The library of today is the home of scholars, filled with light and comfortable seats. There are more computers than books in view and food might even be permitted. While reason generally prevails, a good dose of passion is definitely among the creative forces at work in university communities where debate may be thoughtful and skilful as well as emotional and powerful.

The fifth century Greek painter, Zeuxis, wanted to create the perfect painting of a horse. He studied the anatomy of horses. He watched their habits and he studied art and brush strokes. He worked with different kinds of ink and paint. He painted thousands of horses and was never satisfied that he had captured their essence. One day, in a fit of passion, he threw his wet sponge at his painting and it bounced across the picture creating the impression of motion. His success was due to study and practice but also to passion, the deep desire to succeed and his frustration with his artistic limitations, caused the passionate outburst which assured Xeusis's notoriety even today, many centuries later.

The university needs to make scholars comfortable, to provide them every means of improving their abilities while challenging them to go beyond whatever concepts limit their thinking to the known. While utopian writers take great pains to illustrate their reality, universities today are very real and should perhaps go to greater lengths to describe their existence in virtual reality, in space not yet mapped and in places as yet without name. Symbols are important as they become the basis for the stories our students will tell visitors, the images which inspire us and remind us of our purpose, as well as the foundation for the mythology which will someday inform future generations of our quest.

Rasselas

In Johnson's text by this name, the eponymous hero escapes from utopia and essentially spends the rest of the time attempting to return. In Tuan's terms, "the building is the primary text for handing down a tradition, for presenting a view of reality" (p.112). Perhaps our aging edifices represent well our past. Rather than raze them, we might renew and renovate them, using sustainable architecture as a metaphor for the kind of thinking we wish to encourage. Perhaps rather than expand our campuses from the centres, we might return to the image of the constellation and add stars to the outline we envisage. Perhaps we can make the city sustainable by incorporating spaces it no longer needs as uses change and make them vital to our purpose. Perhaps we might consider learning platforms which are shared with other institutions making our work conquer the challenges imposed by geographical distance and time zones. We may not need as many large lecture halls as students may choose to join class on-line from a variety of locations. On the other hand, we may need more group study spaces as students will require additional small group interaction. Faculty will need offices where they can meet students and work with them individually but those offices should also be equipped with the latest cameras, computers and connections, allowing immediate and easy contact with colleagues and students around the world. Students will require locations where they can connect with other students around the world. For example, when a free-trade negotiation is being conducted by two governments, there is every reason to encourage groups of students to hold their own version of such talks. They will appreciate the timely experience and they just might come up with some ideas which end up being incorporated in the actual negotiations.

The real world can provide an extraordinary campus. Frank Lloyd Wright used to take his architecture students to Arizona where he asked them to go build shelters in the desert to experience the environment before they designed a home as he felt the house should be part of the environment and the environment part of the house. We need to take his thought one step further. People need to be included in this equation. It is not simply the natural environment but the human environment which must be understood.

Batawa

Between Ottawa and Toronto lies the small town of Batawa. Tom and Sonja Bata built a shoe factory there and brought immigrants from Czechoslovakia to work in it. The town flourished until the factory closed about a decade ago due to international competition. The labour market in South America made it impractical to keep the factory open in Batawa. The town began to fail. Young people were leaving and the schools and churches were about to close. Sonja Bata asked Carleton University to join in a project to restore the town. She wanted to create condominiums in the factory and include a branch campus of the university at the site. The university considered that the population was too small to support a branch campus but proposed a distance learning centre which might be combined with a business centre for the local residents and a conference facility. The university sent some 25 students to Batawa to spend the summer in pup tents learning about the community and brainstorming. It was a rainy summer and the townspeople took pity on the cold and damp students, inviting them to their homes for hot meals and showers. They forged excellent bonds and still remain in contact. The students in science created a nature walk and marked the trail with the names of all the plants and rocks. They also created a dinosaur egg park for young children. Students in public policy wrote a successful application for an infrastructure grant to improve the town's water supply. Students wrote sample by-laws to make the community sustainable and environmentally stable. They did business plans for small business development, for waterfront use, for development of the ski hill. This has been a fine example of student engagement with the community. It is also a demonstration of the fact that the community can actually serve as the campus and members of the community can, in turn, become part of the academic community.

Carleton University's current strategic plan is entitled: *Collaboration, Leadership and Resilience: Sustainable Communities and Global Prosperity*. The academic community believes it can make a significant contribution to global prosperity, one community at a time. Should every university adopt a few communities and foster their growth, global prosperity would be attainable.

A New Age of Architecture and New Ways of Knowing

As we embrace the spirit of the present and aim for the success of the future, the new university campus will be a centre which opens to and extends into the surrounding communities: both physically and through technology. The architecture of the future will be warm, human and humane with welcoming places, inviting people to take the time to reflect and to discuss away from the stress of traffic, movement and the surfeit of noise which seems to fill the urban landscape today. The campus will provide a safe and secure environment for discussion and debate, and where the physical surrounding promotes respectful exchanges. The campus of the future will have inspiring spaces which challenge us to contemplate meaning and to strive for excellence. The living and learning environment of the campus of the future will need to be extremely attractive to entice scholars to come to this specific place for the acquisition of knowledge which surrounds us. As Tuan wrote, "Architectural space — a house, a temple, or a city — is a microcosm possessing a lucidity that natural features lack. Architecture continues the line of human effort to heighten awareness by creating a tangible world that articulates experiences, those deeply felt as well as those that can be verbalized, individual as well as collective" (p. 100).

Universities will act as anchors to nascent scholars, rooting them in the wisdom of the past and offering them the means to test theories and to verify supposed "facts" before accepting them. The university will also be the launching pad for ideas and from which new scholars can practice civic engagement and understand their social responsibility. There will be no barriers to the world outside. The gateway must remain open to enter and to exit.

The university will incorporate the latest technology and make it easily usable and flexible so that it can easily be replaced as ever newer means of communications are invented. The university must not perceive itself as the lighthouse sending out a beacon of light to ships that pass through rocky shoals. The university must be the central receiving ground for information from all sources, the processing location and the place where the hierarchy of knowledge in the new information age of massive data and information is created by teams of interdisciplinary scholars from around the world who come to learn together.

The city which supports such an institution or such institutions will extend the network of connectivity into adjoining streets. If, in the 18th century, Paris became known as the City of Light, the city which today supports knowledge collection, creation and application will surely lead the world as the City of Might, the City of Bright! Cities with universities that create the next architecture of and for knowledge will attract bright ideas and minds. Might (power) and the wealth of the future require access to ideas and their organization. These are the keys to successful cities.

References

Cekota, Anthony (1968). *Entrepreneur Extraordinary — The Biography of Tomas Bata.* Rome: University Press of the International University of Social Studies.

Florida, Richard (2013). *The Rise of the Creative Class Revisited.* New York: Basic Books.

Johnson, Samuel (2009). *Rasselas; The History of a Prince of Abissinia,* ed. Thomas Keymer. Oxford: Oxford World's Classics.

Pope, Alexander (2009). *Major Works,* ed. Pat Rogers, Oxford: Oxford World's Classics.

Tuan, Yi-Fu (1977). *Space and Place. The Perspective of Experience.* Minneapolis: University of Minnesota Press.

Wright, Frank Lloyd (2005). *An Autobiography.* California: Pomegranate.

About the Author

Roseann O'Reilly Runte is President and Vice-Chancellor, Carleton University, Canada; and Chevalier of the Ordre des Palmes Académiques.

CHAPTER TEN

KAIST: WORLD-CLASS INNOVATIONS IN TOP-NOTCH RESEARCH UNIVERSITY — CASE OF THE ON-LINE ELECTRIC VEHICLE (OLEV)

NAM P. SUH

Background

Beginning in 2006, the Korea Advanced Institute of Science and Technology (KAIST) developed a "new" strategy to become a leading research university in the world. The strategy had many components. It was decided to increase the faculty size from 400 to 700 professors for 4,000 undergraduate and 6,500 graduate students. The highest standard for faculty hiring and tenure was adopted. A bi-modal education system was introduced to help the students be proficient in both analysis and synthesis. Greater emphasis was placed on "learning" to augment "teaching" and on active learning with fewer lectures and more interaction among students and between students and professors. English was adopted as the language of instruction. And to enhance the scholarly and research reputation of the university, research emphasis was to be on the two ends of the research spectrum — basic research and technology innovation — with a focus on solving some of the most important problems of humanity in the 21st century. Truly interdisciplinary research institutes were created where professors and students from many different disciplines work together without the usual boundaries of traditional academic departments. The net research space available on campus nearly doubled. A new world-class medical facility for students, faculty, staff, and their families was constructed on campus.

At KAIST, we identified four major problems that require innovative solutions in the 21st century: energy, environment, water, and sustainability (EEWS). Based on the report of the Intergovernmental Panel on Climate Change (IPCC) and others, we chose CO_2 emissions as one of the most important environmental problems of the 21st century that must be solved. Since one of the major sources of CO_2 is the internal combustion (IC) engine, KAIST initiated a major R&D project in 2007 to develop On-Line Electric Vehicles (OLEV), which receives electric power wirelessly from underground power supply systems. In addition, we chose to address the potential damage done to the environment when ultra large and deep-water harbours are constructed to accommodate large container ships. As a result, we created the concept for Mobile Harbor (MH). In June 2009, KAIST received major funding for both of these large projects — OLEV and MH — from the Korean Government. In addition to these two major projects, professors and students at KAIST conducted thousands of disciplinary and multi-disciplinary research projects. The result was that the sponsored research volume of the university increased by a factor of 2.4, increasing the overhead income significantly to defray the cost of the new strategic plan.

In 2011, two years after receiving the government funding, we created and implemented a full-scale OLEV system using Shaped Magnetic Field in Resonance (SMFIR), the wireless high-power transmission technology invented at KAIST. OLEV buses receive about 100 kW of electric power wirelessly from underground cables while stationary or in motion. The first OLEV system was installed in Seoul Grand Park. The system, consisting of seven trolley-trams, operates daily and generates a profit. Since then, additional OLEV systems (buses and the underground power supply systems) have been installed in Gumi, an industrial city in Korea, on the KAIST campus, and at the 2012 Yeosu World Expo. Now, the basic core technology of SMFIR is being applied to develop other systems: an ultra-high speed train in Korea, wireless appliances, and others. The idea of shaping magnetic fields for transmission of large amounts of electric power using resonance to capture the transmitted power may find many new applications in the future.

OLEV was an important achievement and has received worldwide recognition. In 2010, *TIME* selected it as one of the 50 Best Inventions in the world and in 2013 the World Economic Forum (WEF) in Davos named it one of the 10 Emerging Technologies of the world.

Research universities rarely undertake large interdisciplinary systems research projects like OLEV and MH for a variety of reasons. However, many of the major problems of humanity require multi-disciplinary and inter-disciplinary approaches. This chapter introduces the rationale for undertaking the OLEV project at KAIST. It describes the enabling technology for OLEV called SMFIR. It covers the genesis of the SMFIR system; the basic theory used in developing these complex systems; and the process of receiving licences and permissions from governments, satisfying the existing international standards and specifications, and dealing with the opposing forces that emerged to derail this project during the early phase of its development. We learned that when conducting a large systems project, one has to be both technically competent and innovative and to protect the project's flank from detractors.

OLEV is a complex engineering system. Having achieved the goal of creating OLEV in two years — from the initiation of the project to installation — we have demonstrated that complex systems can be developed quickly when design principles are rigorously applied rather than depending on experience-based repetitive design/build/test cycles. This project reinforces the experience of other projects that were similarly finished in short times. Axiomatic Design (AD) Theory provided the basis for creating these complex systems. The design of the project is described as well as the basic design of OLEV and SMFIR.

The new policies implemented at KAIST created problems for some senior professors. However, the changes have had an enormous impact on the quality of research and education at KAIST. They have greatly improved the world rankings of KAIST. The changes made at KAIST have also affected higher education throughout Korea.

Introduction

EV will gradually displace many of those that depend on IC engines. It is not the lack of oil, but rather the generation of CO_2 (a combustion product of oil and other hydrocarbons) that will some day impose a limit on the use of oil and IC engines on our streets.

The 5th report of the IPCC[1] from 2013 states that global warming is real and that it has become worse than predicted in its 4th report from 2007. Although there are many who do not share this finding, the risk of ignoring the report's major conclusions is so dire that we must take actions to reduce CO_2 and other greenhouse gases from the atmosphere. Otherwise, we may invite a major catastrophe within this century. For example, the sea level is predicted to rise by 2.5 and 6.5 feet (0.8 and two meters) by 2100 and weather patterns are predicted to change, making dry regions dryer and soaking wet regions. The ocean will become more acidic due to higher concentration of CO_2, which will affect fisheries and other marine ecosystems. And, the circulation of the Gulf Stream of Atlantic Ocean will also slow down, affecting the climates of Europe and America. The CO_2 problem will require global solutions, including the adoption of technologies that can capture and store the CO_2 from power plants, and that can convert CO_2 into useful chemicals. EVs are ultimate solutions in reducing the greenhouse gases emitted by automobiles. There will be more pressure on automotive industry worldwide to replace IC engines with electric motors in the years to come.

To replace the IC engines currently used in automobiles, an EV needs about five hours of 100 kW to 250 kW of electric power. Most automobile companies have adopted rechargeable batteries as the energy source for EVs, typically lithium batteries for their rapid charge and discharge characteristics. Although the idea appears to be simple, it comes with many problems and shortcomings. In addition to needing the infrastructure for charging, batteries present many problems. The failure of "Better Place",[2] the company that employed the idea of mechanical interchange of batteries at "charging stations" to overcome some of these limitations of batteries provides a metric for future EVs.

Commercial EVs are manufactured by nearly all major automotive companies. The most successful of these is the expensive EV manufactured by Tesla. However, EVs are not used widely because of several problems associated with the use of batteries on board. The lithium batteries that are used today are extremely expensive, doubling the price of typical passenger cars. Also they are heavy, large, and dangerous. Lithium is highly flammable and when it comes into contact with water, it can spontaneously react and ignite. The major fire and explosion of a Tela car in 2013, is an example, of what can happen when the lithium battery is punctured. Also the supply of lithium, the main charge-carrying element in the battery, is limited. There are about ten billion kg of lithium reserves in the world that can be economically extracted. If we use all of this to make lithium batteries, we can make about four billion EVs.[3] If the number of automobiles used worldwide reaches the same level as those in advanced economies (one car for two persons), there will be four billion cars on the road, which will exhaust the lithium supply in a few years. It is not hard to imagine what it will do to the cost of lithium.

Right now, governments subsidize EVs since EVs with lithium batteries would cost more than twice the conventional automobiles without government subsidy. When the volume of EVs increases, many components will cost less but the batteries will still be expensive, since the cost of basic raw materials (e.g., lithium, cobalt and others) is likely to continue to increase with the number of EVs manufactured.

The idea of using batteries on board as the power source follows a long tradition. Many vehicles — cars, buses, trains, airplanes, and rockets — have been designed to carry hydrocarbon fuels on board to run the engine. This design concept perhaps started from the horse-and-buggy days when the horse carried the energy in its stomach. Exceptions are electric trams and electric trains, which receive electric energy through mechanical contacts from an external power supply. They typically require overhead wires and tracks, which limit their autonomous manoeuvrability.

In order to overcome the shortcomings of EVs with lithium batteries, we developed the OLEV at KAIST (Figure 10.1). OLEV has a small battery on board but receives all its electric power from underground power supply cables. The small battery provides power on roads without the underground power supply so the OLEV can manoeuvre autonomously. The externally supplied electric power propels the OLEV and re-charges the battery. The OLEV system is designed so that the electric charge in the battery returns to its original charge state when the vehicle makes a round trip. The battery size for an OLEV is typically around 5–20 per cent of the battery needed for traditional EVs. The optimum size is chosen to minimize the overall cost of the OLEV system.

The 2013 WEF selected OLEV as one of the most promising emerging technologies of the world. In 2010, *TIME* selected OLEV as one of the 50 best inventions of the world. The project was being used commercially only two years after its initiation. OLEV is currently serving Gumi, a major industrial city in Korea, as a regular transportation system. Several OLEV trams also provide transportation to the visitors on a commercial basis

Fig. 10.1. Schematic representation of the OLEV bus system (top) and an OLEV commercial bus (bottom) — (Courtesy of KAIST OLEV Project Office)

at the Seoul Grand Park. In addition, the OLEV buses on the KAIST campus provide regular transportation for students, staff and faculty.

It is interesting to note that many electrical engineers dismissed the basic idea of OLEV when it was first proposed without disclosing the details of the technology. They stated that a large amount of electric power could not be transmitted over a large distance wirelessly. Even after we demonstrated the basic concept (without any technical details due to patent related issues), they argued that such technology is not possible. The best explanation for their opposition might be that they have been thinking in terms of inductive coupling used in typical transformers. Our basic invention was conceived in terms of a field effect rather than simple induction, since many functional requirements (FRs) must be satisfied at the same time. My students at Massachusetts Institute of Technology (MIT) and I have successfully used electromagnetic field effects in a number of totally unrelated technological fields in the past.[4]

The design for the SMFIR system that enables the wireless power transmission was successfully conceived and implemented in a mere two years. Many other complex systems in many different fields have been similarly conceived and developed in relatively short periods of time because of the theoretical framework employed in these projects. Based on the framework of AD Theory, complex systems can be conceived and designed without making many mistakes. The future development of EVs of all types should benefit by following the methodologies that are based on AD. The trial-and-error processes that are often used in developing complex systems lead to long development times and high cost. Many of these complex systems have a high failure rate, especially at the early stages of adoption because of poor design of the system. Notwithstanding these success stories, many firms design primarily based on their past experience. Many things our students and researchers designed and implemented were new to them and often new to the world. Yet, they were successfully done at low cost and short times.

In developing large systems, we often overlook the task of satisfying international standards and codes, securing certifications for safety and reliability, and establishing the standards through international and national organizations. It took a long time for OLEV to secure government certifications and permissions. We were fortunate that many government laboratories in Korea helped us in this process.

In developing OLEV, one of the major obstacles was the politics of R&D funding of large projects. A few electrical engineering professors and government officials got together with a politician to derail the development of OLEV at every step of the way. They almost succeeded in killing our project. Also, it is extremely difficult for universities to lead in creating new technological systems for two reasons: lack of expertise in synthesis of large complex systems and the difficulty in securing a large amount of funding. Both of these shortcomings must be rectified in the future if universities are to generate people who can conceive, design and implement large systems, which is often the ultimate purpose of engineering tasks. Also, there has to be more objective and rigorous review of these R&D projects in order to maximize the benefit of R&D investments in these large system projects.

Background on the Creation of OLEV

Many universities cannot undertake large systems projects because it is difficult to secure the funding for design and deployment of large complex systems. This, in turn, forces universities to undertake small, analysis-oriented projects. As a result, many universities do not have faculty members who have expertise and experience in the design and implementation of large complex systems. In that sense, the background story on how OLEV was created at KAIST that is presented here might be useful to policy-makers in government and universities.

The opportunity to conceive and implement OLEV came because I took on a new job. In July 2006, I came to KAIST as its President. Previously, I had been on the faculty at MIT since 1970 except the four years in the mid-1980's when I worked for the United States (US) National Science Foundation as a presidential appointee. It is highly probable that if I had not come to KAIST, OLEV and SMFIR would not exist today. The motivation to work on OLEV was a result of my desire to make KAIST a leading research university in the world. This provided me with enough incentive to pursue the funding required for such a large project, although it is no trivial task to seek such large R&D funding anywhere in the world. Since the amount of funding involved for a university R&D project was rather large (about $23 million in 2009 and another $23 million in the subsequent year), it may be useful to review how the project was initiated and how the funding was secured. It has certain implications on funding university research on large systems and how industrial R&D can be improved through universities' involvement in system design and development.

The three specific events that led to the creation of OLEV were the following:

(1) The strategic decision I made to make KAIST a world-class research university
(2) My appointment as the Chairman of the "Commission for New Economic Growth Engine" by the Ministry of Knowledge Economy of the Republic of Korea
(3) My membership in the National Science and Technology Committee of the Republic of Korea.

As soon as I joined KAIST in July 2006, my colleagues and I developed a strategic plan (through a bottom-up and a top-down process) to make KAIST one of the most distinguished research universities in science and technology (S&T) in the world. The strategic plan dealt with governance, research, education, finance, infrastructure, personnel policy (including the tenure policy for faculty), global relationships, fund raising, and others. To achieve the goal of becoming a major research university, we decided that KAIST should solve some of the most pressing problems of humanity and the world. Hence, a decision was made to undertake major research in EEWS. As part of our research efforts for energy and environment, we chose to lower the CO_2 levels in the atmosphere as an objective of EEWS. In late 2007, we secured special funding to initiate the EEWS program from the Korean Government.[5]

The second event occurred in mid-2008 with the election of MB Lee as the new President of Korea. His government established the Commission for New Economic Growth Engines under the Ministry of Knowledge Economy[6] and I was appointed as the chairman of the commission. The charge given to the commission was to identify new technologies that could become the engines for economic growth of Korea in the 21st century. The implication was that the Korean Government would support the development of promising technologies at significant funding levels. One of the topics strongly supported by many members of the commission was to develop EVs. However, I had reservations about developing EVs that would require large batteries. I did not think the EV would be competitive because of the heavy weight, high cost, and large volume of the rechargeable batteries. EVs were not really a new idea. Automotive companies in many countries had already invested heavily to develop EVs.

As an alternate approach, I proposed the idea of supplying electric power to the vehicle externally without the use of batteries. However, the committee of the Commission that was responsible for this part of the report did not give much credence to my suggestion in the final report. The report gave a greater emphasis to the conventional battery-powered EVs as a promising technology to spur economic growth. This strong push for battery-driven vehicles might have come from those affiliated with Korean industries, since some Korean companies had invested heavily in manufacture of large lithium batteries and EVs. When I, as the chair of the commission, made the final presentation to President MB Lee, I elaborated my ideas for OLEV and MH as examples of promising emerging technologies. After completing the task of the commission, we submitted a voluminous report, listing many technologies that could sustain Korea's economic development. Following the typical fate of most of these reports, I was afraid that they might simply collect dust somewhere in the back room. Fortunately, our work was partially saved by the third event, which gave me an opportunity to secure the funding for OLEV and projects.

I became a member of the National Committee of Science and Technology (NCST), which is chaired by the President of Korea. The function of this committee is to review the budget and the S&T policies of government, and to render advice to the government. In late 2008, the government decided to hold a joint meeting of two national committees, NCST and the National Committee on Green Economy (NCGE), both headed by the President of Korea. During the meeting, President MB Lee asked me to express my views on how Korea should create innovative technologies and promote economic growth. I proposed that the Korean Government should create jobs for scientists and engineers during the economic downturn, similar to the government policy of creating jobs for blue collar workers by undertaking infrastructure projects.

My specific suggestion was that Korea should undertake ten major national R&D projects for two years to create jobs for many unemployed scientists and engineers. I cited what had happened in the US during World War II; the US developed major new weapons during the first two years of the war and won the war during the next two years using the newly developed weapons. I advocated that with significant funding, we could finish these ten projects in two years in the same way that the US did during World War II. President Lee readily accepted my proposal. Since the President of Korea expressed his support in front of all the attendees, including many ministers, I thought that the funding would soon be made available by government. However, I was surprised to learn that none of the ministries had any intention of executing the President's decision.

It took a major effort to create the R&D fund. I visited many ministries to urge them to create a supplementary budget to support ten special

S&T projects to create jobs for scientists and engineers, as per the instruction of President Lee. The officials who finally made the funding possible were the Senior Secretary on Policy to the President and the Director of Policy in the Blue House. They created a supplementary budget of about $270 million for FY 2009 and passed it through the National Assembly. KAIST received about $45 million for two projects – OLEV and MH – for the FY 2009 in June 2009. OLEV and MH each received about $22.5 million for the first year effort, followed by a similar level of funding for the second year. Professor Dong-Ho Cho, Director of the OLEV project, provided outstanding leadership in executing this major R&D project. Over 100 engineers – faculty, students, research and administrative staff – worked on this project.

When I advocated the idea that we should develop OLEV that receives electric power wirelessly from external power sources, many electrical engineering professors in Korea, including many at KAIST, strongly opposed the idea as being unfeasible. They believed that a large amount of electric power could not be transmitted wirelessly over a distance larger than a couple of centimeters. Some professors at other universities actively opposed the funding of the KAIST OLEV project by the Korean Government. To this day, I do not fully understand how they developed such a strong conviction and what motivated them to spare no effort to persuade the government officials to kill the KAIST project. They even enlisted a member of the National Assembly to raise objections at our budget hearings, etc. Some attribute these objections to the fact that KAIST received a rather large amount of funding that might have deprived other universities of the opportunities to get funding for many small projects.[7] What KAIST received is about 16 per cent of the supplementary funding.

My colleagues and I had to overcome these objections without fully understanding the hidden motive of the opponents of the KAIST project. They might have truly believed that the proposed idea could not be translated into real technology, because they were thinking of inductive coupling two adjacent coils similar to what is being done in transformers. However, since I had to comply with the patent law that forbids public disclosure before applying for and securing patent rights, I had to simply assure them that it was going to work. Ultimately, we applied for more than 200 patent applications and many patents have been granted on OLEV. There were similar results for the MH project.

The Design of Complex Systems and AD

OLEV is a complex system that involves many different disciplines from engineering and science as well as the management of people, technology and resources. We have developed OLEV and many other complex systems in rather short periods of time — typically two to three years. In some ways, these are remarkable achievements, when the introduction of so many commercial products, ranging from airplanes to software programs, are often delayed for years because of unexpected problems they uncover after they have done a substantial amount of work. I claim that we can do these things because we minimize the number of mistakes by using the theoretical framework of AD Theory.

The theoretical and operational basis for developing these complex systems, AD, has been applied to many systems, including complex products, software, materials, manufacturing processes, organizations, and many others (Suh, 1990, 2001, 2005). As the name implies, AD consists of two basic axioms that govern all design decisions and processes: the Independence Axiom and the Information Axiom.

In designing complex systems, the customer needs (or goals) must be identified. Based on the defined needs, we have to go through the following sequences:

1. Define FRs and constraints (Cs). This may be the most difficult task in system design. The resulting design must satisfy the FRs. The specified FRs are independent from each other by definition, i.e, they cannot be derived from other FRs.
2. Once the FRs are established, we identify a design parameter (DP) to satisfy each FR. The Independence Axiom states that DPs must be chosen such that the FRs remain independent from each other. As a consequence of this axiom, the number of FRs and DPs must be the same. (The number of DPs cannot be smaller than the number of FRs.) This results in the following relationships: {FRs} = [DM] {DPs}, where [DM] is called the design matrix (DM).

3. According to the Independence Axiom, each FR must be independent from the other FRs at the same level of design hierarchy. This is the case when the DM is diagonal. The result is called an uncoupled design. When the DM is triangular, it is a decoupled design. An uncoupled design is better than a decoupled design, especially at higher levels of design. The [DM] for the case of three FRs and three DPs is illustrated below:

$$\{FRs\} = \begin{Bmatrix} FR1 \\ FR2 \\ FR3 \end{Bmatrix} = \begin{bmatrix} A11 & A12 & A13 \\ A21 & A22 & A23 \\ A31 & A32 & A33 \end{bmatrix} \begin{Bmatrix} DP1 \\ DP2 \\ DP3 \end{Bmatrix}$$

When all the elements of the matrix Aij are zeros, except the diagonal elements A11, A22, and A33, the design is an uncoupled design. This is the best design. If one side of the triangular elements, e.g., A12, A13, A23, are zeros, we have a triangular matrix. This still satisfies the Independence Axiom. However, in this case, we have to choose the DPs in the right sequence to satisfy the Independence Axiom, i.e., DP1 first, then DP2, and finally DP3.
4. FRs and DPs must be decomposed if the DP chosen does not have all the required details. For example, the FRs and DPs for SMFIR at the highest level must be decomposed, because as will be shown, the DPs at the highest level are conceptual and lack actual physical details that can be implemented. However, if the DP happens to be, for example, an electrical motor, the FR and the DP do not need to be decomposed because we can use an existing electric motor.
5. When designing a complex system, FRs and DPs must be decomposed until the design details emerge. The number of decomposition levels can reach ten or more levels. This may also increase the total number of FRs and DPs to a very large number with many different branches, similar to our families. (A family with three siblings establishes three branches when they get married and the grandchildren's generation may establish many more second-level branches at the next level.)
6. In designing a complex system, there may be hundreds of FRs at many levels of the system hierarchy because of the large number of layers

of decomposition required. Furthermore, the overall task must be divided among many groups of people to manage the large number of FRs and DPs, since the possibility that the decision made by one group may affect other unintended FRs in other groups increases, which inadvertently couples the FRs of the highest level. In complex systems, coupling can occur easily but can and must be avoided with vigilance through a systematic design and by checking the system architecture (by assigning an "architect"). Each time there is a coupling, it can take a major effort to correct the mistake. By following AD, we can create a good design without going through the expensive design/build/test cycles to correct the mistakes made.

7. The second axiom, the Information Axiom, enables us to select the best design among several designs that satisfy the Independence Axiom. It states that the system that takes the least amount of information is a better system among all the designs that satisfy the Independence Axiom.

8. The central idea is not to allow any coupling of any of the FRs in the entire system. Many companies develop products by trial-and-error through repetitive design/build/test/redesign/build/test cycles. If the system is a coupled design, it may take several months of intensive work at great cost to correct a mistake created by this trial-and-error process. That is the reason why it takes millions of dollars to develop some new products with long time delays.

9. When the design satisfies the Independence Axiom, the FR-DP relationship becomes that of one-input / one-output rather than a multi-output / multi-input problem. Therefore, any modeling work required for optimization becomes rather trivial even if the relationship is non-linear. Such an uncouple system may even be tuned and optimized even after the system is built.

When there are many FRs and DPs with many layers of decomposition, the use of a computer program makes it easier to track the decisions made by many different groups of engineers and designers working on different parts of the system. A commercial program, *Acclaro,*[8] can facilitate this design process.

The Basic Design of SMFIR

Overall design framework

The basic design of OLEV was done within the framework of AD Theory (Suh, 1990; Suh 2001; Suh, Cho, and Rim, 2010). The FRs at the highest level were as follows:

FR1 = Propel the vehicle with electric power
FR2 = Transfer electricity from an underground electric cable to the vehicle
FR3 = Steer the vehicle
FR4 = Brake the vehicle
FR5 = Reverse the direction of motion
FR6 = Change the vehicle speed
FR7 = Provide electric power when there is no external electric power supply
FR8 = Supply electric power to the underground cable.

The constraints were:

C1 = Safety regulations governing electric systems
C2 = Price of OLEV (should be competitive with cars with IC engines)
C3 = No emission of greenhouse gases
C4 = Long-term durability and reliability of the system
C5 = Vehicle regulations for space clearance between the road and the bottom of the vehicle.

The design parameters for this highest level FRs were as follows:

DP1 = Electric motor
DP2 = Wireless power transfer system
DP3 = Mechanical steering system
DP4 = Hydraulic braking system
DP5 = Electric polarity
DP6 = Motor drive
DP7 = Re-chargeable battery
DP8 = Electric power supply system.

In designing the system, we had to check the relationship between FRs and DPs to be sure that the design was not a coupled design. The DM is shown below:

	DP1	DP2	DP3	DP4	DP5	DP6	DP7	DP8
FR1	X	X	0	0	0	X	X	X
FR2	0	X	0	0	0	0	0	X
FR3	0	0	X	0	0	0	0	0
FR4	0	0	0	X	0	0	0	0
FR5	0	0	0	0	X	0	0	0
FR6	0	0	0	0	0	X	X	0
FR7	0	0	0	0	0	0	X	0
FR8	0	0	0	0	0	0	0	X

In the DM shown above, a capital X is used to denote the fact that an FR is affected by the DP. The matrix indicates that this design is a decoupled design at the highest level. This is an acceptable design, but the FRs must be satisfied by following the right sequence. For example, we must set DP2, DP5, DP6 DP7 and DP8 before we set the value of DP1 to satisfy FR1. Once the design is finalized, the Xs can be determined through modeling and analysis, but during the early stages of design, it is sufficient to know that there are relationships. Uncoupled or decoupled designs makes the entire design a collection of one-input/one-output problem. Therefore, optimum values of DPs to satisfy a given set of FRs can easily be determined either analytically or experimentally. If the design is coupled and violates the Independence Axiom, the resulting multi-input/multi-output problem cannot be easily managed or controlled to satisfy the FRs. At this stage of design, it is more important that the design is approximately correct than precisely wrong (paraphrasing the statement attributed to Warren Buffet). As we proceed to the lower-levels of design, the system finally becomes "precisely correct" in satisfying the highest-level FRs.

Each task of the complex OLEV system was given to different technical teams headed by senior members under the organizational framework established by the project director. Each week, we held one or two meetings with all the engineering and management staff to review and discuss the progress of each team and the overall project. The "Architecture Group" was given the task of checking the system architecture to be sure that all the designs done at all levels did not create a coupled system at the system level to avoid inadvertent coupling of the FRs of the system (Hong and Park, 2011). A group headed by a civil engineering professor designed a safe and reliable structure for the underground power supply system that could withstand the weight of vehicles, heavy rain, and temperature fluctuations. Another group dealt with the management of power that was delivered to the vehicle between the motor and battery. Another group designed the power receiver system that captures the power delivered to the vehicle by magnetic field at resonance. Initially, we converted a hybrid bus (a bus with a diesel engine and an electrical motor) designed by an industrial firm to OLEV.

The most challenging part of the project was the transfer of large amounts of electric power over a large distance (~ 20 to 30 cm) wirelessly, i.e., FR2 and DP2. From the beginning, we thought that we could use a field effect to transmit the power wirelessly.

Field effect as the basis of transferring electric power

The idea of using the field effect for wireless power transfer is, in some ways, a natural extension of the earlier work I had done with my students and colleagues at MIT. At MIT, we created many innovative processes and products using electric and electromagnetic field effects. For these inventions and discoveries, my students and I received many US patents, e.g., technology for creating a "perfect mixture" of powders that overcomes the entropic limitations (Suh and Tucker, 1977); a charge-decay non-destructive testing technology (Suh and Tse, 1984); technology for mixing highly viscous liquids in electric fields (Suh, Rotz, Erwin, Melcher, and Hoburg, 1979); curing composites rapidly using high frequency electric fields (Haven and Suh, 1983); and desalination of seawater through transportation of ions in electric field effects (Suh, Kim, Lee, Ishan and Heo, 2007).

To send a large amount of electric power over a large distance wirelessly (without electric conducting wires), it is natural to think in terms of the field effect, either electric or magnetic fields. The central idea is to transmit electric or magnetic power by establishing either electric or magnetic fields from a set of electric or magnetic poles.

Decomposition of FR2 and DP2 (Design of SMFIR)

We needed to decompose FR2 and DP2 to develop a means of transmitting power from the underground cables to the vehicle.

FR2 = Transport electric power from underground power supply system to the vehicle
DP2 = Power supply system.

We named this wireless electric power transmission system "SMFIR". Figure 10.2 shows the conceptual design that satisfies FR2.

The idea is to create a magnetic field above the ground that can reach the vehicle. Magnetic fields will not be affected by ice or many other materials that may be on the surface of the road.

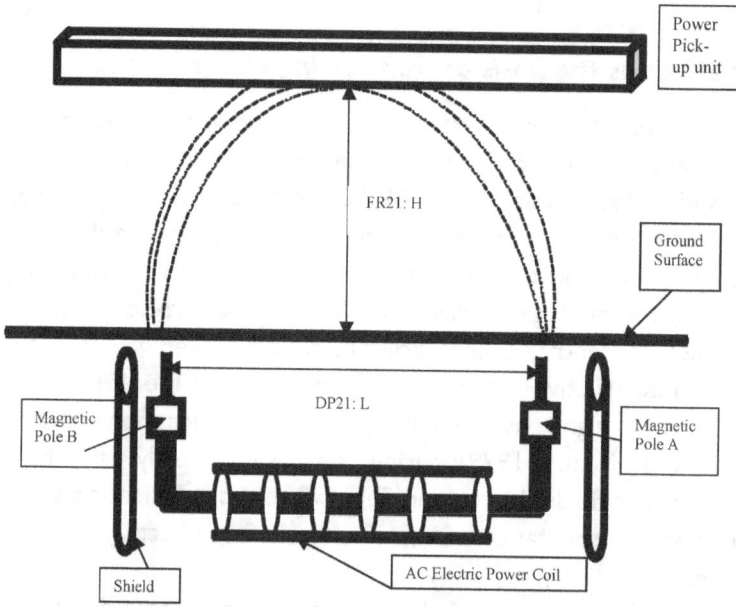

Fig. 10.2. Concept for sending power over a distance H wirelessly. First, a magnetic (or electric) field is created above ground. Once the field shape is determined, the field strength can be adjusted. The field is then captured at the bottom of the vehicle.

The second-level FRs are obtained by decomposition of FR2 as follows:

FR21 = Create a magnetic field above the ground
FR22 = Control the shape of the magnetic field
FR23 = Control power level of the magnetic field
FR24 = Pick-up the energy of the magnetic field by the vehicle
FR25 = Confine the electromagnetic waves between the vehicle and the underground power supply system.

The second-level DP2 are chosen as follows:

DP21 = Electromagnet design (ferrite core inside electric field)
DP22 = Distance between the magnetic poles (L)
DP23 = Amplitude of the electric current that generates the magnetic field around the ferrite core under the ground
DP24 = Resonating magnetic energy pick-up unit on the vehicle
DP25 = (Passive or active) shield for stray electromagnetic field.

The constraints that the design must not violate are the following:

C1 = Maximum allowable EMF level of 62.5 mG
C2 = Maximum weight of the pick-up unit
C3 = Electric shock resistance of the system
C4 = Temperature rise should not exceed 20C
C5 = High magnetic permeability of the core material m
C6 = Minimize the power loss.

The DM for this second-level FR2s and DP2s is given by the following DM, which may be represented as:

	DP21	DP22	DP23	DP24	DP25
FR21	X	0	X	0	0
FR22	0	X	0	0	0
FR23	0	0	X	0	0
FR24	0	0	0	X	0
FR25	0	0	0	0	X

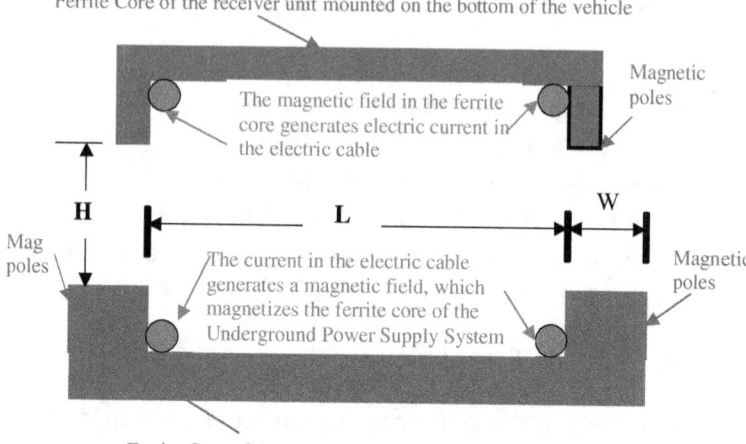

Fig. 10.3. Schematic design of SMFIR. To have the strongest field extend from the underground magnetic pole to the pole of the pick-up unit on the vehicle (FR21), L must be much larger than H, i.e., L ≫ H.

The design at the second level of FR2 and DP2 is almost an uncoupled design. Figure 10.3 shows the schematic arrangement of the SMFIR design that is given by the DM.

To satisfy FR21, DP21 is the ratio L/H, which must be much larger than 1, i.e., L/H ≫ 1. FR25, the shielding of EMF, can be satisfied by either an active or passive type of shielding arrangement. The passive shielding consists of putting a barrier in the ground and grounding the EMF picked up around the receiving unit. The active solution is to generate a signal that is opposite to the EMF coming out of the receiver unit. The design of DP25 is given in Kim, et al. (2013).

The current that flows in the electric cable loop generates a magnetic field in the ferrite core by aligning magnetic domains. Because the ferrite core has low magnetic permeability, the magnetic field is concentrated in the ferrite core. One end of the ferrite core becomes the S pole and the other N pole. Since the electric current that flows in the electric cable is alternating current (AC), the magnetic field above the ground also oscillates and the magnetic poles alternate between N and S. To create a magnetic field that is strongest above the ground, pointing toward the vehicle rather than directed toward the magnetic poles, the distance, H, from the magnetic pole in the ground to the poles of the pick-up unit on the vehicle should be much smaller than the distance, L, between the magnetic poles of underground power supply system, i.e., $L \gg H$ (see Figure 10.3).

Ahn, et al. (2012) numerically determined the magnetic field between the underground power supply system and the pick-unit at the bottom of the OLEV, which is shown in Figure 10.4. This is a dual rail system, i.e., two of the units shown in Figure 10.4.

The idealized flow of the magnetic field is shown in Figure 10.5.

Having determined that the overall design that was going to work, we needed to determine the elements of the DM through modeling to develop optimum solutions. Obviously, the modeling should be based on the magnetic field emanating from the poles of the ferrite buried

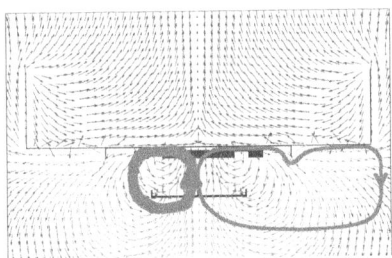

Fig. 10.4. Simulation of the magnetic field between the underground power supply system and the pick-up unit mounted at the bottom of the vehicle. The ferrite core is a dual rail unit, a superposition of two of the units shown in Figure 2. (From S.Y. Ahn 2013).

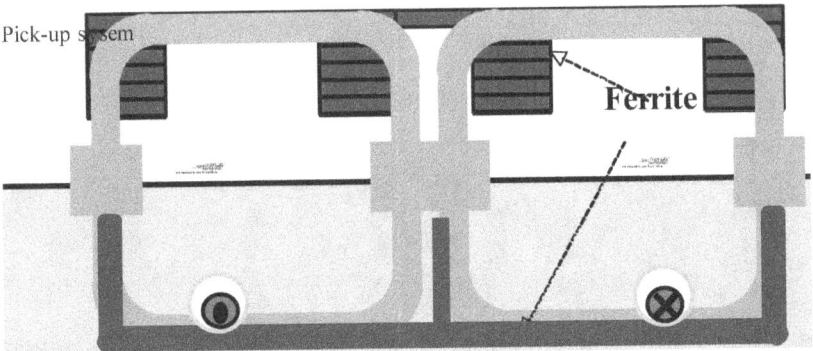

Fig. 10.5. An idealized magnetic field flow of the dual rail system. The blue ferrite core is under the ground with an electric coil. The ferrite core in the pick-up unit on the top controls the shape of the magnetic field. (Courtesy of D. H. Cho)

underground and how they induce the magnetic field in the ferrite core of the pick-up unit mounted under the vehicle. This would involve fairly complicated modeling that will require a numerical solution. To simplify the analysis, Kim, et al. (2013) modeled SMFIR as two parallel coils in close proximity as shown in Figure 10.6(a). The power transferred to the pick-up unit (the load) and the efficiency is shown in Figure 10.6(b). The resonant frequency is tuned to 20 kHz by varying the capacitance of the pick-up unit.

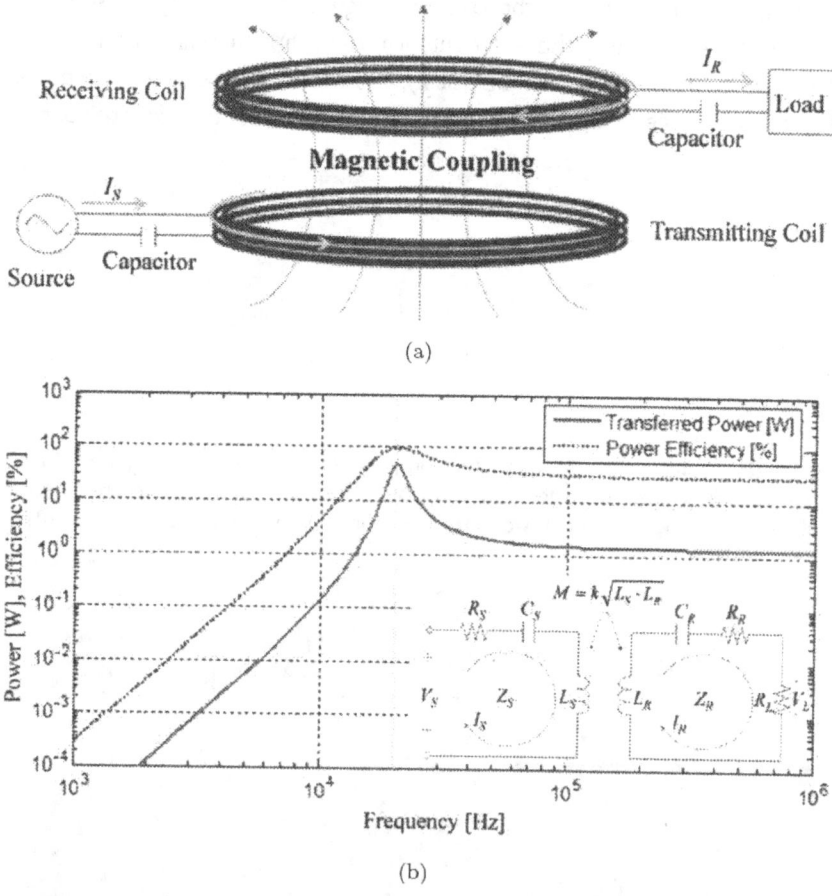

Fig. 10.6. (a) SMFIR is replaced with two parallel coils with power input to the lower coil and power output at the upper coil in order to simplify the analysis. (b) The equivalent circuit model and power transferred and efficiency as a function of frequency. The resonant frequencies of the coils are tuned to 20KHz and the power transferred to the load is 50 W at the resonant frequency (from Kim, et al., 2013).

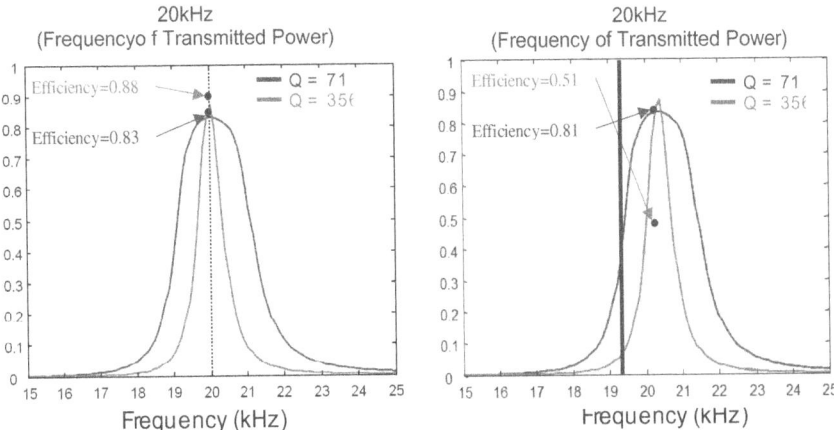

Fig. 10.7. Power transfer efficiency as a function of frequency and the Q factor. At resonance, the efficiency is highest. A large Q factor results in higher efficiency as well. (from Ahn, 2013).

In order to make the system most efficient, the Quality Factor (Q) should be large. The coil configuration and materials were fine-tuned to make Q as large as possible. For the OLEV bus system, the resonant frequency chosen was 20 kHz. The efficiency of the system decreases when the system is not at resonance and when the Q factor is small. Figure 10.7 shows that the higher the Q factor, the higher is the efficiency. Also the power transfer efficiency is the highest at the resonance frequency as expected.

To minimize the EMF outside of the bus, both passive and reactive shields were tried. However, the passive shield, which was done by grounding the bus to the road, was too cumbersome. Therefore, reactive shield was adopted. This was done by using the measured field to create an opposing magnetic field. As shown in Figure 10.8, it reduced the EMF to a value much less than the internationally accepted standard of 62.5 milli-Gauss (mG) (which is equal to 6.25 microtesla, μT).

Comparison of cost of OLEV against other transportation systems

Cho, et al. (2013) analysed the total cost of four different bus systems: diesel buses, compressed natural gas (CNG) buses, OLEV buses, and plug-in electric vehicle (PEV) buses. The analysis is based on the proposal

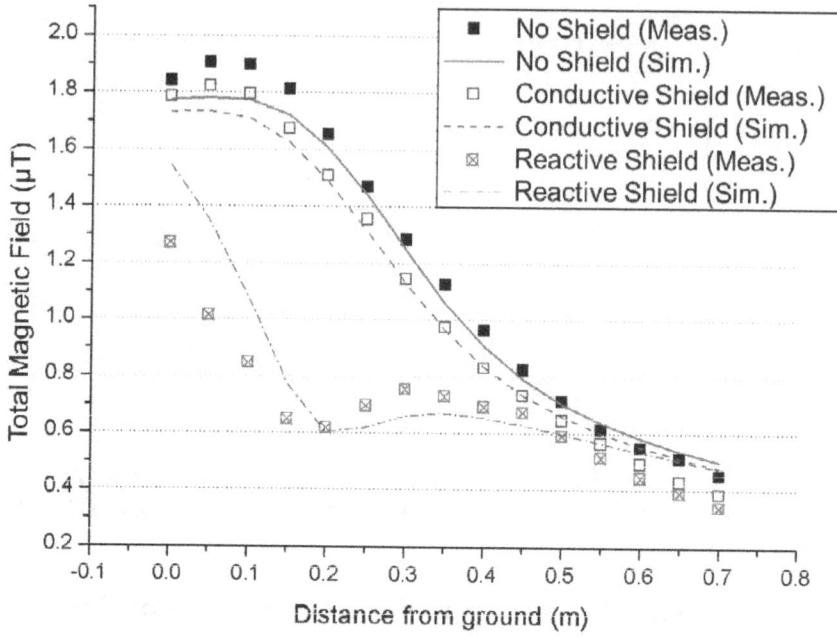

Fig. 10.8. Effect of reactive shielding (*Source*: S. Ahn, et al, "Design and Analysis of a Resonant Reactive Shield for a Wireless Power Electric Vehicle". IEEE Trans. on Microwave Theory and Techniques. Submitted, 2013).

submitted to the government by a city in Korea for a bus rapid transit (BRT) system. They assumed that the length of the bus line is 20 km and the buses run in every four (4) minutes or at ten (10) minute intervals, requiring 15 buses except the case of a PEV system which requires an additional seven (7) buses due to the 30 minutes of battery charging time. The assumed amortization period was nine (9) years. They considered the total operating cost, which included the cost of the buses, the infrastructure cost, fuel cost, and CO_2 cost. In calculating the CO_2 cost, it was assumed that 50% of electricity is generated using nuclear power plants and they used the formula advanced by a national environmental research institute in Korea. Figure 10.9 shows the costs of the various systems. Among these, the OLEV bus system costs the least, although the initial bus cost is greater for the OLEV than the diesel or CNG bus. The PEV bus is the worst of the four systems because of the higher cost of the bus. The operating cost of diesel and CNG is higher because of the fuel cost.

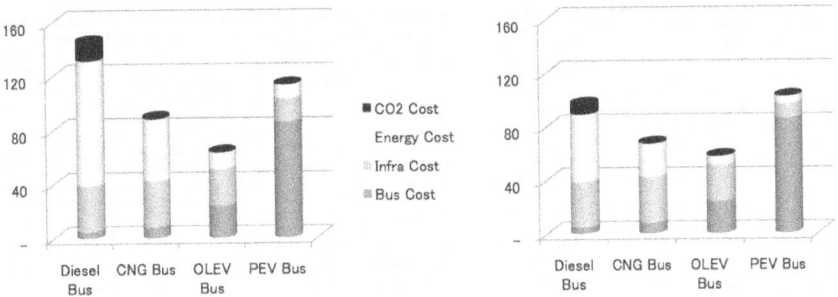

Fig. 10.9. A comparison of the operating cost of diesel, CNG, OLEV and PEV buses. The figure on the left is for one dispatch every four minutes and the figure on the right is for every 10 minutes. The vertical axis is millions of U.S. dollars (from Cho, 2013).

Fig. 10.10. Tram tested in Korea. (The frequency of power supply is at 90kHz.) — (Courtesy of KAIST OLEV Project Office)

Other Applications of SMFIR

In addition to the OLEV buses, the SMFIR technology was applied to a tram that runs on rails (Figure 10.10).

Also, the National Railroad Research Institute in Korea is developing a high-speed train that can reach a cruising speed of 450 km/hr. Since it runs on rails, we expect to get a higher efficiency of up to 90 per cent for OLEV trains, since the pick-up unit can be closer to the emitting unit (Figure 10.11).

Fig. 10.11. High-speed train to be constructed using SMFIR. Because of the elimination of overhead electric wires, the infrastructure for the tunnels can be much smaller than the current tunnels by about 30 per cent. (Courtesy of KAIST OLEV Project Office)

In addition to these transportation-related applications, various organizations are pursuing other applications of the SMFIR technology such as home appliances.

Conclusions

1. Leading world-class research universities must make significant major contributions to humanity through their scholarly, research, and educational activities. KAIST has adopted the strategy of solving some of the major problems that humanity has to solve in the 21st century as a means of elevating its educational and research capabilities. Through the OLEV and MH projects, KAIST has achieved its distinction among world-class research universities. Its world ranking in engineering has come up to 23rd in the world.

2. EVs will gradually displace vehicles with IC engines in order to deal with the environmental issues caused by CO_2.
3. OLEV is an efficient, competitive, reliable, safe, and environment-friendly technology that will gradually replace vehicles with IC engines. An OLEV bus system is the most cost effective in comparison to diesel, CNG and PEV bus systems.
4. SMFIR, the wireless electromagnetic power transfer technology, can be applied to many other systems such as high-speed trains and appliances.
5. Complex systems can be developed quickly at minimum cost if the project is executed following the principles of AD. We have developed OLEV and many other complex systems in many fields successfully in two to three years.

Acknowledgement

The author is grateful to President MB Lee, Minister Jae Won Park, and Minister Jin Shik Yoon of the Republic of Korea for their support of this project. Professor Dong Ho Cho rendered an invaluable leadership in directing this project both technically and administratively. Key leaders of the technical team were Prof. JH Kim, Prof. SY Ahn, Prof. T.S. Lee, Prof. G.J. Park, Prof. IS Suh, Prof. I.G. Jang, Professor Y. J. Jang, Prof. CT Rim, Prof. HK Lee, Res. Prof. GH Jung, Res. Prof. UY Yoon, JG Shin, SY Shin, YS Kim, SW Lee, Dr GH Jung, Dr BW Park, BY Song, and Visiting Prof. SJ Jeon. Also I would like to thank all the members of the OLEV project team for the successful execution of the OLEV project. Dr SM Hong, President of the Korea Railroad Research Institute, has provided the leadership in executing the high-speed train project. His contributions are gratefully acknowledged. Finally, the author wishes to thank Professor Mary Kathryn Thompson for going over the manuscript.

Notes

1. IPCC was established by the World Meteorological Organization (WMO) and the United Nations Environment Programme (UNEP) in 1988 and won the Nobel Peace Prize in 2007 for its work on the environment.

2. *Better Place* was a venture-backed international company that developed and sold battery-charging and switching services for electric cars. It was formally based in Palo Alto, California, but the bulk of its planning and operations were steered from Israel, where both its founder Shai Agassi and its chief investors resided. (Wikipedia).
3. Eric Eason, Stanford student paper (30 November 2010). Wikipedia.
4. In the past, we used electromagnetic "field effects" in the following inventions (most of them patented): mixing of powder to a "perfect" mixture, curing of composites using internal "heat sources", NDE based on the electric charge decay rate, mixing of viscous liquids, and desalination.
5. I am grateful to Prime Minister DS Han for this funding.
6. The commission had about 200 members in three major committees and its various sub-committees. Each committee held open forums to solicit ideas from about 3,000 engineers, scientists, and business leaders in Korea. The commission was supported and guided by the senior civil servants of the Ministry of Knowledge Economy. The commission received many suggestions. However, most of the ideas were technologies that had already been invented or had gone into manufacturing in other countries. Real original ideas were few. President of Korea Myung Bak Lee was somewhat disappointed that there were not too many novel ideas that were identified that were truly novel.
7. A similar argument was advanced when the US National Science Foundation started the Engineering Centers Program in 1985. In both cases, we received funding through a special supplementary funding process.
8. A product of Axiomatics Software Design, Inc. (DBA Axiomatic Software Solution, Inc.).

References

Ahn S.Y., Suh N.P., and Cho D.H. (April 2013). "The All-Electric Car You Never Plug In", IEEE Spectrum.

Ahn, S.Y. (October 2013). "Overview of Wireless Power Transfer Technology". Presentation made at the IEEE Conference on Intelligent Transportation Systems, Hague, The Netherlands.

Cho, D.H. (October 2013). "WPT Concept and Applications". Presentation made at the IEEE Conference on Intelligent Transportation Systems, Hague, The Netherlands.

Haven, R. and Suh N.P. (27 December 1983). "High Frequency Electric Field Curing of Polymeric Composites". U.S. Patent 4,423,191.

Hong, E.-P. and Park, G.J. (2011). "Collaborative design process of large-scale engineering systems using the axiomatic design approach". *Proceedings of the Institution of Mechanical Engineers, Part C: Journal of Mechanical Engineering Science* 225, no. 9, pp. 2174–2188.

Kim J.S., Kim J. H., Kong S.Y., Kim H.S., Suh I.S., Suh N.P., Cho D.H., Kim J.H., and Ahn S.Y. (2013). "Coil Design and Shielding Methods for a Magnetic Resonant Wireless Power Transfer System". Invited Paper, Proceedings of IEEE.

Seppala, T.J. (4 October 2013). "Tesla Model S catches fire after battery puncture, Musk responds". <engadget.com>

Suh N.P. and Tucker, III, C.L. (12 July 1977) "Method and Apparatus for Mixing Particles". US Patent 4,034,966.

Suh N.P., Rotz, C., Erwin L., Melcher, J.R. and Hoburg, J.H. (20 November 1979) "Fluid Mixing Apparatus". US Patent 4,174,90.

Suh N.P., and Tse, M. (17 April 1984) "Method for Non-Destructive Detection and Characterization of Flaws". US Patent 4,443,764.

Suh N.P. (1990). *The Principles of Design*. Oxford University Press.

Suh N.P. (2001). *Axiomatic Design: Advances and Applications*. Oxford University Press.

Suh N.P. (2005). *Complexity: Theory and Applications*. Oxford University Press.

Suh N. P, Kim S.-G., Lee T., Ishan B., and Heo G. (filed 19 December 2007). "Method and Apparatus for Permeating Flow Desalination". USSN 12/002,664.

Suh N.P., Cho, D.H. and Rim, C.T. (2010). "Design of On-Line Electric Vehicle". Presented at the 20th CIRP Design Conference 19–20 April. Nantes, France.

Suh N.P. (28 March 2011). "Design of Wireless Electric Power Transfer Technology: Shaped Magnetic Field in Resonance (SMFIR)". Proceedings of the 2011 CIRP Design Conference at KAIST, Korea.

About the Author

Nam P. Suh is Cross Professor Emeritus, MIT and was President of KAIST (2006–13).

CHAPTER ELEVEN

CAMBRIDGE: FROM MEDIEVAL MARKET TOWN TO UNIVER-CITY

GORDON JOHNSON

HRH Raja Dr Nazrin Shah, in his keynote address to the conference,[1] drew on a wide range of academic research, mainly in the fields of development economics and geography, to argue that wealth is created in cities, and that, within an urban environment, universities can play a distinctive part in the process. He also argued that there were other non-economic benefits stemming from universities, and that fruitful interactions between universities and the societies in which they were located are an essential ingredient in promoting human welfare, enhancing human experience, and tackling inequalities in economic, social and political organization.

The conference sought, through historical examples, modern case studies, campus and city planning, and the uses of new technologies, to explore the ways in which the contemporary university might be structured and led so as to contribute effectively to meeting current challenges. More ambitiously, the ultimate aim was to see how, in a considered way, networks of universities, crossing nations and cultures, might be put together, facilitating the exchange of ideas, stimulating innovation, and developing cross-cultural understanding: in particular, to see how to encourage in a conscious way, the coming together of individually distinguished university departments for a concerted international and multi-disciplinary attack on defined major problems.[2]

In earlier times, such developments were largely serendipitous and were often achieved by the haphazard movement of peoples, driven to migrate by economic necessity, lured by the profit of long-distance trade, war, or motivated by religious evangelism. Exploration of the seas led to more than the discovery of markets, as goods carried ideas and technologies with them round the coasts and across the oceans; and, over centuries, people traveled thousands of kilometers over topographically inhospitable inner Eurasia, creating the "silk roads" that linked China and eastern Asia with Iran and the Mediterranean. We are more and more aware of how significant these connections have been, and in our contemporary era, where means of communication have been so radically revolutionized, the possibility of creating flexible networks of univer-cities, engaged separately and together in the task of improving life, is an exciting prospect, worthy to be pursued with vigour.

The purpose of this chapter is to explore more generally the complex relationship of university to society, and it draws upon a particular example: that of the University of Cambridge (with an occasional reference to Oxford — until the 19th century, these were the only universities in England), which has been in existence in some form or other for 800 years. It would, however, be a mistake to think that Cambridge has remained the same over all those centuries. In fact, it has had a chequered history; but a striking feature of its longevity as an institution has been its capacity to change, often quite radically, as circumstances have demanded. At heart, the university has remained true to the purpose of serving society; but the ways in which it has done so have differed according to time and need.

Essentially, universities perform the following, not always totally compatible, functions. First, they exist as great repositories of knowledge; they have a duty to pass on that knowledge from one generation to another — i.e., to teach. But they are also charged with the discovery of new knowledge, a continuing critical evaluation of what has been learnt in the past combined with innovative enquiry that leads to new understanding — i.e., to conduct research. Both functions, teaching and research, involve the dissemination of knowledge, but that knowledge is only of value if it is truly tested, critically examined, and responsive in some degree to contemporary interests. The university is, therefore, a repository of time-valued knowledge, a place of discovery of new knowledge, and an institution that publishes that knowledge: an Oxford scholar put it succinctly in the late 19th century when he maintained that a university consisted of a library and a press.[3]

None of this is without controversy. What should be taught and what should engage the brightest minds as fields of research are constantly subject to on-going discussion, and knowledge is not simply incremental. Moreover, universities, and what they do, are not without cost. If they are to perform at all, they need resources to do so, and whether these are provided as a public good or as private benefaction, to satisfy an immediate utilitarian purpose or to serve distant and often intangible aims, who is to pay, and how much, and for what, raise interesting political, economic and ethical questions and involve the most intimate interaction with society at large. In modern parlance, universities have many stakeholders, each requiring different, sometimes conflicting, things from the institutions they are willing to support; and that investment will not only be financial but will also embrace social, political and cultural capital, very broadly defined.

For universities to work well, then, they must be, and be seen to be, an integral part of society — here is no ivory tower, distant from the pressures of everyday life. But, paradoxically, they also need to have some immunity from those same pressures if they are to perform effectively. Universities require a substantial element of freedom to determine their own structures of management (which should be light and tolerant), to have a major say in deciding their own academic and intellectual priorities, and to be relatively free of short-term external demand. They are institutions that foster creativity and, as such, are engaged in activities that will not always produce immediately visible results. They will thrive best in an environment that discourages formal hierarchy and supports enquiry into the unknown. In short, they are to be judged by long-term results and are to be trusted to hold fast to their key purpose — a quest for knowledge and understanding.[4]

From one aspect, the university will appear as being conservative: it is holding to traditions, passing on what has been refined over the years and is known to be of interest and value. But it also inculcates a skeptical and critical way of thinking: what is known is constantly tested and subverted; the universe is constantly unsettled and expanded. The teacher and researcher is at once an embodiment of authority of what is agreed *and* a radical questioner of that authority. No wonder that what is taught and what are the best topics for research are often furiously debated, leading to bitter conflicts in the quest for status and resources. In the simplified rhetoric about the purpose of universities, there emerge many false dichotomies: between straightforward utilitarian objectives (we need doctors, or architects, or priests, or a solution to a particular economic or technological problem) and the pursuit of knowledge for its own sake; between instantly applicable knowledge and "blue sky" thinking; and, most perniciously in our own times, between "science" and the "arts" — as if all knowledge were not in the end related to human well-being. It is this that belies the statement, often wrongly attributed to Henry Kissinger, that university politics are so vicious because so little is at stake. On the contrary, university politics are so passionately fought because so much is at stake.

A prominent feature of university activity is its competitiveness: universities compete for the best teachers and the best students; their governing bodies press academics to ensure their institutions rank high on published league tables. Scholars closely guard their own patch, keeping others out until they are ready to publish their results, to be first in the field and, therefore, well placed to carry off prestigious prizes and new funding. Departmental and personal rivalries lead to entrenched positions, often bolstered by strongly expressed ideologies as ideas and approaches seek to differentiate themselves from others and gain ascendancy. A pernicious consequence is a reluctance sometimes to recognize or value other work, and the development of webs of patronage when it comes to making new appointments that, reinforcing particular positions, inhibits new departures.[5]

But in fact, survival depends as much on co-operation and collaboration as on narrow competitiveness: it is the paradox of the battle between the selfish gene and the well-being of the whole body. In the modern world, the genius of individuals stands more clearly on the achievements of the many. Laboratories may well work apart, or scholars plough their own furrow, but they will be looking to identify and solve similar problems, pursuing similar lines of enquiry in areas that are of particular interest and importance in the here and now. This makes it all the more interesting to try consciously to evolve a culture that will combine fierce judgments about excellence and the promotion of what is best with as free a flow as possible of ideas and thinking, and an exchange of skills, particularly between theoretical and applied sciences.[6]

Medieval Cambridge: Religious Origins

In strict historical terms, it is not possible to date exactly the founding of the University of Cambridge. Over the years, various possibilities with varying degrees of credibility have been put forward, from Athenian philosophers fleeing from the sack of Troy in the company of the Spanish Prince Cantaber, to the seventh-century Sigebert, King of the Angles who remained embedded in the University's annual prayer for its benefactors until 1914. But during the past century, a general consensus has emerged that, if one wanted a founding date, AD 1209 is as good as any. It was in that year that the scholars of Oxford, which was well established as a centre of learning, fell foul of royal authority: students were tried in civil (as opposed to ecclesiastical) courts, and some were executed. King John, at the height of his conflict with the Papacy, attacked church institutions and scholars fled from Oxford. Some of them came to Cambridge and put themselves under the protection of independent or semi-autonomous ecclesiastical authorities in the town. Over the ensuing century, the University of Cambridge gradually took institutional form and acquired appropriate royal and ecclesiastical recognition. It received charters and other documents recognizing it and its colleges as separate legal entities, granting them legal and fiscal privileges, and encouraging their endowment.

The medieval town of Cambridge was a significant place and had for some time been active on religious, charitable and educational fronts, with many churches, religious houses, hospitals and schools located there. Until the national expulsion of the Jews in 1290, there was a prosperous Jewish financial quarter in the town handling much of the region's banking. It was, for the time, a wealthy place. Although small, and built on the constricted area of a meander of the river Cam, surrounded by flood plain and marsh, Cambridge owed its prosperity to being the link between complementary agricultural economies. It was the natural market place for the nearby hamlets and villages, thus fulfilling from an early date a regional role in the economy. The higher land to the south and west was good for grain, while to the north and east the fertile lands of the fens supported garden products, cattle, and a miscellany of "fen products" — wild fowl, osiers for basket weaving, sedge and reed for housing, eels and fish. The agrarian products of this part of England came naturally to Cambridge to be part-processed and to be transported on: either by the roads, that connected Cambridge with the south-east, the north, and the west, or, very significantly, by water through the Ouse river system, to King's Lynn, the great port on the North Sea, serving other parts of England and northern Europe. At times of population growth and agricultural expansion, Cambridge was a centre for trade, an inland port, attracting a great deal of business. And through the early modern period, the town was host to the annual Stourbridge Fair, one of the largest trade fairs in Europe. This concentration of wealth underpinned Cambridge becoming a religious, educational and cultural centre. The prosperity of the town, its local and regional economic strength, and its strategic links with other parts of England and Europe provided the conditions necessary for its emergence as a "univer-city".

The two old universities in England, Oxford and Cambridge, grew in an ecclesiastical and monastic context. They depended on the accumulation of privileges taking them and their colleges (each with its own independent charitable status) out of the legal structure of much local and national government. They drew resources from the state, via the Crown, and from the private benefactions of ecclesiastical authorities, wealthy families, or in the case of Corpus Christi College in Cambridge, a group of trade guilds based in the town. Support took the form of money for building and the assignment of land, rents and fines that provided recurrent income to cover the cost of living. At the time, the purpose of these institutions, in which such heavy investment was made, was to serve God and their benefactors. The colleges were religious houses with an obligation to hold regular services and to pray, in perpetuity, for the souls of their benefactors.[7] The scholars, to whom these religious obligations were entrusted, were of necessity literate and tended to be recruited from among poor but intelligent boys. For those able to excel in the skills of literacy, the colleges were means of social mobility and the prospect of promotion beyond the university, particularly to high office in the church, at Court, or in the households of landed families.

The colleges formed communities with clear hierarchies, based on age and status; but in other respects, they were little republics: those who had attained full legal status within the community regarded themselves as equal to each other in terms of rights and privileges. This was reflected in the constitution of the wider university: it was a sort of federal organization. The central authority recognized those institutions that were formally part of it, defined the terms of admission to various levels of university membership, and awarded degrees; but the constituent parts had great autonomy and despite an established hierarchy of office and status, ultimate authority rested in the hands of the many senior members.

Early Modern Cambridge: In Service of the Tudor Church and State

England in the 14th and 15th centuries was subject to dynastic wars and economic disasters: virulent plague may have carried off as much as a third of the population. But towards the end of the 15th century, the kingdom moved, albeit hesitantly, to greater political stability, the economy stabilized and the population began to grow. During the ensuring century, under the Tudors, the two English universities grew in importance. As Renaissance and Reformation took hold, Oxford and Cambridge were touched by the new learning, spreading from Europe, and became key centres of cultural and theological debate. More practically, there was increased demand for literate men to fill administrative positions in Church and State, to service the growing number of thriving country estates, and to meet increased demand for clergymen, lawyers, doctors and schoolmasters.

Indeed, from the closing years of the 15th century until the opening decade of 17th century, huge new investments were made in the two English Universities. Their constitutions and privileges were confirmed and refined; their colleges were multiplied, endowed and re-endowed; their senior people were men to be reckoned with in court and country. Of course, this was not a simple or uncontroversial development. The Tudor sovereigns forged their new state (this "empire" as Henry VIII would grandly term it) through ruthless deployment of violence, breathtaking audacity with regard to other people's property — estates were confiscated, monasteries and other religious houses closed and their resources re-directed to other objectives — and an extraordinary development of government and administration.

In Cambridge, King Henry VII's mother, the Lady Margaret Beaufort, led the way, endowing St John's and Christ's Colleges, a Professorship of Divinity, and funds to support a preacher. She was influenced in her benefactions by John Fisher, typical of an emerging elite of scholars and statesmen who rose to eminence through new literacy. Fisher, born in 1469, the son of a Yorkshire merchant, came via his local grammar school to Michaelhouse (later absorbed into Trinity College), one of the Cambridge colleges, where he took avidly to new scholarship in Latin, Greek and Hebrew. He was ordained a priest at an early age and during a distinguished life held, among other appointments, the Presidency of Queens' College, Cambridge and the Chancellorship of the University. He was long-serving Bishop of Rochester and, significantly for our purposes, chaplain, confessor and executor of the Lady Margaret. He influenced her in the disposition of her benefactions and after her death, he saw that her wishes were carried out.[8]

In the bitter politics of Reformation England, Cambridge, as an institution, played its cards well. After a certain amount of agonizing, the academics lent their support (in advance of Oxford doing so) to King Henry VIII's controversial divorce and to his claim to be Head of the Church. In 1546, Henry added to the wealth and standing of the University, pre-eminently by creating (out of existing institutions and other people's money) Trinity College. But he remained canny about financial matters and colleges. In the previous year, an Act had been passed dissolving all major chantries and colleges and placing their resources at the disposal of the crown. Cambridge responded to this potentially devastating move with some skill, turning it to advantage. The King was persuaded not to send to the University an external committee of enquiry to assess the situation but to appoint a local body to do so. This committee consisted of three Heads of colleges who used their influence, through men who had been tutors to the royal household, to gain the support of Queen Katherine Parr to preserve their endowments. They surveyed the colleges' lands and income, and set out the good work that flowed from the prudent use of the funds. They made a good case for the value of what the University provided, stressing the modest nature of the investment underlying it. The King accepted their response, though observed (perhaps not without wit) that "he thought he had not in his realm so many persons so honestly maintained in living by so little land and rent".[9]

In fact, very substantial resources were accumulated and concentrated during a century of dramatic economic and social change in England. Beginning with St Catharine's Hall in 1473 through to the establishment of Sidney Sussex College in 1594–96, nine new colleges were founded or re-founded, bringing the total number of colleges to 16, a figure that was to remain constant until the eventual opening of Downing College in 1800. The colleges admitted young and ambitious students and supported by means of endowed fellowships more senior scholars who devoted their intelligence and research to the controversial issues of the day. Books and manuscripts were collected and deposited in college libraries. In 1534, the King allowed the University to print books approved by the Chancellor or his deputy and three other senior academics, and to sell them anywhere in his realm. In fact, this privilege was not wholly operative until 1584, but since then, Cambridge University Press has published something every year.[10] Books for teaching and scholarship needed in the early part of the century came from outside Cambridge, indeed, many from the continent, demonstrating again the importance of Cambridge's easy and established links with northern Europe in particular.

That academics were disputatious and did not always support a correct establishment view of things was to be expected; and some paid for the fruits of their learning with their lives. But it is clear that through these tempestuous years, Cambridge contributed in major ways to the general good of society. The fact of so many benefactions, the placing of so many Cambridge-educated men in positions of influence in church and state, its peopling of the professions, its promotion of scholarship and learning, testify to the importance of the University in English life. Many benefactions assumed that the best source for a literate elite would come from among intelligent but poor boys, without other means of support and no prospect of inherited station or wealth. Thus a service was bought that had other social, and indeed charitable, benefits. But by the end of the century, the sons of gentry and prosperous families became students as well, not expecting thereby to earn a living, and thus changing the nature of the place. Cambridge became yet another power base of the socially privileged.[11]

The vibrancy of academic life and recognition of its usefulness brought with it issues of management and control. The new colleges all had a statutory framework, and from the time of Queen Elizabeth, a reformed legal structure was imposed on the University. The underlying political principle in all these measures was very simple: for the granting of resources and privileges, benefits had to accrue and someone had to be made accountable. Scholars may prefer total freedom, but there had to be limits. In the colleges, Heads of House were given greater powers over their Fellows and students, and in the University, the Chancellor and Vice-Chancellor were similarly empowered to control and censor. However, these powers, though ferocious in form and content, were not used in an active or directional manner. The legislation allowed intervention and held some particular authority responsible, if ever thought necessary. There was built into these Tudor constitutions (and which remained fundamentally unchanged until the 19th century) a paradox that remains at the heart of University organization to this day: how to reconcile short-term utilitarian demands and to secure the results the patron asks for, with the need to allow freedom of enquiry and criticism of the status quo? At one extreme is a push for managerial direction from above, at the other is a policy to give free rein to the academics and allow dynamism from below.

The concentration of wealth and scholarly interests in Cambridge in this period had one further consequence: the academic sector became the predominating interest in the town and its economy. Many and bitter were disputes as the town authorities fought to restrain the growing legal privileges of the University and to retain overall control of local government and finance. Town and gown sat in uneasy relationship with each other; but what was undeniable was that the colleges had now become the principle economic drivers of local development. They occupied physically the stretch of river from the main bridge upstream to the Mill pool. Although the Mill pool itself was to retain commercial importance until the 19th century — it allowed the growth of the University Press between Mill Lane and Silver Street, and flour was milled there until the 1920s — the expansion of the colleges along "the Backs" restricted commercial and industrial activity downstream and to the north and east of the historic centre. The colleges were the main employers of labour, much of which was poorly housed in cramped conditions within the confines of the old medieval town; and the University would use its influence locally to prevent growth inimical to its own perceived interests: in the 1840s, the University, out of concern for the moral welfare of its undergraduates, ensured that the railway station was built inconveniently far away from the centre of the town, and in the 1950s, a new planning regime sought to prevent the expansion of Cambridge city in order to preserve its qualities as a "university town".

Cambridge Emerges as a Centre of International Scholarship

The 17th century saw a leveling off of activity: student numbers stabilized; theological controversy remained keen. The political strife of mid-century did not help and Cambridge, though in the main more Puritan and Parliamentarian than Oxford, boxed skillfully to avoid excessive retaliation from whichever party attained an ascendancy locally or nationally. But the second half of the century witnessed a flourishing of scholarly activity. There was a fresh impetus across western Europe to research — particularly in subjects like mathematics, astronomy, physics, and chemistry which ushered in a new intellectual and cultural world; and this was accompanied by similar creative movements in philosophy, literature and critical approaches to ancient Greek and Latin texts that lay the foundations for what became termed as the "European Enlightenment". The effect of all this was to steer thinking away from religion and theology, and to usher in (albeit in slow and complicated ways) a more secular and aggressively rational approach to the study of the natural world and the social order. Ironically, for some considerable time to come, many of the leading scholars would still be clergymen, and their formal education limited to ancient disciplines.

Within Cambridge, this intellectual revolution is best symbolized by the work of Isaac Newton, a Fellow of Trinity College, whose research and publications laid the basis for scientific understanding until the 20th century. The son of a farmer (whose father died before his birth), Newton gained admission to Cambridge in 1661, when he was 19 years old. He paid his way through college by undertaking menial duties, before being awarded a scholarship in 1664. Although his formal studies at school and at Cambridge were in Latin and classical philosophy, Newton had a particularly mathematical bent and early began research in calculus, optics and the laws of gravity. Newton's work in these subjects was encouraged by the Lucasian Professor of Mathematics (and later Master of Trinity), Isaac Barrow, theologian and scholar, who had spent time travelling in Europe meeting leading intellectuals of the day. In 1669, Newton succeeded Barrow as the Lucasian Professor. He published the first edition of his *Principia Mathematica* in 1687, and a major work on *Opticks* in 1704; but his prolific publication of scientific papers began in the mid-1660s.

Newton was recognized in his time as being quite exceptional, but he lived and worked among fellow scholars of great distinction, exchanging views in the recently founded Royal Society, and corresponding privately with each other — both within and beyond the University. Moreover, the Fellows of the Royal Society, and the leading academics in the Universities, did not, at this period, recognize any rigid divisions in knowledge: for them all knowledge was fair game and there was a commendable inquisitiveness that recognized no disciplinary frontiers. Newton himself pursued what are now perceived as rather eccentric interests in alchemy, and conformed to conventional religious beliefs.

The second half of the 17th century was a period of great scientific and literary output. There was international interest in establishing and publishing better editions of classical texts, based on the collation of variant readings and deploying new theoretical approaches to understanding the texts. The giant in this field was Richard Bentley, who was to spend most of his life in conflict with his colleagues, particularly when he was Master of Trinity (1699–1740), on both intellectual and secular matters. There was also a new interest in exploring non-European languages and cultures, particularly through the medium of Hebrew, Arabic and Persian, and a reviving curiosity about the natural world, the arts, modern literature, politics and philosophy. In all these areas, the printing press enabled scattered scholars to communicate with each other and to extend their discussions beyond the small circles admitted by personal correspondence. In Oxford, Dr Fell took hold of the printing operation in midcentury. He acquired new types for the Oxford Press and sought out oriental fonts and other symbols. In Cambridge in the 1690s, Richard Bentley revived the University Press, providing for it a better structure, and raising funds to buy new typefaces and to publish uneconomic academic work, including books and pamphlets using non-standard fonts. Texts of great complexity were set in the printing house, including in 1713, a second, and much revised, edition of Newton's *Principia*. While the Bible and Prayer Book, together with local ephemera and school texts, had hitherto been the main business of the University presses, it now became part of their purpose to print new scholarship. Both authorship and readership of such work was international, and thus developed a strand of university activity that transcended the interests of the local scholars in Oxford and Cambridge and brought into being a nascent international academic community.[12]

The outburst of intellectual activity that touched many in the Cambridge colleges helps to put Newton's great personal achievement into perspective. It also helps to explain why his work became so influential: it was part of a greater academic enquiry, drawing from, and contributing to, the work of others. His contribution amounted to an intellectual revolution that could not be gainsaid: scholars across Europe recognized his claim, in *Principia*, that he had "laid down the principles of philosophy; principles not philosophical but mathematical; such, namely, as we may build our reasonings upon". From this period stems the dominance of mathematics as *the* intellectual discipline in Cambridge. Of course, it did not sweep all before it: although it became central to the award of a Cambridge degree. But, almost paradoxically, during the 18th century, the University functioned more and more as part of the established Church of England. It qualified priests (though not through any particular theological or pastoral education) and provided jobs for them: there was a steady movement of graduates from colleges to parsonages, from Professorships and Masterships into Deaneries and Bishoprics. Edward Gibbon's virulent criticism of the Oxford and Cambridge of his time are well known. He attacked the indolence of the dons, who "supinely enjoy the gifts of the founder…. From the toil of reading or thinking or writing they had absolved their conscience, and the first shoots of learning and ingenuity withered on the ground without yielding any fruit to the owners or the public". Other European universities had branched out into new fields of study where professors were in control of their subjects; but in Oxford, professors were of no account, holding their posts as sinecures, their influence on students as nothing compared to the tutors in charge in the colleges. Cambridge, he admitted, seemed not to be quite so degraded being "less deeply infected than her sister with the vices of the cloister ... and the name and philosophy of her immortal Newton was first honoured in his native academy". Gibbon's strictures pointed to a growing complacency in the relationship between University and society: and since the former occupied a privileged, wealthy, and monopolistic position, the time was ripe for re-appraisal.[13]

The Emergence of the Modern University

The modern transformation of the ancient English universities was radical and thorough, but it took a long time to achieve. Entrenched within the established church, and drawing on historic endowments, 18th and early 19th century Cambridge seemed content to transmit with blind deference from one generation of students to another, the accepted wisdom of the past. It admitted men only, and to qualify for any degree they had to be members of the Church of England. Academics tended to be critics, compilers and commentators rather than original thinkers aiming to challenge and enlarge the limits of the human mind. Innovation in social studies or the natural sciences and technology had no part in the formal activities of the colleges, though some attempts were made to stimulate research by the establishment of new chairs or through support for institutions like the University Library, the Botanic Garden and museum collections. Research was conducted privately and discussed through exchanges in numerous learned societies founded in this period, and through personal correspondence: it was not a mainstream activity of the University as such.

As agricultural and industrial changes transformed the British economy and society, however, the failings of the old universities came more and more to the fore, and critical and covetous eyes were cast on their privileges and wealth, enjoyed without adequate relevance to contemporary needs. If Oxford and Cambridge would not move with the times, then new universities in dynamic cities rather than old colleges in provincial backwaters would be created. First in London, with agnostic, if not atheistic, University College (1826), and the more godly King's College

(1829), followed by Durham (1832), as the Bishop sought to avoid a more devastating expropriation of the wealth of his See, the process gained momentum: Manchester (1851 — but with a significant technological institute founded in that city in 1824), Liverpool (1881), Birmingham (1900), Leeds (1904), and Sheffield (1905) came into being, driven by local initiative and funded by local wealth; open to all and with a modern curriculum that paid attention to the economic and social needs of thriving industrial cities.

Cambridge changed slowly (and Oxford even more so), though to be fair, a good deal of the demand for change in those seats of learning came from within the universities themselves: there was never wanting a class of critics who thought that the University should be doing more, or that part of its task was to think broadly and explore. Biblical and textual studies became exposed to discoveries in geology and archaeology; and gradually during the 19th century, new subjects were introduced into the curriculum: in Cambridge, Mathematics and Classics were followed between 1851 and 1920 by undergraduate courses in Philosophy, Natural Sciences, Law, History, Theology, Oriental languages, Modern and Medieval European languages, Engineering, Economics, English and Geography. Each new introduction was accompanied by controversy, and not all subjects achieved the status that continued to be afforded to Mathematics and Classics. Even within those branches of knowledge, the content of the curriculum or what was thought important in new scholarship was contested: Cambridge Mathematics fighting off (too successfully as it turned out) developments in the subject originating in Europe, and Classics split between those who saw its educational worth as being solely a discipline of language and those who wished to broaden its remit to include the whole history, culture, religion and art of ancient Mediterranean civilizations.[14]

Disputes within disciplines, and the relationship of disciplines one to another, were also related to the purpose of a University education: who was being educated and what for? This in turn raised the question of access to Cambridge and in the course of time barriers on the grounds of religious affiliation or of gender were removed; so too, though in no straightforward way, there was a return to the medieval idea that Cambridge, though an expensive place, was not to be the resort of wealthy youth only, and endowments, coupled in the 20th century with an influx of public money, provided opportunities for admission on intellectual merit and potential — though how these could adequately be determined remained problematical.

Perhaps the greatest change, though, came in how the academic community saw itself. The critical idea grew that the Fellows of the colleges were not part of the professional Church, nor were the Universities fundamentally religious institutions. Rather, they had a responsibility to teach students for the modern world, and to take a leading role in research. An explicit commitment to the latter was prompted in part by the establishment of specialized research institutes in European, especially German, and later in North American, universities. Cambridge became, step by step, a more secular place; its academics thought of themselves as a new species of professionals; subjects multiplied and became more specialized, and changes were pushed forward in relation to social and economic imperatives. Several factors were at work: first, there was the intellectual excitement of the chase as modern life threw up more opportunities and challenges; and as the store of knowledge increased its interpretation became more exacting and excitingly questionable; then there were benefactors willing to fund new developments; and finally, the State, influenced by a variety of concerns, willing, as much as ever the Tudor monarchs had done, to legislate, finance and intervene, to ensure the universities pulled their weight. Royal Commissions, designed to change structures of governance, to over-ride local legislation, and to alter arrangements for funding, reported on Cambridge in 1852, 1874 and 1922; and the remainder of the 20th century saw the progressive intrusion of public policy into the University as it became part of a system of national higher education.

Towards a Univer-City

The Cambridge of today is essentially the creation of the past half century. What was still in the 1940s and 1950s, a small and exclusive type of liberal Arts College with some quite exceptional internationally renown research attached, located in a modest provincial town, has become a much larger institution, still distinguished for its undergraduate teaching but driven more and more by research imperatives and situated in an entrepreneurial and rapidly growing city. By almost any measure, Cambridge University has more than doubled in size since the 1950s: whereas then the resources devoted to teaching came to around three-quarters of the whole, now, with far greater wealth, research accounts for upwards of three-quarters of the University's annual budget. Research, increasingly specialized and expensive, has grown in volume and importance so as to alter balances within the University in radical ways. Similarly, the city has grown beyond recognition: no longer just a "university town", it thrives as a local and regional economic and administrative hub, with a buoyant economy and displaying increasing national and international importance.

Throughout the 20th century, but especially in the second half, the University and the colleges became perpetual building sites. Moreover, they burst out of their quarters within the old town. Until the 1960s, most colleges and Departments were within easy walking distance of each other, facilitating a convivial social life. But the die was cast as early as the 1930s when the University Library, housed in the centre of town, was relocated to a green-field site so far away across the river that it was thought readers would be greatly inconvenienced with regard to their lunch. The Library was followed by the Chemistry Laboratories which occupied new premises to the south of Lensfield Road in the 1950s, and when the Veterinary School was established in open fields far to the west, a local joke was that one needed to get there by hired autobus. The colleges redeveloped their historic sites to accommodate increased numbers of undergraduate students, partitioning rooms, shoe-horning three people into sets that had once held only two, and even squeezing new buildings into existing sites. But this proved an inadequate response and after 1954, 11 new colleges were created one way or another located in the suburbs and beyond.[15]

In this expansion, there was some loss of intimacy; but this did not just stem from physical sprawl. The arrival of graduate students, about a thousand by the mid-1960s, over 6,000 by the end of the century and the hiring of more lecturers, professors, librarians, administrators and technicians meant that more and more people fell out of the conventional collegiate structure. The University Library's tea room served a broader function than just providing a quick bite to eat, and the laboratories began to provide social facilities for their members. Faced by demands for economy in the 1980s, the Head of one laboratory reported that the last place he would look would be in the provision of tea and cakes for his students and staff, and the Computer Laboratory became famous for its "real time" image of its coffee pot so that people could see from their offices who had turned up and join them for a chat. This showed that more emphasis was being placed on talking to colleagues in your own field, and, indeed, as a reputation for outstanding research became more and more the main criterion for appointment and promotion, finding ways of networking with colleagues internationally became a regular way of doing things. This powerful change in academic culture permeated the arts, humanities and social sciences also. There had been no demand in Cambridge for specialist Faculty buildings for Mathematics, Classics, History, Law, English etc, but by the early 21st century, they had all come about. Of course, they did not replace the traditional collegiate ways, but added to them; and while there were gains (as the changes worked their way in, colleagues often expressed amazement at the benefits of being able to meet and talk to others in the same subject), there were also losses to be guarded against: most significantly a loss of easy communication with scholars in other fields.

A further great shift in the past half-century has been the pressure to centralize and to manage resources in transparent and accountable ways. Here, the principal funders of the University — the state, either directly by way of annual grant or indirectly via Research Councils, philanthropic charities and wealthy individuals — have all been keen to see that the resources they provided have been well-managed and applied strictly to the purposes for which they were allocated. Moreover, the special legal privileges that universities, particularly Oxford and Cambridge, sheltered under for so long, have gradually been whittled away: national legislation governing health and safety, or employment and wages, for example, have been applied with increasing rigor; many of the more picturesque rights have quietly disappeared. University politics have never been so lively or so contested.[16]

The impact of the modern university is not easily judged. In one critical sense, its graduates are the fruits of its labour. They are so varied and make such diverse contributions to society that their value is difficult to measure and is conveniently overlooked. But the development of advanced economies has gone hand in hand with the rise in general levels of literacy. As recently as the 1950s and 1960s, the proportion of English children leaving formal education aged 16 or 18 was as high as 90 per cent. After World War II, Britain, following North America, recognized the need for a vastly increased number of more highly skilled workers. State schools were reformed, and the school-leaving age was raised. By the 1950s, this drove an expansion of the university system, and by the end of the century the aim in almost every developed country was to see that a third, or even more, of the population continued in some form of post-school education, and every country in the world set a premium on developing mass literacy and the skills that would follow. Expansion of universities and other institutions of higher education, however, proved a costly business, falling mainly on the tax payer. How, and for what purpose universities were funded, thus, became a live political issue.

One way of approaching this issue was to see how universities interacted with the broader economy: what contribution their research made to immediate economic growth and how connected they were with business and industry, both locally and nationally. In 1983, a report, commissioned by the British Prime Minister, was published on fostering links between higher education and industry. It noted in passing "that something interesting seemed to be happening in Cambridge by way of development of small firms that were connected with the University and in which Barclays Bank was playing a significant role. The observation was made that a study of this 'Cambridge phenomenon' would be useful in order to document what was actually going on, and why, and to disseminate more widely such reasons as there might be from the Cambridge experience."[17]

Since 1960, Cambridge and its immediate hinterland have witnessed significant sustainable economic growth based on the service and high-technology sectors of the economy. This "phenomenon" is directly related to Cambridge being a univer-city. Detailed study showed how, in complex ways, the interactions between an ancient university in a medieval market town had created for contemporary times a dynamic engine for intellectual exploration and economic growth. A key report of findings was published in 1985 and an updated analysis in 2000. By the mid-1980s, there were over 350 small, independent, businesses clustered around Cambridge, focused mainly on computing hardware and software, scientific instruments, electronics, scientific consultancy and R & D, and biotechnology. They accounted for nearly 20 per cent of employment in the area. By 2012, the number of companies had risen to about 1,400, employing some 48,000 people, accounting for almost a quarter of all jobs in the region.[18]

The "historically pervasive influence of the University on most aspects of life in Cambridge" is reckoned a key component to this development:

> It has set a tone and style of quality, individualism and confidence; and, especially because of the collegiate structure, it has created a unique environment for social and inter-disciplinary contact within the entire academic and research community and, increasingly, now also extending to the local high technology and business communities. The concept of "networks" goes a long way towards explaining how Cambridge has operated as a university and market town in the past, and now also as a high technology business centre.[19]

These explicit attitudes grew out of the University's tradition of fostering maximum academic freedom, and they gave essential stimulus to the dynamism of the University in the second half of the 20th century. But it is important to recognize also that without a parallel development of the city, and of the region around Cambridge, the University initiative would not have had so great an impact. Indeed, deeper study of the "Cambridge Phenomenon" showed how vital the contributions of business and entrepreneurship were in driving things forward. Without a reassertion of the independent economic vitality of the city, the University would not have had the incentives to develop in the way it did. The pressures for growth had proved relentless. Cambridge developed as a regional centre for health and other services. People were drawn to it by the prospect of interesting and fulfilling jobs, and because it offered an agreeably high quality of life.

A number of intangibles come into play. Cambridge and the surrounding region remain overall a beautiful part of England. The presence of so many opinionated and well-educated citizens makes for lively local politics and diverse interest groups. There are many opportunities in Cambridge to hear lectures, to make and listen to music, to look at and enjoy art, to participate in sport, to explore religion, and simply to have easy access to books and learning. In the univer-city, the Arts, Humanities and Social Sciences, as much as technology and material possession, stand in the very centre: libraries, museums, galleries, concert halls, and the vibrancy of research in the Humanities are all essential for the good life: they create a style of living associated throughout the ages with cities.

The Univer-City in a Global Context

What then, are the implications of all this for the formation of networks of univer-cities across the Asia-Pacific, and beyond, where learning, research and enterprise rather than silk are the currencies of exchange? Perhaps the most interesting feature of Cambridge University's long history is that it has been effective in bursts: it met an initial need to nourish the religious culture of the 13th century; it re-invented itself to serve a different Church, an expanding state, and a growing economy in the 16th century; it flourished in a the context of the European spirit of enlightenment in the late 17th century; and, with recurring frequency it has re-created itself over and again from the 19th century to the present day.

This brings us back to the purpose of a university and to its relationship with society: to provide literacy at the highest possible level; to transmit, but not uncritically, the knowledge and received wisdom of the ages; to research, enquire and explore; to be intellectually creative. The conditions needed to meet these requirements are places where a sufficiently large number of highly diverse and intelligent people, committed to an academic vocation, can live and work. There must be enough of them to spark debate and to engage in mutual dialogue, and their concept of knowledge and its purposes must be broad. They need to be open-minded and be prepared both to inherit from the past and to be excited to probe the future. They will have their own specialist interests and, indeed, will have developed special knowledge, methodologies, and ideas in order to think effectively, but they must be willing to brush up against different cultures and disciplines. Specialist institutes, whether in science, technology or the arts, have their place, but they are in reality but part of a wider interconnected whole. They need to have exacting standards and to be committed to seeking that which is true; though they must recognize that they draw from others, both past and present, and that the pursuit of truth is a never-ending work in progress. Specific projects change in nature, disciplinary boundaries shift and change; knowledge occupies a vast uncharted zone through which we pick our way with trepidation.

For a university to be truly effective, it must be grounded in its own contemporary society and be responsive to the challenges facing that society. So to be located in a city — a place of economic, social and political activity, to be touched by the dynamism of that place and to interact with it, is essential also: the medieval market town of Cambridge was such a place; 21st century Cambridge has become such a city. But university and city are not locked together in any narrow geographical, political or utilitarian purpose. The univer-city looks to broader connections — within the region, the nation, and beyond. And this is where the concept of a necklace of such cities, each a separate jewel of worth but strung together across the world has such force behind it. Modern communications make more possible, without at all replacing the need for direct human contact, the easy and rapid dissemination of information. That information still has to be measured and assessed, and its validity and usefulness tested. Here, univer-cities, with their economic power, intellectual excellence and cultural diversity, can purposely be connected for the good of everyone.

Acknowledgement

I am grateful to Peter Carolin and Anthony Teo who commented on an earlier draft of this essay.

Notes

1. See Chapter 2 in this volume.
2. An example of a problem-solving collaboration is that of the recent agreements between complementary Departments in Cambridge, the National University of Singapore and Nanyang Technical University to work together on a range of energy-related issues. Such long-term strategic alliances between western and Asian research-intensive universities are becoming increasingly common. The links between Cambridge and Singapore rest on long-standing flows of students, the informal networks of alumni, and support received by Cambridge and its colleges from friends in Singapore. Significantly, Wolfson College, Cambridge, numbers among its Honorary Fellows benefactor Dr Lee Seng Tee, alumnus the Hon Tharman Shanmugaratnam, and former Visiting Fellow, Professor Wang Gungwu.

3. Fredrick Yorke Powell, Regius Professor of History, quoted in Nicholas Barker, *The Oxford University Press and the Spread of Learning, 1478-1978* (Oxford: Clarendon Press, 1978), p. 49
4. Without an understanding of the electron, revealed most clearly by J.J. Thomson through work in the Cavendish Laboratory in Cambridge in 1897, the 20th-century as we know it would not have been possible. But the Wikipedia entry for "electron" shows just how extended and drawn out were both the theoretical work behind the "discovery" of the electron, and then its subsequent application.
5. Dharma Kumar, herself an alumna of Cambridge University, exasperated by "the quaint Cambridge belief that practically all the light (and none of the heat) on Indian history emanates from that beautiful town" went on, in a magnificent swipe that enabled her to take down simultaneously two academic communities prone to a sense of excessive self-worth: "Situated on a narrow river, centre of scholarship, austere, puritanical and parochial — surely Cambridge is the Pune of the West", *Indian Economic and Social History Review*, 1979, vol. 16, p.435. Sanjay Subrahmaniam led me to this delicious quotation. Sometimes truly outstanding departments tend to clone themselves and thus make it difficult to adjust to new developments: Cambridge's Department of Physiology, for example, a world-leader in the 1950s, did not adequately recognize the opportunities offered to the subject of the emerging field by molecular biology.
6. The myth of the lone genius is most effectively exploded in Lord Broers' Reith Lectures: Alec Broers, *The Triumph of Technology* (Cambridge University Press, 2005), especially pp. 23–39. The later 19th-century and early 20th century saw much movement of ideas and skills between the new Cavendish Laboratory at Cambridge and the scientific and technological departments at Manchester and elsewhere. Rutherford (from New Zealand) and J.J. Thomson, both claimed as "Cambridge men", had Manchester experience, and Clerk Maxwell, another in this distinguished galaxy of "Cambridge" scientists, set out from Edinburgh. Indeed, the pattern of diverse professional backgrounds is common among the most eminent scientists and scholars from the earliest periods. The Cavendish's great scientific achievements would not have been possible without the technical support and practical inventiveness of Horace Darwin (son of Charles) and his colleagues who founded the Cambridge Scientific Instrument Company in 1878: M.J.G. Cattermole and A.F. Wolfe, *Horace*

Darwin's Shop: A History of the Cambridge Scientific Instrument Company 1878–1968. (Bristol & Boston: Adam Hilger, 1987) This small, highly specialized, company is recognized in Cambridge today as being an essential progenitor of the "Cambridge Phenomenon". A further striking example of the complexity of discovery is that of the unraveling of the structure of DNA. The famous Crick and Watson paper, published in *Nature* in 1953, rested on work done in the Cavendish Laboratory, in the Computer Laboratory, in the Department of Chemistry, and in the MRC's Laboratory of Molecular Biology; but it also depended on work being done in London University (especially the findings of Rosalind Franklin) and on significant input from Oxford and elsewhere.

7. For example, King Henry VI founded King's College in 1441. Its iconic chapel was central to its purpose. The original endowment was for the support of a Provost and 70 poor scholars. The college occupied what had been a commercial quarter on the bank of the river.

8. There are good articles about John Fisher in Wikipedia and the *New Oxford Dictionary of National Biography*. His importance to Cambridge is easily found in Elisabeth Leedham-Green, *A Concise History of the University of Cambridge* (Cambridge: Cambridge University Press, 1996), pp. 40 ff. Fisher's eminence and learning did not, in the end, save him from controversy, and because he sided with the Queen in the matter of Henry VIII's divorce and refused to accept Henry's claim to be Head of the Church, he was executed on 22 June 1535. The success of subsequent Tudor propaganda — effectively excluded Fisher from the history of Cambridge until the 20th century.

9. Quoted in Elisabeth Leedham-Green, op.cit., p. 49.

10. M. H. Black, *Cambridge University Press 1584–1984* (Cambridge: Cambridge University Press, 1984); David McKitterick, *A History of Cambridge University Press*, 3 vols (Cambridge: Cambridge University Press, 1992, 1998, 2004)

11. Quentin Skinner, 'The Generation of John Milton', in David Reynolds, ed., *Christ's: A Cambridge College over Five Centuries* (London: Macmillan, 2004), p. 45.

12. For Oxford University Press the 17th-century see Barker, op. cit. and Ian Gadd, ed. *The History of Oxford University Press, Volume I: Beginnings to 1780* (Oxford: Oxford University Press, 2013); for Cambridge University Press, see Black, op.cit. and McKitterick, op.cit. volume 1; Gordon Johnson, *Printing and Publishing for the University: Three Hundred Years of the Press Syndicate* (Cambridge: Cambridge University Press, 1996), pp. 10–16. There is a superb

early 19th-century biography: James Henry Monk, *The Life of Richard Bentley, D.D.*, 2nd edition (London: Rivington, 1823).

13. The quotations from Gibbon are taken from Betty Radice, ed., *Edward Gibbon, Memoirs of My Life* (London: Folio Society, 1984), ch. 3. There are many editions of Gibbon's *Memoirs*, which have a complex publishing history. The Folio Society's text is that of the Penguin edition.

14. Gordon Johnson, *University Politics: F.M. Cornford's Cambridge and His Advice to the Young Academic Politician* (Cambridge: Cambridge University Press, 1994; Centenary edition, 2008).

15. The list of colleges in order of foundation is conveniently given in Leedham-Green, op.cit., pp. 223–224. Among those founded since 1954, Darwin, Wolfson and Clare Hall were specifically designed for post-graduate students. By the second decade of the 21st century, Cambridge University has expanded to the west and is about to grow further to the north-west. The Veterinary School, once in the heart of the countryside, is now hemmed in by new laboratories, occupying an area greater than the historic confines of all the colleges and University Departments.

16. The University's rights over the town were gradually eroded during the 19th century. The Vice-Chancellor's entitlement to license the Colleges for the sale and consumption of wine survived until the end of the 20th century.

17. Nick Segal, "The Cambridge Phenomenon: The Growth of High Technology Industry in a University Town", *The Cambridge Review*, March 1985, p. 39.

18. The original report is Segal Quince Wicksteed, *The Cambridge Phenomenon* (1985) and revisited in 2000. The reports are accessible at <www.sqw.co.uk>. There is an extensive literature, helpfully commented on in SQW's Viewpoint Series, Issue 12 July 2011, by Christine Doel and Chris Green. There is a coffee-table book, Kate Kirk and Charles Cotton, *The Cambridge Phenomenon: 50 Years of Innovation and Enterprise* (London: Third Millennium, 2012). Similar clusters of academia and business, on a larger scale than that at Cambridge, are found in California and in the Boston-Cambridge region of Massachusetts. Elsewhere in the UK there are similar developments around, for example, Oxford, Glasgow and Manchester. And one should not overlook the importance and tremendous potential of London, with its considerable university sector and concentration of libraries, art galleries and museums, and the new development of entrepreneurial research and business clusters in the King's Cross area and the rejuvenated Docklands.

19. Nick Segal in *The Cambridge Review*, March 1985, p.41. The University had earlier proved a magnet for a broad range of "external" research interests. For example, the Babraham Institute, established by the then Agricultural Research Council in 1948, and the Medical Research Council's Laboratory of Molecular Biology. These, and other similar independent organizations, funded and governed outside the University have significant interactions with it. More recently, public funds, private benefactions, medical charities and business investment are creating Europe's most advanced research campus for the life-sciences located with Cambridge's regional hospital on the south of the city.

About the Author

Gordon Johnson was President of Wolfson College Cambridge (1993–2010); Deputy Vice-Chancellor; Chairman, Cambridge University Press; and Director, Centre of South Asian Studies.

CHAPTER TWELVE

TUNISIAN SCIENTISTS' EXPERIENCES IN SINGAPORE: ON THE NEW SILK ROAD?

LILIA LABIDI AND ANTHONY SC TEO

Introduction

Since the beginning of the 2000s, young Tunisian scientists — breaking with the dominant tendencies among the élites in formerly colonized countries where the main exchanges continue to be with the former colonial power — are creating new dependency relationships and choose new roads for their travels. Speaking Arabic and French and proficient in other languages — such as English, German, Spanish that they have learned in secondary school[1] and then improved at the university level — there are now some 13,000 Tunisian students in US, Canadian, German, and French universities.[2] Since 2000, a new trend has emerged, with young Tunisians making virtual connections or travelling on new roads, renewing their taste for voyages, discovery, and scientific exchange, and setting themselves up in various Asian countries, like Japan, India, Taiwan, and Singapore.[3] In this chapter, we will see how scientific tastes developed among Tunisian youth, the role of exemplary scientific figures in the general culture, and how the desire for discovery among the Tunisian scientific community led to an attraction for travel.

These Tunisian scientists, who now travel, have many predecessors: the Phoenicians of long ago, who were represented in the Iliad and the Odyssey as craftsmen, seamen, and merchants and who established trading posts all around the Mediterranean; and the Carthaginians, with their maritime technology and knowledge of the seas, who sought to discover new lands. One was Hannon, who followed the Atlantic coast of Africa up to the Gulf of Guinea; another was Himilco who followed the European coast towards Great Britain; and others from the Maghreb who, later,

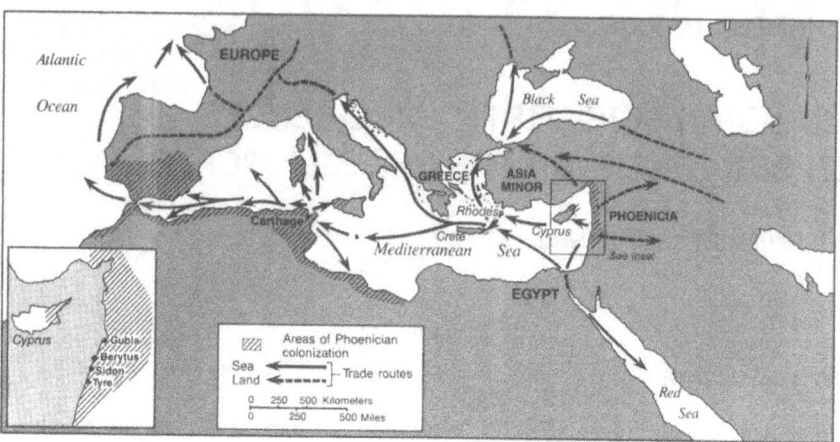

Map 12.1. Phoenician Trade Routes. *Source:* Collelo, T, ed. (1989), p. 6.

starting from their pilgrimages to Mecca, followed the Silk Road, leading to cultural, commercial, and scientific exchange with the civilizations of China, India and Southeast Asia; or who, via trans-Saharan trade, established links between the Mediterranean and West Africa, tracing routes between Morocco and Niger, between Tunisia and Lake Chad, between Niger and Egypt — routes that continue to this day to nourish the imagination of society.

Heirs to this culture of the *Rihla* as a rite of passage and a means for exchange, a group of Tunisian scientists started arriving in Singapore from around 2010, bringing with them different projects — some to finish their PhD degrees, others doing research in university laboratories, still others as specialists in international companies. They have all come from the smallest country of the Maghreb with a history of several thousand years and where human habitation has been traced back to the Paleolithic period. It has been a cradle of civilization — known for being the breadbasket of the Roman Empire — and today is known for its citrus fruits, olive oil, dates, mass tourism and extensive beaches. Perhaps less well known is the importance of Tunisia's phosphate resources that were discovered in 1885 and that today produces eight million tons annually, placing it 5th in the world in natural phosphate

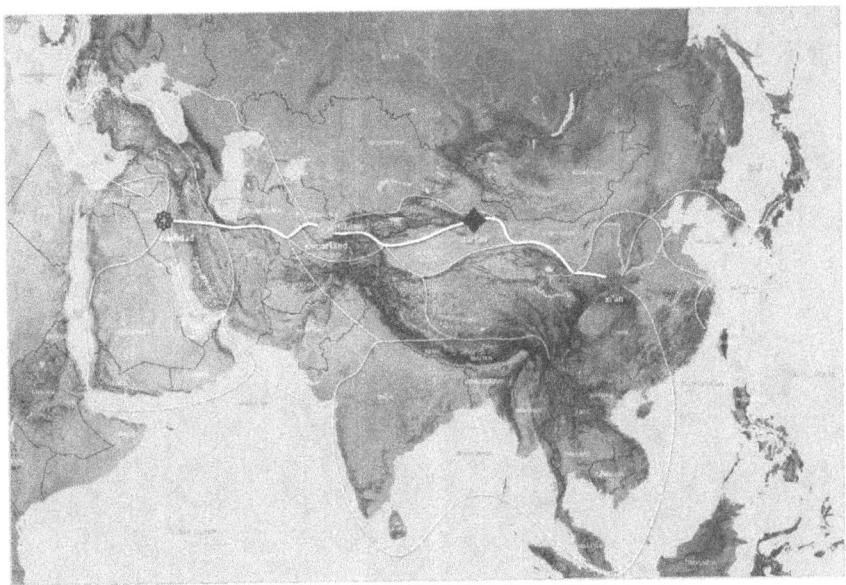

Map 12.2. Silk Road: Land & Sea Routes. *Source:* American Museum of Natural History.

production and 2nd in exploiting more than 80 per cent of its production, which is exported towards the five continents via the ports of Sfax, Gabès and Skhira.

Taste for Science

What are the origins of the taste for science among the Tunisian scientists? They have been socialized in an environment where the discourse of science pervaded their culture. The temple of Eshmoun, God of Medicine and Health, is built on the hill of Byrsa in Carthage, and several scientific books were produced during the Punic period. Libraries older than the one in Alexandria existed in Carthage. Archeological monuments of the Roman period show thermal baths existing in Bulla Regia, Carthage, Dougga, Makthar, Sbeitla, and so on. Esculape — the Greek god of medicine whose statue was discovered at the Bulla Regia site — was adopted as the god of medicine. Several famous doctors practised in Carthage

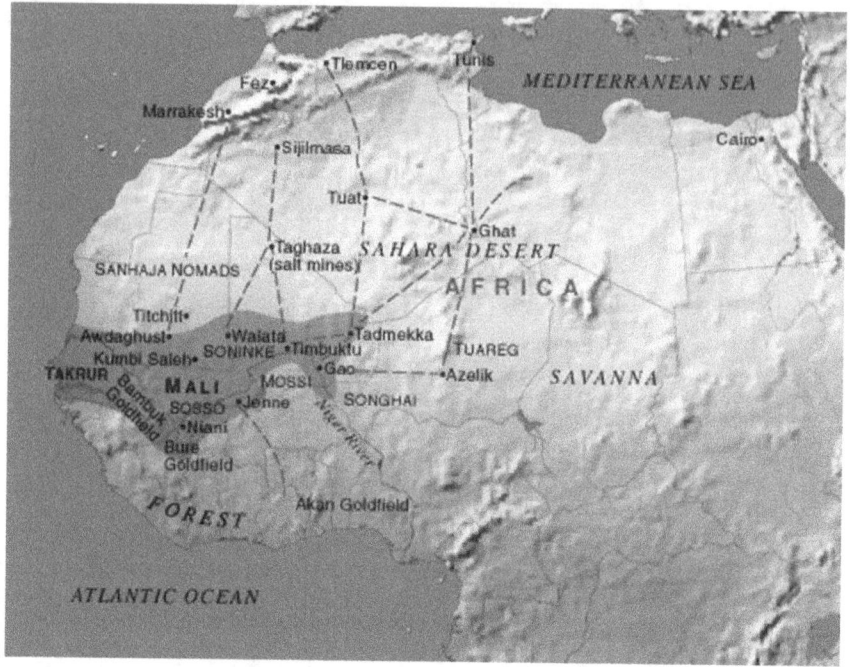

Map 12.3. Trans-Saharan Trade. *Source:* The Metropolitan Museum of Art.

and in Kef during this period. Later, during the Islamic period, a prestigious medical school was established in Kairouan and, in the same city, Oqba Ibn Nafi founded one of the most important mosques in the Maghreb, in 670, which gave inspiration to Fatima Mohamed Al-Fehri (d. 880) to establish Qarawiyyin University in Fes, Morocco, in 859. The *hammam*, as the *madrasa*, were annexes of the mosques and were places for cleanliness and purification. They were as important as the hospitals, which were called *adl-Dimnah* ("Bimaristan", a Persian word, was the name given to hospitals in the Mashreq).

Al-Kairouan hospital, built in 830 by Prince Ziyadat Allah I, was followed by others in the 9th century in cities like Sousse, Tunis and Sfax. In addition to rooms for patient care, the hospitals also contained rooms devoted to courses, a library, and a prayer room. Ahmed Ben Miled, a doctor and historian (1902–94), mentions in his work *Histoire de la médecine Arabe en Tunisie* a map that shows the existence of a psychiatric hospital in Kairouan during that period.[4]

The names of a number of doctors who worked in Tunisia and who contributed to the spread of medical knowledge are part of collective memory. Ishaq Ibn Omrane, doctor and pharmacist who came from Baghdad in 887, is known for having directed medical education at *Beit El Hikma Raqqada* in Kairouan.[5] Works such as *Kiteb El-Fuqara* (*Medicine for the poor*), among others, by Ahmed Ibn Jazzar (who was born in Kairouan

Scene from a 15th century persian manuscript of a Hammam. *Source:* Time Life Books, *The Rise of Cities* (Amsterdam: Time-Life Books B.V., 1991), p. 74.

in 898 and was a doctor and pharmacist), were used in teaching in a number of European universities up until the 17th century. The Nobel Prize awarded in 1928 to Charles Nicolle, Ernest Conseil, and Charles Comte for their work at the Sadiki Hospital in Tunis on the transmission of typhus by lice also galvanized youth. Since the 1960s, national radio and then television broadcast campaigns addressing children's vaccination, diarrhoea, birth control, road safety, organ transplants, anti-smoking, nutrition, protection against AIDS, have contributed to the presence of the discourse of science in public space making a deep impression on that generation's imagination.

The arts, too — literature and cinema — contributed to spreading new images of scientists. Characters in TV films and novels were doctors, engineers, teachers, and so on, and this was also true in other countries of the region. The novel *Chrysalis* (*La Chrysalide*) by the Algerian Aicha Lemsine has a young female doctor as protagonist,[6] showing us a young woman who makes new choices with regard to her milieu, taking her life into her own hands. In the Moroccan Driss Chraibi's *Civilization, my Mother!* (*La civilisation, ma Mère!*), we see the reaction of the mother of two children — characters in the novel — to the arrival of the radio and telephone into her home.[7] The novel, structured as a diptych — one part is "Being", the other "Having" — shows how an illiterate woman succeeds "in humanizing the same objects that have intensified the alienation of European and American women".[8] These works among many others were catalysts for readers, both male and female.

All these factors and some others contributed to producing a culture turned towards the sciences, giving birth to passions among Tunisians, who came from a country of relatively limited resources but benefitted from a universal educational system since 1956, enabling Tunisia to reach a relatively high ranking among countries after just a few decades.[9] The budgetary expenditures (operating and capital) devoted to basic and secondary education increased, up to nearly 20 per cent of the state budget in 2005 (although

Table 12.1. Evolution of Number of Tunisian Pupils Enrolled in Primary Education (Grades 1–6).[10]

School Year	Schools	Classrooms	Pupils	Teachers
1983–1984	3,066	36,160	1,191,408	33,026
2008–2009	4,513	45,374	1,006,488	59,011

this had decreased to 16.25 per cent in 2009), allowing many children to be educated for free, year after year, in continually improving conditions.

We should point out here, that whereas the number of schools, classrooms and teachers has been increasing, the number of pupils is decreasing, because of the reduced numbers of children in the population due to birth control programmes introduced in the 1960s. Compulsory education improved the supervision of children, with 99 per cent of children of both sexes in school for the first year, and 97.7 per cent at the age of 11.[11] The percentages for those between 12 and 18 years of age, both sexes combined, was 68.4 per cent in 1998/99, rising to 75.5 per cent in 2008–09.[12] A higher percentage of students leave school during adolescence than during the early years of schooling, but this percentage was lower in 2008–09 (approximately 25 per cent) than it was a decade earlier (when it was more than 30 per cent).[13]

Table 12.2. Evolution of Number of Pupils Enrolled in 2nd Cycle of General Basic Education (Grades 7–9) and in Secondary Education (Grades 10–13).[14]

School Year	Schools	Classrooms	Pupils	Teachers
1983–84	335	10,801	364,492	17,943
1993–94	665	17,618	605,935	26,817
2003–04	1,161	33,103	1,076,238	55,717
2008–09	1,325	36,245	1,006,143	71,880

This system enabled the number of university students to increase from 28,618 in 1978–79 to 350,828 in 2007–08. For the same years, students receiving degrees rose from 4,162 to 60,840.[15] Tunisian higher education has 13 universities and a *Direction générale des études technologiques*, 193 higher education establishments in 2010–11, a virtual university since 2002–03 and has, since the 1980s, increasingly turned towards information technology, with 15.5 per cent of the total student population, or more than 55,000 students, following a course of study in communications technology in 2009–10.

The number of student visas given by France (Tunisia was a French Protectorate from 1881 to 1956 and France remains Tunisia's leading commercial partner, both in imports and exports[16]) to Tunisian students went from 2,595 in 2005 to 3,233 in 2011, of which 34 per cent were in basic or applied sciences, 50 per cent were for graduate studies, with women constituting one-third of this population (34 per cent).[17] Europe remains the main destination for highly educated migrants from the Arab world, whose numbers doubled during the 1990s from 2.5 to 4.9 million. Fifty per cent of Arab students registered in the Organization for Economic Cooperation and Development (OECD) countries are registered in France, and this is tied to the preponderance of students coming from the former French colonies of the Maghreb (Morocco, Algeria, Tunisia).[18] A recent study by the Arab League, in September 2008, points out that emigration of degree holders from the Arab countries amounts to a significant brain drain and these numbers continue to increase.

Demographers estimate that 54 per cent of Arab students trained in the West will not return to their home countries,[19] so Tunisia is not alone in this situation.

Table 12.3. Origins of Foreign Students in French and British Universities, by Geographical Zones.[20]

Origin of students	France (%)	United Kingdom (%)
Africa	48	9
Europe	24	26
Asia (including China, India, Oceania)	16	38
North and South America	7	9
Middle East	5	18

Table 12.4. The 10 Nationalities with Highest Representation in French and British Universities.[21]

Rank	France	United Kingdom
1	Morocco 26,998	China 45,356
2	China 20,852	India 25,901
3	Algeria 18,780	Ireland 15,261
4	Tunisia 10,812	USA 13,895
5	Senegal 9,298	Germany 13,625
6	Germany 6,918	France 12,685
7	Cameroun 5,655	Greece 12,626
8	Lebanon 5,609	Nigeria 11,783
9	Vietnam 5,133	Malaysia 11,727
10	Italy 5,009	Cyprus 9,795

Tunisia numbers more than 20,000 engineers and scientists, of which more than 9,500 have degrees in the IT sector, for a population of 10.78 million. With the percentage of university students at 4 per cent of its population, Tunisia is in the range of OECD figures.[22]

Voices were raised during the regimes of Habib Bourguiba and Zine El-Abidine Ben Ali against the policies of tying the country closely to France, including sending many of its students there. Paradoxically, when the liberal state chose liberal economics and individual initiative between 1987 and 2002, it became interventionist whereas between 1956 and 1986, when it had been authoritarian and planning-oriented, the initiative allowed to Tunisian scientists was greater and the managers and teachers reproduced the French model in a variety of scientific fields.[23]

Competition for qualified care-givers has upset the health systems in a number of countries. In Tunisia, whereas the overall density of medical personnel has evolved in a positive direction, this has not affected all regions of the country equally. The district of Tunis numbers 111 specialists and 96 general practitioners per 100,000 inhabitants, the northwest has only 17 and 40, the centre-west 12 and 36, and the southwest only 16 and 51, with a trend towards feminization in the last three regions. For Tunisian doctors practising abroad, the breakdown according to type of practice has favoured general practitioners (their proportion went from 23.3 per cent in 2000 to 53 per cent in 2009, whereas specialists decreased from 76.7 per cent to 47 per cent over the same period). In Tunisia, the rate of non-practising doctors rose from 4.6 per cent in 2000 to 15.2 per cent in 2009, due to budgetary restrictions, among other reasons.[24]

Western countries in need of health workers attract them from countries where English is spoken — like India, Egypt, and the Philippines — to

Table 12.5. Number of engineers per 100,000 inhabitants.

Country	Engineers per 100,000 inhabitants
Tunisia	44, in 2008
France	86, in 2006 (OECD)
South Korea	165, in 2006 (OECD)

240 *Univer-Cities: Strategic View of the Future*

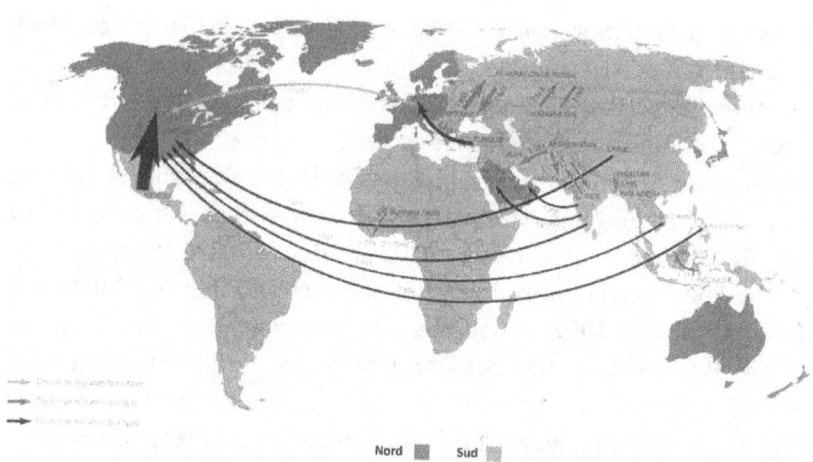

Map 12.4. Principal routes of migration. *Source*: World Migration Report 2013.

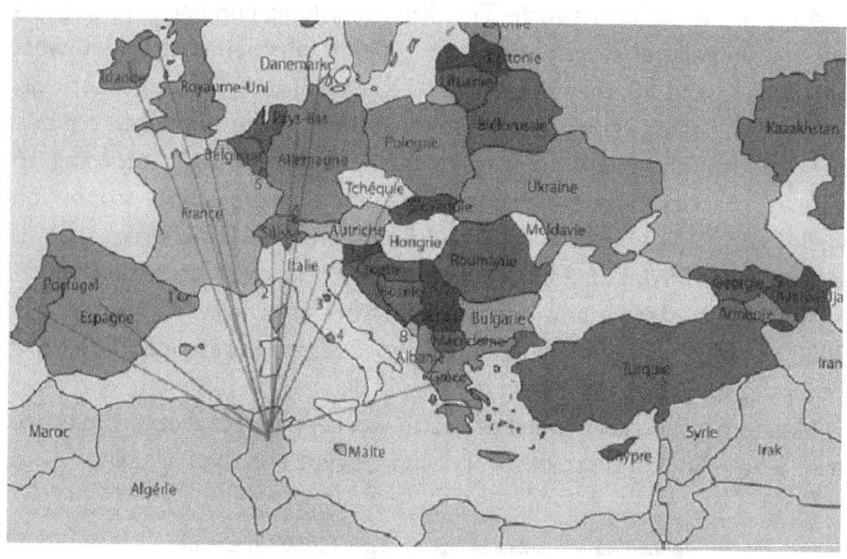

Map 12.5. Tunisian students and scholars in Europe.

fill the gaps. We hear of some 100,000 nurses from the Philippines, some of whom have been trained as doctors but who find it more remunerative to work abroad as nurses than in their home country as doctors. We see that also in some Gulf countries, Tunisian nurses are regularly sought after, creating insufficiencies in advanced Tunisian hospital services where the replacement personnel have less experience and expertise than those leaving, confirming the hypothesis that the international migrant tends to be increasingly well educated. A World Bank study estimates that 10 per cent of university-educated populations worldwide are lost to emigration.[25]

This situation is relevant not only for the countries of the South. A number of countries of the North, like Italy and the United Kingdom, are also faced with a dilution of scientific competence and are not succeeding in attracting scientists. In some countries, we hear of a negative balance in the circulation of brain power, as in Japan, Holland, Italy, Mexico, and Poland.[26] For every trained scientist/technologist entering Italy or Ireland, one and a half leave and, in the case of Mexico, five leave; the figure is more than three for Poland. In addition, the definitions of geo-political regions have evolved. The 2010 United Nations Development Programme (UNDP) classification using the Human Development Index (HDI) in health (life expectancy at birth), education (average length of schooling and number of attendees), and income, shows 42 countries having a high HDI and thus considered to be among developed countries or countries of the North. These include Saudi Arabia, Bahrain, Brunei, Kuwait, Oman, Qatar, and Singapore.

New Scientists, from Ibn Battuta to Ahmed Zuweil

We will discuss here why this group of Tunisian researchers based in Singapore, in the context of the "Arab spring", chose paths other than the common European ones, linked to the experiences others of similar origin have had of this region — scientists and researchers like Claude Cohen-Tannoudji, born in Algeria; Ahmed Zuweil, born in Egypt; Rachid Yazami, born in Morocco, all of whom are distinguished by their creativity in scientific fields — and how they follow in the footsteps of Ibn Battuta, who left his native country at the age of 21 to discover the world and to gain knowledge, leading him from Morocco to Southeast Asia and to China.

Among the internationally recognized researchers born in the Arab world and who have been welcomed in Singapore we find Claude Cohen-Tannoudji, whose family name alone resonates with the history of the region. His family, fleeing the Spanish inquisition, came to Tangiers, leading to the name Tannoudji, then based itself in Tunisia, before settling in Algeria in the 16th century, where he was born in 1933 in Constantine. Cohen-Tannoudji received the Nobel Prize in physics in 1997, along with Steven Chu and William D. Phillips, for their work in developing ways to freeze atoms with the aid of laser beams.

There is also Ahmed Zuweil, born in Egypt in 1946, who received the Nobel Prize in chemistry in 1999, for his work on the transition states of a chemical reaction with the aid of femtosecond spectroscopy. His work also earned him other distinctions such as the Nile Necklace award, Egypt's highest; honorary doctorates in Lebanon, China, India, South Korea, and Japan; and he holds an honorific chair at the United Nations University and is member of several science academies, such as those of Malaysia and France.

Finally, Rachid Yazami, born in Fes, in Morocco, has held the Tsang Man Chair Professorship in Energy in the School of Materials Science & Engineering at the Nanyang Technological University in Singapore for some years now. A research director at the CNRS, he co-founded at the California Institute of Technology (Caltech) a CNRS-Caltech joint laboratory on materials science for energy storage applications, including in lithium ion batteries and in hydrogen storage. In 1980, Prof. Yazami invented the graphite anode (negative electrode) used in the 8 billion lithium ion batteries produced in 2012. This discovery was the turning point in rechargeable lithium battery technology. Rachid Yazami has published more than 200 articles and other works and is an inventor involved in over 70 patents related to battery technology. He has received several scientific awards, including from NASA, NATO, IBA, the Japan Society for the Promotion of Science (JSPS), the Hawaii Battery Conference and is the winner of the 2012 IEEE (Medal for Environmental and Safety Technologies) and the 2014 Charles Stark Draper Prize for Engineering.

Europe continues to be the continent that attracts students and most Tunisians who are highly educated. Whereas the Arab world attracts five times as many highly-educated individuals as the US and Canada, students are more attracted to North America than to the Arab world. Asia and Australia attract twice as many of the highly-educated and students as the African continent.[27]

Tunisian men and women scientists in Singapore number about 45.[28] Among them are technicians who have been living in Singapore with their families for several years; others are students or researchers in the sciences, information technology, or in the financial sector. Some have Tunisian citizenship, others are of Tunisian origin but have another nationality, most commonly from Europe. With a variety of careers, they have chosen to stay for some years in Singapore, where science and spirituality co-exist in this "univer-city". The universe of science and the city of the scientist are just what Ibn Battuta was looking for during his voyage, and he stopped each time he thought he found it, whether with a Sufi master, a *faqih* or an *&alim*. We will show how these Tunisians found

Table 12.6. Sample of Tunisian Scientists Interviewed, who Have Arrived in Singapore since 2010–11.

Name	Specialty	Institution and function	Year of arrival in Singapore
Dr M. S. M. Unmarried	Marine biology	Private sector (DHI), Senior Ecologist	2010
Dr K. L. Married	Electro-magnetism	Public sector, Temasek Laboratories NUS, Research Scientist	2011
Dr A. L. Married	Biology, immunology	Public sector, A*Star, Principal investigator, technologist.	2010
M. S. Unmarried	Molecular and cellular biology	Ph.D., Public sector, Laboratory of Cancer and Genetics and Therapeutics	2011
O. M. Unmarried	Human genetics and molecular biology	Public sector, A*Star, Institute of Medical Biology, Laboratory of Human Embryology & Genetics.	2012

in this univer-city a site where knowledge could serve equitable development. Looking at this sample of researchers, we see that the earlier they arrived, the higher they are in the hierarchy and the more articles and presentations they have published or delivered at scientific events taking place on several continents.

The imaginary of these scientists is marked by the travels undertaken by people like Ibn Fadlân, Ibn Jobair (who travelled for 27 months), Ibn Battuta, and Ibn Khaldoun. The story of Ibn Battuta (1304–68), born in Tangiers, is the longest. The recounting of his *Rihla, Tuhfat al-nuzzar fi aga'ib l-amsar wa gara'ib l-asfar*, testifies to the taste he developed for travelling. The reader discovers not only the author's universe but also encounters the ulama of the period, such as Abdullah al-Zubaidi and Abdullah al-Nafzaoui in the Maghreb; Shaykh Soufi Burhanuddin in Alexandria; Shaykh Abdulrahman Ibn Moustapha whose teaching he followed; Ibn Taymiyah whom he meets; Shaykh Qutbuddin Hussain in Isfahan, Sit Zahida, a woman master of a Sufi group whom he visits in Baghdad; Shaykh Malik al-Zahir in Sumatra, and so on.

His travels across the Islamic world take him from the Maghreb to the Nile valley, Gaza, Hebron then Jerusalem, Tyre, Sayda, Beirut, and Syria, Iraq, and Iran. During his second pilgrimage, he goes along the southern coast of the Arabian peninsula to Yemen, Mogadiscio, Mombasa, Zanzibar, to Kilwa and the African coast of Swahili culture. With his third pilgrimage, he explores Turkey, the Black Sea, Central Asia, India, Ceylon, Sumatra, Malaysia, and China up to Beijing. He makes his last trip from Morocco across the Sahara to Mali, showing the international dimension of the Islamic world where the dinar, proof of its economic power, was accepted as currency throughout his travels.

His voyages were made possible by his education in Islamic Law, *fiqh*, and by his urban education where he learned how to conduct himself. He was comfortable in discussion with ulama, with sufis, or with qadis. When Ibn Battuta began his voyage to Mecca, he was 20 years old, and he stopped there for three years. He went further on the Silk Road, stopping in the Maldives and in Delhi, where the Sultan named him a Supreme Court judge. He joined caravans — these could bring together some 30,000 people with travel provisions, and included imams, judges, doctors, and soldiers. Confident of his training in Islamic law, he benefitted, over three decades, from the hospitality of kings, ulama, and Sufi sheikhs going from the Maghreb to Mashreq, to East Africa, Central Asia, India, China, and Sub-Saharan West Africa, travelling about 120,000 kilometers[29] — what some writers estimate as equivalent to 44 different countries today — sometimes with descriptions of places that might be conflated. Of course, all this movement had a great impact on his private life, with multiple marriages and divorces, even while these were carried out according to Islamic law. He thus accomplished what the anthropologist Claude Levi-Strauss called a voyage in time, space, and social hierarchy.[30]

Another interesting aspect of the *Rihla* is its transcription by Ibn Juzzayy at the request of the Sultan of Morocco, Abu Inan of the Merinid dynasty, a period characterized by peace and where Europe did not exist as an important space, where the Mediterranean was only of minor significance, and where the known world featured China, India, Arabia, Greece, and Byzantium. For historians, Ibn Battuta's text reflects the cohesion of the Maghreb's Malikite rite, heir to Islam as a faith and worldview and an attitude simultaneously personal and social. This helps us understand Ibn Battuta's curiosity towards religious practices and hadith interpretations in the face of events and human situations. He related some observations on the behaviour of populations he met, on how the *waqf* functioned, enabling the poorest to undertake the *Hajj*, to collect a marriage chest for poor girls, to pay a prisoner's ransom, or to finance the upkeep of travellers.[31]

What should we retain from Ibn Battuta's *Rihla* (which, by the way, was translated into French only in 1858 and a century later into English)? It allows us to see the traits that enabled him to travel over a period of 30 years, as though he was in his own space. Several writers, among the historians, Islamologists, geographers, and literary figures, agree that certain factors contributed to the success of this kind of voyage, among them the unity of judicial knowledge like the Shari'ah, having the Arabic language in common, and the network and commercial routes that were protected by the rulers of the period, whose prosperity depended on international commerce. The competition among leaders contributed to the mobility of researchers, architects, doctors, engineers, poets, teachers, etc., who could find employment in different fields, facilitating the diffusion of knowledge and faith. Spirituality cemented ties among Arabs, Persians, Turks, Indians, Malays, Chinese, Africans, and so on, favouring the

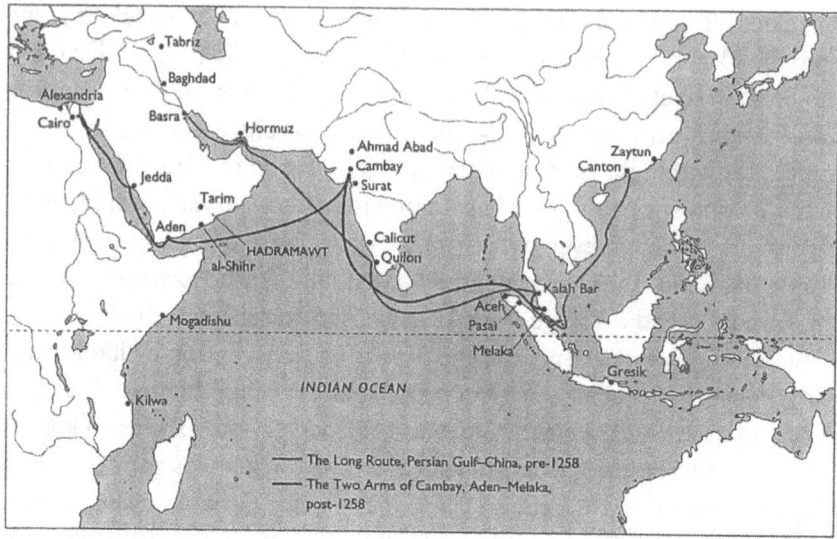

Map 12.6. Hadrami Indian Ocean Trade Routes. *Source*: Ho, 2006: xvii cited by Jacobsen, F.F. 2009: 12.

migration of ulama who could find rest stations set up for travellers where they could recover their energies.

Rest stops for pilgrims along the routes, like those constructed by Zubeida, the wife of Haroun al-Rashid, when she celebrated her Hajj in 799, contributed to the spread of knowledge, with pilgrims able to advance their education by spending time with learned men in the mosques which, in the cities, also had madrasa. These sites were also spaces for the circulation of ideas and of peoples — "univer-cities" — where instruction was given in secular fields like astronomy, geometry, and philosophy, and were so numerous in Cairo, for example, that they could not be counted, as Ibn Battuta reports.[32]

This tradition of travel was cultivated from the first centuries of Islam, with Arabs and Persians present throughout Southeast Asia and controlling the routes between East Africa, Central Asia, South and Southeast Asia. Later, in these areas, the Hadhrami founded organizations and modern schools, contributing to educational reform and the schooling of girls, to the introduction of secular subjects into the curriculum, and elaborating new means for transmitting knowledge, for developing the press, constructing routes, providing water, electricity, and public buildings.[33]

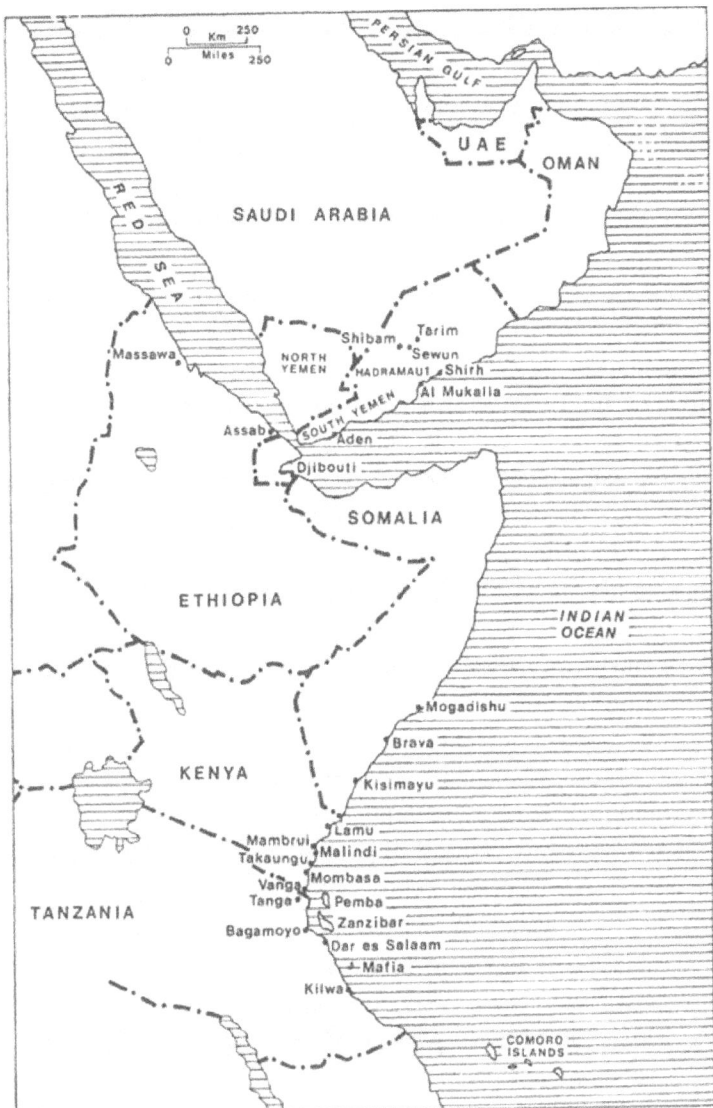

Map 12.7. Hadrami settlement sites in E. African Coast. *Source:* Guennec-Coppens, F.L. 1989: 187.

How did those who left their country experience their migration towards Southeast Asia? Hadhramis wrote about their experiences settling in countries in this part of the world and, by analogy, they can help us understand the psychology of the Tunisian scientists who moved into similar areas. A study by the anthropologist Engseng Ho examines a document that borrows the form of the *Rihla* — the voyage of a person who leaves Hadhramout seeking his fortune — and this is the *Maqama dham al-dunya* by Ahmed b. Muhammad al-Mihdar (d.1887). The author of this document uses the rhetorical figure of a parable in presenting a meeting with a woman to symbolize the world that he was looking for.[34]

Today, if the attraction of scientific research is carried by the desire for discovery, progress in communication and transportation lessen the discomfort of distances and, as Abdelmalek Sayad argues, the new virtual routes open the way to a "co-presence" here and there, reducing the disadvantages tied to migration without at the same time making the advantages disappear.[35] Ons Mamai, who introduced us to the community of Tunisian scientists in Singapore; Linda Sellou and Kenza Maher, whose life stories we collected in 2012 and 2013; Mohmed-Sofiane Mahjoub, Larbi Anis, and Karim Louertani, whom we met in person; and Mzoughi Slim, who answered our questionnaire by email — all have itineraries influenced by virtual routes, thanks to which they discovered the laboratories and universities they are affiliated with in Singapore. They all participate in the circulation of knowedge and in the exchanges among members of a scientific community wherever the individuals may be located and, on the other hand, modern communication technology enables them to remain in contact with family still in Tunisia, or in the suburbs of Paris, or in Morocco, without the full negative effects of separation.

Their curiosity is directed, as with Ahmad Zuweil, towards questions like, *"Why?"* and *"How?"* Socialized in a post-independence context where minds were "decolonized", even at a very young age Ahmad Zuweil was comfortable in dialogue with eminent figures like Gamal Abdel Nasser — he was 10 years old when he wrote Abdel Nasser a letter and received a response, which he has kept to this day. He is marked by the solidarity and community that structured his life, how the inhabitants of his city that did not have a bank used a communal savings system ("tontinette"), a solidarity structure where each member contributes a sum and where the person most in need receives the total, while at the same time being obligated to contribute in the same way for the other members. His second memory relates to his community where the mosque and religious leaders of his neighbourhood played an important role in his life, and where he was proud to be recognized, as his father was, by the booksellers situated near the mosque.

When he enters university, he is determined to achieve very good grades. As he finishes, it is 1967 and the year of the *Naksa* — the Arab defeat in the June 1967 war with Israel — but his grades are very good, 93 out of 100. His success is celebrated with an uncle who played an important role in shaping him, and with his family, who organize a large gathering to mark the event. In his research, he discovers the freedom to choose his subjects, his methodology, and his collaborators. But very quickly, he also perceives the weaknesses of the institution — uneven quality and training of teachers, absence of logistic support, the tragic political history and context of Egypt and the Arab world in 1967 and 1968. The oppressive reality around him — war, humiliation, despair, and the closing of university doors — pushes Ahmed Zuweil to look towards more distant horizons. He decides to leave Egypt and go to the USA, where he studies for the doctorate at the University of Pennsylvania. He succeeds in obtaining the fellowships needed for his research, universities begin to notice him, colleagues make requests of him, students seek his advice and help. His research grows more successful, the most prestigious periodicals publish his research results; between 1983 and 1987 he receives four of the most important awards in his field; and in 1999 he is awarded the Nobel Prize. He attributes the failure of scientific development in the countries of the South to what he calls the "institutional cultures" — relations not based on collegiality, rivalries that undermine enthusiasm and leave little room for creativity, and pushing the most motivated individuals to leave.[36]

Recently he pointed out that without the Arab scholarly works and translations from Greek philosophy and without the Arabs' original work in astronomy, European development might not have taken place for another 500 years. He continues, arguing that the progress achieved during the time of Muhammad Ali only 200 years ago put Egypt in such strong position that the Japanese and Koreans at the time studied how the Egyptian economy worked. What then happened in the last century? Colonization, counter-productive alliances of certain social classes with the colonial powers, illiteracy among peasants and among women weighed down development. Policies set up following independence led to much frustration. After having looked towards the West and then

Table 12.7. Routes Taken by a Group of Tunisian Scientists, now Based in Singapore.

Name	Specialization	Arab world	Europe	USA/Canada, South America, Australia, New Zealand	Asia
Dr M. S. M.	Marine biology	Tunisia	Spain, France, Greece, Denmark	Ecuador	Singapore, China, Taiwan, Japan
Dr K. L.	Electro-magnetism	Tunisia	France	USA, Canada	Singapore
Dr L. A.	Biology, immunology	Tunisia	UK, Scotland, Ireland, Germany, Poland, Switzerland, Spain, Portugal, Italy, Greece, France	Australia	Singapore, Korea, Japan
M. S.	Cancer Genetics and Therapeutics	Tunisia	France	—	Singapore
O. M.	Biologist	Tunisia, Dubai	France	—	Singapore

towards the East, finally the end of the Cold War arrived. The absence of jobs and opportunities continued to lead to frustration, allowing groups to use religion for their own needs and leading to failure in developing scientific research.

Zuweil proposes that the solution requires new educational institutions, liberal trade, and that this will lead to democracy, not the other way around. Finally, he recommends that establishing equitable policies and constructing peace between Palestine and Israel would free people's minds and create discipline, and that this would make a big difference.

He suggests promoting an Education Jihad and education in the modern sciences, setting up in each country centres of excellence in science and technology and four or five model universities, to pull the caravan and transform the frustration of youth into positive energy, to build a different future.[37]

The New Silk Roads

What trends can be seen in the scientific *Rihla* of the Tunisian researchers? On the basis of our small sample, the women of the Maghreb seem not to neglect the underprivileged regions of their own countries and are attracted by the Arab world and Africa. While the main country serving as a model for Tunisians' education continues to be France — commanding the French language being a skill one should not underestimate — the scientific exchanges occurring via participation in conferences, seminars, internships, etc., increasingly take place in a variety of European countries and in North America. Finally, new routes have opened up to these audacious researchers from the Maghreb, primarily towards North America and Asia.

There is nothing surprising in seeing these researchers going to the USA, a country that attracts 42.4 per cent of highly skilled labour flows. English-speaking countries like Canada, Australia, and Great Britain continue to be attractive for scientists. Also, it is not surprising that a number of countries are working to set up policies that will attract researchers and, consequently, the countries attractive for scientists are not only the traditional ones but also new countries that offer attractive conditions for those fleeing corruption, harassment, discrimination, racism, unemployment, and other forms of frustration. But these new countries must still set up practices that will spread knowledge of their advantages and their policies. The number of Tunisian high-level employees working in the private or public sector, or who are students, and who are on the Asian continent or more specifically in Southeast Asia, constitutes a community too small to change the general pattern. However, the activities of Tunisians who are in these areas can contribute to expanding exchange between the continents which will no doubt bear fruit in the future, enriching the dialogue among scientists.

252 Univer-Cities: Strategic View of the Future

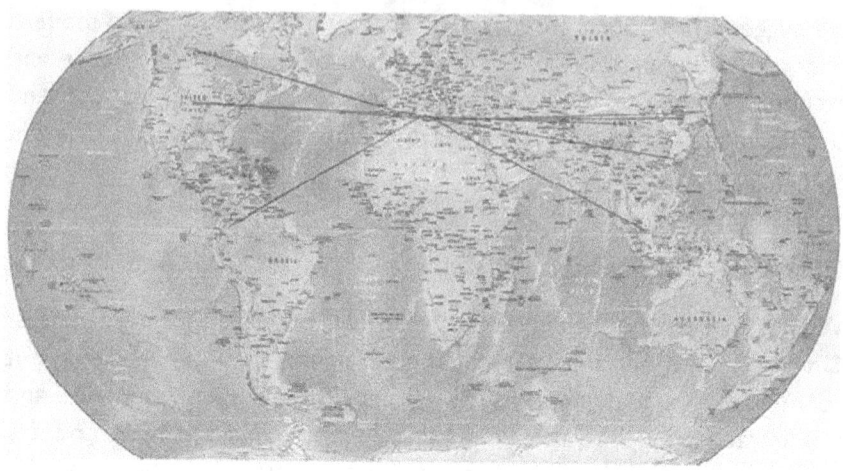

Map 12.8. Tunisian scientists and new routes

Table 12.8. Countries Visited by Women Scientists/Researchers from the Maghreb now Working in Singapore, or for Academic Conferences.

Name	Specialization	Arab world, Africa	Europe	USA/Canada, South America, Australia, New Zealand	Asia
Dr L. S. (French, of Algerian origin)	Chemist	Egypt, South Africa	UK, Switzerland, Ireland, Holland, France, Malta	Puerto Rico	South Africa, Brunei, Malaysia, Singapore, China
Dr K. M. (Moroccan)	Chemist	Morocco, Tunisia, Cameroun	Sweden, Austria, Poland, Turkey, Germany	Canada, USA, Australia	South Korea, Singapore, Japan
O. M. (Tunisian)	Biologist	Tunisia, Dubai	France	—	Singapore

Conclusion

The way in which Tunisian researchers in Singapore talk about Singapore recalls some of the different characteristics mentioned by Ibn Battuta on his voyage from the Maghreb to Southeast Asia and China, a voyage on which he paused each time he found a master of knowledge. Remember, he said that there were so many laboratories/madrasas in Cairo that they could not be counted. These universities, laboratories, polytechnics and research programmes existing in Singapore and, more broadly, in Asia in what we are calling here "univer-cities" — offering an architecture of knowledge and creativity, unified by scientific and technological expertise, a shared language (English), a network based on collegiality and an education founded on intellectual rights — all define the New Silk Roads for researchers from Tunisia. The concept "univer-cities" evokes for us the spaces that are like the pilgrims' "rest stops" constructed by Zubeida (Haroun al-Rashid's wife), and refers to a potential space, a transitional space, that is neither internal nor external (a psychoanalytic notion taken from D.W. Winnicott). Singapore, situated at the crossroads of continents, possessing one of the world's most important shipping ports, famous for its political stability, with English as its language of commerce and facilitating its relationship with other continents, has committed itself since the 2000s to the knowledge economy, setting as one of its priorities research that would spur innovation in areas useful to the nation.

The portion of the nation's budget devoted to research has supported this commitment, rising from 1.34 per cent of GDP in 1996 to 2.65 per cent in 2008, and rising 20 per cent over the period from 2011 to 2015. To attract researchers to Singapore, measures have been adopted like finding employment for the researcher's spouse and providing housing for the family and educational structures for children. However, whereas these and other similar measures attract established researchers, some policies, such as limited-time contracts, lead to dissatisfaction among young researchers we have interviewed. These young researchers, who are at an age where they want to begin building a family, suffer from the insecurity of employment and have difficulty planning for the future.[38]

Taken all together, this system has enabled Singapore, in a few years, to attract a number of researchers comparable to figures in some northern

European countries, to more than triple the number of its publications between 1996 and 2008, and to rank 11th worldwide in the citation frequency of its scientists' publications.[39] Therefore, this concept of transitional space, a kind of paradise for science researchers — young researchers and established ones, winners of the Nobel and other prizes — where they can launch their own research groups, surround themselves with highly-qualified colleagues, find adequate financing, establish ties with other research laboratories, and in this context foster innovation in fields that are useful to the nation, has enabled the National University of Singapore and Nanyang Technological University to rank among the best in Asia. We also see how this space of fantasy and creativity serves as a cultural experience, where the researcher can have, at least for a specified period of time, the possibility of undertaking fundamental scientific and cultural experiments to aid the spread of knowledge for the construction of a more equitable world.

Acknowledgement

We would like to thank Retna Devi, research assistant at MEI, for her invaluable help in putting together the maps and for her overall assistance.

Notes

1. Tunisia chose to introduce French in the third year of primary school. In secondary school students study English and any other language of their choice in addition to Arabic and French. This enables students who reach the baccalaureate to speak at least four languages.
2. Agence de Promotion de l'Investissement Extérieur — FIPA Tunisie.<http://www.investintunisia.tn/site/fr/article.php?id_article=178>
3. Ibid.
4. Ahmed Ben Miled, *Histoire de la médicine Arabe en Tunisie*. (Tunis Cartaginoiseries, 2012), p. 193.
5. Sleim Ammar, *Histoire de la psychiatrie maghrébine*. <http://www.arabpsynet.com/Archives/OP/OP.Ammar.PsyHistory..htm>
6. Aicha Lemsine, *La Chrysalide*. (Paris: Ed. des Femmes, 1979).

7. Driss Chraibi, *La civilisation, ma Mère!...* (Paris: Denoel, 1972).
8. Hédi Bouraoui, "Ambivalence structuro-culturelle dans 'La civilisation, ma Mère!'... de Chraibi". *Modern Languages Studies* 10, no. 2 (Spring 1980): 59–68.
9. Table: Index from 1 to 7, with a higher score indicating a more favourable situation."Report on Global Competitiveness 2011–2012", World Economic Forum of Davos.

Country	Quality of the public education system		Quality of education in math and science	
	Rank	Score	Rank	Score
Switzerland	1	6.0	4	5.8
Belgium	6	5.5	2	6.3
Germany	17	4.9	48	4.4
United Kingdom	20	4.8	43	4.5
France	34	4.5	15	5.1
Tunisia	41	5.0	18	5.1
Czech Republic	49	4.1	66	4.1
China	54	4.0	31	4.7
Portugal	76	3.6	105	3.3
Hungary	80	3.5	37	4.6
Italy	88	3.3	74	3.9
Romania	90	3.3	45	4.5
Morocco	93	3.3	65	4.1
Turkey	94	3.3	103	3.4
Spain	98	3.2	111	3.3
Greece	120	2.9	61	4.1
South Africa	133	2.3	138	2.1
Egypt	135	2.3	132	2.4

10. Munther Masri, Mohamed Jemni, Ahmed M. Al-Ghassani, Aboubakr A. Badawi. "Entrepreneurship Education in the Arab States (Jordan, Tunisia, Oman and Egypt) and Regional Synthesis Report". April 2010. (UNESCO-UNEVOC, Germany), p. 39.
11. Ibid.

12. Ibid.
13. We should also mention that schooling, obligatory since 1991, was strengthened by a law in 2002 that attempted to diminish differences between the sexes and regions by fining parents if their child under 15 years of age was withdrawn before finishing the first nine years of basic education, with the fines going from 20 to 200 dinars (and reaching 400 dinars in cases of recidivism). Several studies show that girls, although more successful than boys in exams at the end of the primary school cycle, also more frequently leave school in rural areas than boys do. Among the reasons given for this are distance and the girls' domestic and agricultural work. In 1998, 7 per cent of girls between 10 and 14 years of age, 22 per cent of girls between 15 and 19, and 26 per cent of girls between 20 and 24 who lived in rural areas worked in the households of families in the capital city (see Bénédicte Gasteneau, "Les facteurs de la déscolarisation en milieu rural tunisien. L'exemple de Kroumirie et d'Elfaouar", p. 113. <http://www.cicred.org/Eng/Seminars/Details/Seminars/education/ACTES/Com_Gastineau.PDF>)

    The film *Poupées d'argile* (*Clay Dolls*, 2002), by the Tunisian filmmaker Nouri Bouzid, deals with the situation of these rural girls who are exploited both by urban families and their own families, with their meagre earnings being used to finance the education of their brothers or to construct dwellings for the rural family. However, when it comes time to inherit, these women, who have contributed to improving their family's situation, inherit only half of the share of a brother.
14. Munther Masri, et al., op. cit.
15. Hassen Boubakri, "Migration pour le travail decent, la croissance économique et le développement: le cas de la Tunisie". *Cahiers des Migrations Internationales*, no. 102 (2010): 21, 22.
16. <www.ambassadefrance-tn.org/echanges-commerciaux-franco>
17. Les étudiants tunisiens en France. (13/9/2013)<http://www.ambassade-france-tn.org/Les-etudiants-tunisiens-en-France>
18. Hassen Boubakri, "Migration pour le travail décent, la croissance économique et le développement: le cas de la Tunisie". *Cahiers des Migrations Internationales*,

no. 102 (2010): 24. <http://www.ilo.org/public/english/protection/migrant/download/imp/imp102f.pdf>
19. Hani Fakhouri, "The Brain Drain in the Arab world". <http://mid-east-today.blogspot.sg/2009/11/brain-drain-in-arab-world>
20. OCDE, Ministère des Affaires étrangères, France, 2011.
21. Ali Ben Makhlouf, "Communication and the dissemination of ideas" in *Arab Muslim Civilization in the Mirror of the Universal: Philosophical Perspectives* (Paris: UNESCO, 2010), pp. 53–60.
22. <http://pro.01net.com/editorial/532469/les-ssii-francaises-puisent-dans-les-ressources-strategiques-de-la-tunisie/>(9/5/2011)
23. Vincent Geisser, "Les diplômés scientifiques tunisiens: la 'voie moyenne' des études à l'étranger". *Revue des mondes musulmans et de la Méditerranée*. 101–102 (9/11/ 2013). <http://remmm.revues.org/51>
24. Hajer Aounallah-Skhiri, Hager Lazaar-Ben Gobrane, Mohamed Hsairi, Noureddine Achour, Béchir Zouari, Taoufik Nacef, "Démographie médicale en Tunisie: état actuel et perspectives". *La Tunisie Médicale* (2012) 90, no. 2: 166–71. <http://www.leaders.com.tn/article/les-tunisiens-a-l-etranger-les-cadres-et-les-professions-liberales-en-progression?id=2149>
25. Dr Mohammad Reza Iravani, "Brain drain problem: A review". *International Journal of Business and Social Science* 2, no. 15 (1/8/ 2011).
26. Simona Milio and coll., "Brain drain, brain exchange and brain circulation. The case of Italy viewed from a global perspective". <www.lse.ac.uk/businessAnd-Consultancy/LSEEntreprise> (March 2012).
27. Table: Tunisians abroad by gender and activity.

Country	Total	Men	Women	High-level employees	Liberal professions	Students
Algeria	16,402	8,778	7,624	949	583	336
Libya	87,177	68,571	18,606	5,866	6,987	680
Saudi Arabia	18,582	11,800	6,782	4,679	2,236	32
United Arab Emirates	13,842	8,251	5,591	8,377	380	40

(Continued)

Country	Total	Men	Women	High-level employees	Liberal professions	Students
Kuwait	2,230	999	1,231	1,131	590	13
Qatar	3,039	1,921	1,118	507	5	77
Total Arab World	154,714	108,380	46,334	24,166	12,186	1,887
Total Europe	911,378	578,993	332,385	29,793	39,202	38,250
Total Americas	29,074	17,907	11,167	5,437	3,105	4,896
Japan	659	490	169	132	25	109
China	196	132	64	27	64	58
Indonesia and Southeast Asia	159	107	52	27	52	2
Australia	644	419	225	382	75	0
Total Asia and Australia	1,767	1,214	553	589	217	192
Total Africa	1,279	915	364	361	281	89

Source: *Les Tunisiens à l'étranger: Les cadres et les proféssions libérales en progression. (22/4/2010)* These statistics only take into account Tunisians who have registered at the Tunisian embassy in the host country. <http://www.leaders.com.tn/article/les_tunisiens_a_l_etranger_les_cadres_et_les_professions_liberales_en_progression?id=2149> (accessed 11 January 2014).

28. According to Ons Mamai, a Tunisian scientist in Singapore (personal communication).
29. V. Monteil cited by A. Miquel. "L'islam d'Ibn Battuta", *Bulletin d'études orientales*. T. 30. Mélanges offerts à Henry Laoust. Vol. Second (1978), pp. 75–83.
30. Levi-Strauss, *Tristes tropiques* (Paris: Plon, 1955), cited by A. Miquel in "L'Islam d'Ibn Battuta", *Bulletin d'Etudes Orientales*. T. 30. Mélanges offerts à Henry Laoust. Vol. Second (1978), pp. 75–83.
31. Ross E. Dunn. *The adventures of Ibn Battuta: A Muslim Traveler of the 14th Century* (Berkeley: University of California Press, 1986); G. H. Bousquet. "Ibn Battuta et les institutions islamiques", *Studia Islamica* no. 24 (1966): 81–106; V. Monteil. (réimpr. augmentée d'une préface et de notes par) *Ibn Battuta. Voyages d' Ibn Battuta*. Arabic text accompanied by a French translation by C. Defremery and B. R. Sanguinetti (Paris: Anthropos, 1968).

32. Ali Ben Makhlouf, "Communication and the dissemination of ideas" in *Arab Muslim Civilization in the Mirror of the Universal: philosophical perspectives* (Paris: UNESCO, 2010), pp. 53–60.
33. Frode F. Jacobsen, *Hadrami Arabs in present-day Indonesia: an Indonesia-oriented group with an Arab signature* (New York: Routledge, 2009), p. 46.
34. Engseng Ho, "Hadramis abroad in Hadhramaut: The Muwalladin". In Ulrike Freitag and William G. Clarence-Smith, eds. *Hadramis traders, scholars and statesmen in the Indian Ocean* (Leiden, New York, Koln: E.J. Brill. 1997), pp. 131–46.
35. Staphane Dufois, *Les diasporas* (Paris: PUF, 2003).
36. Ahmed Zuweil, *Rihlatoun âbri alZamen. alTarik ila Jaizat alNobel* (Cairo: AlAhram, 2003).
37. Road map to a Muslim Renaissance. An interview with Nobel laureate Ahmed Zewail, *New Perspective Quarterly*. Fall 2004. <http://www.digitalnpq.org/archive/2004>
38. In "Wanted: Local talent in varsities", Charissa Yong and Andrea Ong discuss how the large number of foreign faculty members in departments like Political Science and Public Policy at NUS and in International Studies and Communication and Information at NTU has led to frustration among local faculty, some of whom see this as "discriminatory hiring". This question has been raised six times in Singapore's Parliament since 2012, and it has also been discussed on social networks and in newspaper columns (*The Straits Times*, 5 April 2014).
39. According to the *l' Observatoire des sciences et techniques*, as cited in David Larousserie, "Singapour eldorado scientifique". (*Le Monde*, 9 February 2013.)

References — Sources for Maps and Images

Map of Phoenician Trade Routes. Source: Collelo, T., ed., *Lebanon: A Country Study* (Washington, D.C, 1989 : Library of Congress) p. 6. Cited by Cartoko: A map database, *Phoenician Colonization and Trade Routes* <http://www.cartoko.com/2010/05/phoenician-colonization-and-trade-routes/> (accessed on 11 November 2013).

Map of Silk Road: Land & Sea Routes. Source: American Museum of Natural History, *Map of the Silk Road Routes*. <http://www.amnh.org/education/resources/rfl/web/silkroadguide/map-routes.php> (accessed on 11 November 2013).

Map of Trans-Saharan Trade. Source: Department of Arts of Africa, Oceania, and the Americas. "The Trans-Saharan Gold Trade (7th–14th century)". In *Heilbrunn Timeline of Art History*. (New York, 2000: The Metropolitan Museum of Art)<http://www.metmuseum.org/toah/hd/gold/hd_gold.htm> (accessed on 11 November 2013).

Map of Principal Routes of Migration. Source: International Organization for Migration, *World Migration Report 2013* (September)<http://www.iom.int/files/live/sites/iom/files/What-We-Do/wmr2013/fr/WMR2013_PPT_FR_final.pdf>(accessed on 11 November 2013).

Map of Tunisian Students & Scholars in Europe using *Carte de l'Europe* by University of Kentucky <http://fr201.files.wordpress.com/2013/04/carte-europe-pays-1.jpg> (accessed on 11 November 2013).

Map of Hadrami Indian Ocean Trade Routes. Source: E. Ho, *The graves of Tarim : genealogy and mobility across the Indian Ocean* (Berkeley: University of California Press, 2006) Cited by Jacobsen, F.F. *Hadrami Arabs in present-day Indonesia: an Indonesia-oriented group with an Arab signature* (New York: Roultedge, 2009), p. 12.

Map of Hadrami Settlement sites in E.African Coast. Source: F.L. Guennec-Coppens, "Social and Cultural Integration: A Case Study of the East African Hadramis", *Africa: Journal of the International African Institute*, 59, no. 2 (Cambridge University Press: 1989): 185–195.<http://www.jstor.org.libproxy1.nus.edu.sg/stable/1160487> (accessed on 11 November 2013).

Map of Tunisian Scientists and New Routes using *Physical Map of the World 2012* by Perry-Castaneda Library Map Collection.<http://www.lib.utexas.edu/maps/world.html>(accessed on 11 November 2013).

About the Authors

Lilia Labidi is Visiting Research Professor at the Middle East Institute, National University of Singapore (NUS), and former Minister for Women's Affairs in the Tunisian Cabinet post-Arab Spring.

Anthony SC Teo is Co-author and Chairperson of the Univer-Cities Inaugural Conference 2013; Adjunct Professor, Lee Kuan Yew School of Public Policy; Founding Board Member, Middle East Institute, NUS; and Chevalier of the Ordre des Palmes Académiques.

CHAPTER THIRTEEN

UNIVER-CITY OF MELBOURNE: CASE OF MEDICAL REGIONALITY

SHANE HUNTINGTON AND STEPHEN K. SMITH

Introduction

The city of Melbourne is one of the most spread-out cities in the world relative to the size of its population. With a little over four million people, Melbourne is the second largest city in Australia and the capital of the State of Victoria. But unlike many of its European counterparts, it does not have thousands of years of history, nor has it seen destruction and rebuilding consistent with war, or the changes that necessarily come with shifting sovereignty. But Melbourne did have a head-start when it was initially founded in 1835. The richness of cultures from the northern hemisphere enabled the key decision-makers of the day to invest early in an institution of higher learning: something they considered to be a key component of a democratic and modern society. So despite Melbourne's relatively short history, we find that its relationship with the University of Melbourne (UM) dates back to the earliest days of the city's formation.

In this chapter, we will discuss the early developments in the city of Melbourne, along with the establishment and challenges faced by a new university in a fledgling city. We will explore this history through the lens of one of the university's most significant contributions to the city — the provision of medical training programmes and biomedical research. The landmark changes to the degree structures at UM will also be discussed, along with the recent results of graduates entering the workforce from the new education model in medicine. At the end of this chapter, we will look to the future and new partnerships that are developing between the University, the city's public and private hospitals, its partner research institutions, and the city of Melbourne itself.

From Colony to City

Although founded in 1835, the town of Melbourne did not become a city until 1847 when it was given the accolade by Queen Victoria. The city's growth rate had been rather standard for a colony of the time. It had ample land and water resources and by the year 1850, had some 20,000 residents. But unlike the great cities of the northern hemisphere, Melbourne lacked some of the key features that its residents would have encountered in London. It did not have a public library nor any type of exhibition space, and Melbourne as a city was unable to provide any form of higher education. So residents who were interested in a profession would be required to take the long and arduous sea journey back to Europe or the United Kingdom (UK) in order to receive training. Even today, the trip from Melbourne to the United States (US) or Europe is considered long — but in the mid-19th century, long was measured in months.

In August 1851, an event occurred that would not only redefine the city of Melbourne itself but would also lead to the establishment of multiple satellite cities within a few hundred kilometres of Melbourne. Two men named James Reagan and John Dunlop were camping at a creek west of Melbourne's city centre — a place that the traditional owners of the land called Ballaarat. They soon discovered that the area had an unusually high amount of gold. Of course, at that time, they had absolutely no idea that they had discovered what would soon become the richest goldfield the world had ever seen. Within just one month, nearly 1,000 miners had established themselves in Ballarat and were digging for gold. Within two years, this number extended to 20,000 miners who represented nationalities from all over the world.

By the end of 1851, Melbourne's population was greater than 77,000; an increase of over 300 per cent on the pre-gold numbers. Within just six years, this number would grow to more than 400,000 with some 140,000 of the residents living in tents. For a very brief period, the city of Melbourne was actually the second largest city after London in the entire British Empire.

The civic challenges of population growth of this magnitude seem almost unimaginable to us today. With our current state population growth sitting close to 2 per cent, we often hear about the challenges of housing and supporting citizens with adequate transport and health care.

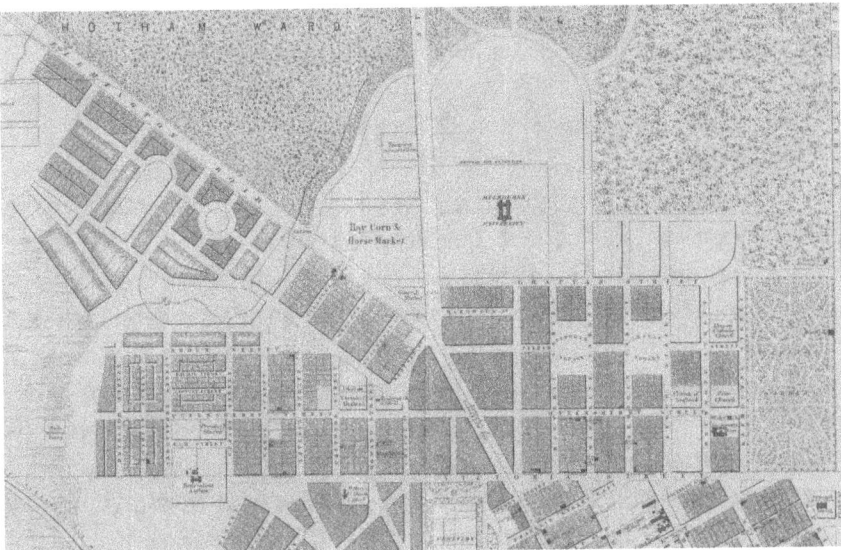

Fig. 13.1 Melbourne and its suburbs 1855 [cartographic material]/compiled by James Kearney, draughtsman; engraved by David Tulloch and James D. Brown. (Note: this is not the full map of Melbourne)

Fortunately back in the early 1850s, key individuals in the city of Melbourne understood that a great city needs not just population but education institutions and facilities to draw its citizens together. Lieutenant Governor Charles La Trobe was such an individual. He had been the primary driver in the campaign to build Melbourne's first public hospital from 1841 and saw the success of these endeavours in 1846 with the laying of the hospital's foundation stone. Of course during this period, prior to the gold rush, the acquisition of public funds for such projects was difficult to say the least. Once the gold rush had begun, the public purse began to swell making key projects for the city more attainable. In 1852, a group of citizens petitioned Charles Latrobe to establish a university for the city. It is perhaps no coincidence that the inauguration ceremony of the University of Sydney happened in October that same year. Swift action was taken to correct this cultural imbalance between Australia's two major cities and on 3 November, the Auditor General Hugh Childers was instructed to set aside £10,000. In 1853, Charles Latrobe made the enlightened decision to set aside land for two institutions that he considered to be most important assets of any great city: a library and university. The University was officially established in 1853 with a 39-year-old judge named Redmond Barry being appointed as its first Chancellor.

The land that was set aside for UM was situated on the very outskirts of the city, some 2 km from the City's Town hall. Construction of the university's first building, the quadrangle, commenced in 1854. Those familiar with the Old Quad today will notice a slight difference in colour in the stones used on the south face of the building. This difference is due to the fact that the building was not completed with its fourth side for more than 100 years. Although somewhat distant from the centre of the city, the requirement for large areas of land meant that university grounds had to be established on the border of existing city buildings. To put this in perspective, just across one of the main roads next to the University was the area designated for the hay, corn and horse market. Because of the extremely large quantities of livestock, it was critical that this market be placed within proximity of the city but far enough away from residential properties to avoid any safety concerns. We will come back to the relevance of this market on numerous occasions during this chapter.

As one would expect, in the early years of UM student enrolment, numbers were very low. In fact, in some years, the number of members on the university council actually exceeded the total number of students enrolled at the University. The first teaching staff at UM were selected by a committee that had been set up in London. There were initially four appointments: a Professor of Latin, Greek and ancient history; a Professor of mathematics and natural philosophy (physics); a Professor of natural science; and a Professor of modern literature and history, political economy and logic. These professors were extremely well paid, receiving some £10,000 each, the equivalent of three times the salaries of their London equivalents. They also received free accommodation on university grounds. The problem with these initial appointments, however, was that they did not link well with the needs of the colony. The University's Chancellor Redmond Barry clearly understood that in order for the support of the University to be maintained, it would have to be relevant to the colony. At the time, the University only offered one degree, the Bachelor of Arts, which had little value to the professional requirements of the city of Melbourne. Fortunately, Barry pushed for new courses to be established in law and medicine. The law school was established to enroll students in 1857. The medical school which was slower to be established took its first students in 1863. By this stage, UM was no longer struggling to achieve student numbers in double figures: in 1865, it had enrolled 56 students which within a decade would expand to close to 200.

It is important to note that the establishment of the medical degree at UM presented some very significant challenges. At that particular time, students who did medical degrees at Oxford, Cambridge for Trinity universities in the UK would not be automatically able to practise medicine when the degrees were completed. Instead, they would need to have awards bestowed upon them by institutions such as the Royal College. As one might imagine, it was completely impractical for Melbourne students to take the long sea voyage back to England in order to meet this requirement. In order to address this need, the Chancellor Redmond Barry in collaboration with the Vice-Chancellor, Anthony Brownless, constructed a specific course that would enable local graduates of medicine to immediately begin practising in the profession without the need to return to England. Bypassing of the traditional system was not initially accepted by Melbourne's doctors or lawyers, but significant negotiations enabled Barry and Brownless to push through their proposals. For the first time in its history, Melbourne was now able to produce its own professional requirements. Other degrees in areas such as engineering were soon to follow and the university was intricately connected to the city.

Part of the purpose of this chapter is to give some insight into the development of what is now known collectively as the Parkville biomedical precinct, an area which contains certainly some of the most prestigious institutions in Australia and arguably in the world. But at this point, we are a long way from development of a precinct and it is important to have an understanding of the many undertakings that were required in order to reach the current day success. As mentioned earlier, the land immediately adjacent to the UM site in the 19th century was utilized as the city hay, corn and horse market. Keep in mind at this point in time, Melbourne's population was growing rapidly and the city was slowly but surely reaching out and meeting the University and even extending beyond its boundaries. With growing residential properties in the area, it became very clear that livestock and the general populace did not mix well in city streets. To address this concern, the city embarked on a major undertaking in 1888 to construct a wall made of brick to essentially cordon off the market area from the surrounding population. To this day, a large portion of this brick wall has been preserved and can be seen in several parts of the Parkville biomedical precinct. Of course, around the turn-of-the-century, there were no medical buildings owned by the University located on the southwest corner of the campus.

The medical building had been instructed on the opposite corner of the campus in 1863. Like many of the buildings of the University that preceded and followed, the medical building faced inwards towards the centre of the campus presenting its back to the city. The position of the medical school gave a significant separation from the existing quadrangle building. There were significant differences in architecture and the two parts of the university were even separated by a lake. In the southern hemisphere, the teaching period is predominantly over the winter months and stories persist of students who were forced to traverse the lake as a form of punishment; an experience that at the time would have been extremely cold and dirty.

As one might expect, the expansion of the medical faculty began in earnest after the turn-of-the-century. Early maps of the University indicate that the medical faculty took up the entire northeast corner of the campus. Although it is difficult to tell today, this part of the campus was not originally included in the government grant for the site in 1853. In fact, the entire eastern side of the current campus was not originally part of the University. The slow but sure acquisition of this area of land which started with the construction of the medical building did not actually end until 1989 when the University amalgamated with the Melbourne College of Advanced Education. The southwest corner of the campus, where all the current medical buildings sit, was predominantly unoccupied with the exception of five individual professorial lodgings.

So what over the next 50 years would cause all the University's medical buildings to move from the northeast corner of the campus to the southwest? This transition arguably is the largest one the University campus has ever seen, and the medical faculty gave up some of the University's most prestigious buildings in order to achieve it. The answer of course brings us back to the links between the University and the city of Melbourne.

In order to train medical practitioners, the University relied on the Royal Melbourne Hospital to provide clinical training for its graduates. Logically, the original hospital was built in the centre of the city of Melbourne on the corner of Lonsdale and Swanston streets. This hospital served the city for many years but in 1892, a Royal Commission condemned the building. This was no surprise as for some time, the overcrowding of the hospital and the inadequate facilities had reached crisis point. At this stage, even prior to the end of the 19th century, there were a number of calls to move the hospital to a new location, and also that it should be closer to UM's medical school. Unfortunately, however, this was only one proposal that was put forward and it did not receive unanimous support. Ultimately, the decision in 1908 was made to rebuild the hospital on its existing site in the city. The foundation stone for its new building was laid and in 1913, the hospital's new building opened.

This new hospital serviced the city for some 30 years until in September 1935, the state government decided to invest in a statewide hospital rebuilding programme. Despite significant financing problems which were ultimately resolved by philanthropic donations from the general public, the Royal Melbourne Hospital was again to be rebuilt and this time at its current Parkville site. The foundation stone of the new hospital was laid in November 1941. Unfortunately, the original plans for public use at the hospital had to be put on hold due to World War II. During the war, the hospital facilities were made available to the US Army and were essentially occupied until March 1944. It was at this time that the Royal Melbourne Hospital formally moved, and finally, after almost 100 years was located proximate to the University.

In the decades that followed, the medical faculty slowly but surely began moving its various departments from the northeast corner of the campus to the southwest corner across the road from the Royal Melbourne Hospital and its clinical schools. Biochemistry, Microbiology and the Howard Florey Institute took the lead and were finally followed by the Medical School in 1969.

In 1963, the Royal Children's Hospital also moved into the Parkville precinct area. With two of the country's most prestigious hospitals sitting alongside the country's top university, the new critical mass of medical excellence in Parkville had been created. Today, the Parkville Precinct draws together more than 10,000 researchers and provides care to some half a million patients each year. The University has departments in more than ten of the best hospitals in the city of Melbourne, many of which are located in or around the Parkville biomedical precinct.

Despite more than 150 years of interaction between the city of Melbourne and the University, and in many ways the "growing up" of the two together, the real influence from the University on the city itself has primarily happened in more recent times. It is this economic and planning impact that we will now turn our attention to.

The Impact of Universities on the City of Melbourne

When discussing Melbourne as a city, it is important to clarify what exactly we are talking about. For the sake of this chapter, we will describe the complete metropolitan city of Melbourne simply as "Melbourne". In contrast, when we are speaking of the municipality of Melbourne which refers to the central business district and surrounding suburbs only, we will refer to the "City of Melbourne". It is the latter that we will focus our attention on in this discussion.

In total, Melbourne is home to some eight Universities and over 200 educational institutions. Like many similar cities around the world, Melbourne appropriately describes itself as a Knowledge City. The economic, social and physical impact of the tertiary education sector on the city is extraordinary. The primary reason, but not the only reason, for this impact is the large numbers of international students that come to Australia for an education.

Unlike the US and Europe, Australia is relatively new to the international student market. Over the last decade, however, the growth in this market for Australia has been substantial. The primary driver for this increase has been the reduction in government funding for Australian Universities over the same period. Fees for all courses for domestic undergraduate students have been tightly regulated and research is far from fully funded. Additionally, Australian Universities do not have the strong philanthropically derived endowment base enjoyed by leading Northern Hemisphere institutions. International student income, on the other hand, is in no way regulated by the Australian Federal Government and thus provides local universities with an opportunity to successfully address reductions in government funding. So great is this change in funding structure that UM in 2005 started referring to itself as a "public-spirited" institution rather than using the traditional "public" label to more correctly describe the type of institution it had become. Today, almost 30 per cent of the University's students are international and the revenue derived from these students accounts for almost 20 per cent of the total for the University. The international student market has become an integral part of the Australian tertiary landscape and presents a significant risk to many institutions that are critically reliant on this source of revenue.

Australia is actually the third most popular market for international students; quite an accolade given the country's entire population is just shy of 23 million — smaller than the State of Texas and 50 per cent of the population of Spain. In 2013, Australia was home to over 525,000 international students, making up close to 2 per cent of our population. In total, this "student market" generates in excess of A$16 billion for Australia annually (2011–12 export data). International education is Australia's fourth largest export industry.

In our home state of Victoria, this figure is estimated to be around A$4 billion and leads to the employment of some 38,000 full-time staff. Over 60,000 international students live in Melbourne and on average, these students spend more than A$42,000 each year — a major contribution to the local economy. The City of Melbourne in 2012 had more than 42.5 per cent of its residents attending an education institution, well above the national average of 30 per cent.

UM has a limited number of residential colleges that are far from adequate to accommodate the near 12,000 equivalent full-time international students. As a result, the property market proximate to the University has changed significantly over the last decade. The proliferation of students dwellings has been substantial. In 2002, the number of purpose-built student dwellings was 2,050. By 2010, this had grown by 133 per cent to reach a total of 4,785. With this growth rate, student dwellings represent the fastest growing category of residential dwellings in the City of Melbourne. Many of these high-rise apartment blocks, the height of which seems only limited by planning restrictions, also have numerous retail spaces — changing the distribution of such spaces in the precinct considerably.

But how do we account for this extraordinary period of growth in the Australian international student market? In the past, this could have been partially linked to the weak Australian dollar which made Australian tertiary programmes significantly cheaper than their northern hemisphere counterparts. Certainly this argument worked well between 2000–02 when the ratio of the dollar to the greenback was essentially 2 to 1, but since then, the Australian dollar has progressively gained ground. Most recently, the dollar has been so strong that many of Australia's key export industries have suffered as a result, but tertiary education remains strong.

There are other key factors that drive the international student market for Australia. Firstly, and perhaps most importantly, Australia is a safe and stable country for citizens regardless of origin. Melbourne in particular is one of the most cosmopolitan cities in the world and has repeatedly won the award for the World's Most Liveable City. This driver was tested in recent years when the perceived safety for Indian students was questioned after a number of violent altercations in Australian capital cities. Universities with significant exposure to the Indian student market had crucial revenue placed at significant risk primarily due to disproportionate media reporting of these events. Throughout the period, Melbourne remained one of the safest cities in the world for all its residents.

Australia is also in an ideal location both geopolitically and geographically to address the Asia-Pacific market. As a western nation, we present an ideal training ground for students from neighbouring Asian countries while still being "in Asia". Our strong links to the western world, especially in terms of scientific collaborations makes Australia an ideal location to study and do research. Recent research by the New South Wales State Government also indicates that international education would grow by 2.2 milion in 2005 to 3.7 million in 2025 with China, India, Malaysia and Indonesia to account for 60 per cent of this growth. Melbourne would expect to take the lion's share of this growth.

Of course, the majority of students at the University are domestic. For 160 years, the University has closely linked its professional programmes with the needs of the City and the country more broadly. The services sector in Australia, and in particular in Victoria, is a dominant industry and our tertiary programmes continually support this sector. In the case of the medical services, the University is intimately involved in providing doctors and other healthcare providers to the entire sector. There is no closer link for the University with industry than the one we have with the healthcare sector.

The strength in biotechnology that the university has generated for the City is also borne out by the number of biotechnology companies that exist in the State. In fact, Melbourne is home to 50 per cent of the top 20 biotech companies that are listed on the Australian Stock Exchange. In total, there are some 140 biotech companies in the state.

Transforming Australia's Education Landscape

In 2005, UM recruited a new Vice-Chancellor, Profession Glyn Davis. As is often the case with new senior positions, this appointment set in train what is now culminating in a decade of reform for the University, most prominently in our educational programmes. Australia has an educational model that is quite distinct from the systems found in the US and Europe. Here, the majority of university students are at an undergraduate level with very few enrolled in postgraduate study. The majority of professional degrees (for example in medicine, law and engineering) are undergraduate programmes of varying length depending on the institution. In 2005, the medical degree at UM, the MBBS, was a four-year underaduate programme.

The University recognized that there were numerous issues with this model. Firstly, the prominence of the Bologna Model in Europe designed to develop a standardized educational system was foremost in mind. Our students were not transferable after undergraduate study to these institutions nor were they well prepared for graduate schools in the US. This lack of student mobility would ultimately lead to a devaluation of our programmes.

Secondly, in Australia, the number of students and how much you charge them at undergraduate level is tightly regulated. In some areas like medicine, this makes good sense, at least on the numbers side, but in other fields, it is very problematic. The issue is compounded by a historical funding model that essentially pays every university the same amount for courses that are vastly different. For example, the model assumes that the cost of provision is identical whether you are at the number 1 (one) institution in the country or the number 50. There is no connection between quality and resourcing. So essentially, labour demand does not drive the numbers and provision cost does not drive the resourcing. The graduate space on the other hand is deregulated both with regards to number and price; offering the freedom for universities to essentially direct their own destiny and plan for growth, where appropriate.

Thirdly is the issue of educational choice. In the Australian system, students were (and in many cases still are) essentially choosing their careers at age 16. The secondary school programme in Victoria involves a two-year assessment structure that runs through the 11th and 12th years of secondary school. Students essentially make their career choices in year 10 as a result, especially where mathematics and other prerequisites are required for tertiary programme entry. This does not lead to the best outcomes for students or institutions and prevents students from exploring relevant knowledge before choosing a career path.

As a result of these drivers and others, UM split off from the educational norm that was dominant across Australia and introduced what was commonly known as "the Melbourne Model" — the name of which was supplied not by the institution itself but by a local newspaper. To introduce the model, the University embarked upon a plan that would slowly but surely shift the student body from being predominantly undergraduate to one that was at the very least, evenly split between graduate and undergraduate.

Because of the long pipeline of students travelling through the system, the University first needed to adjust its undergraduate programmes. With careful planning, it went from having almost 200 undergraduate offerings to just six. These "new generation degrees" offered students the specialization that they had received in the past, but with the added requirement that they take a number of "breadth" subjects to widen their understanding of available options. This created a triad of exit pathways for students at the end of their first degree. They could either enter the workforce, enter a professional graduate degree, or move into a research higher degree programme.

At the same time, appropriate graduate schools were established to cater for professional programmes such as Medicine, Law and Engineering. This new structure enabled students to essentially change direction part way through their tertiary education, or even enter the University's graduate school programmes after having done undergraduate programmes at other institutions. Although this is the norm in the US, for example, it is almost unheard of in Australia. Student mobility in Australia is historically very low, especially between the different states. UM has broken free of this traditional educational model and now draws in a much wider student cohort.

One of the great criticisms universities can receive about their professional degrees is that graduates are not considered "work ready" by industry. In the case of medical degrees, this is of critical importance as it pertains to the safety and effective treatment of patients. Achieving work ready status was a key attribute of the development of the new Doctor of Medicine (MD) programme at graduate level for Melbourne.

The MD requires students to gain a total of **67 graduate attributes** that are considered highly valuable for them to be successful contributors to the medical profession. These graduate attributes were carefully established as a result of the University engaging with the various stakeholders relevant to the profession. Patients, bioscientists, doctors, nurses and allied health professionals, health bureaucrats and population health practitioners were all involved in detailed concept mapping programmes to determine the key attributes that our graduates should have. Essentially, the graduate attributes fell into six domains — self, knowledge, the patient, the profession, systems of healthcare, and society.

The goal of the MD is not only to supply industry with "work ready" professionals, but also to train a higher level of healthcare professional. One of the phases of the programme, for example, provides students with a genuine research experience. This gives them an understanding of the importance of research in clinical application and enables them to potentially contribute to producing new original knowledge during their studies.

Ultimately, the new MD programme regards students as early professionals and treats them with an approach commensurate with this status. This means a more active form of learning is required, resulting in more onerous teaching requirements. But the result is a cohort of more well-rounded and experienced graduates that are not only ready for the profession they are entering, but have the potential to be transformative to that profession.

Professor Mark Cook, Chair of Medicine and Director of Neurology and St Vincent's Hospital Melbourne describes his experience with the MD students:

> There has been a major change in my experience of dealing with the students in the Melbourne MD course. I hadn't been convinced that it would change the nature of the students, or how they interacted with teaching staff. I was wrong on both counts. The students are better informed, more mature, and far more sophisticated in their approach to clinical problems. They have a much better grasp of complex clinical situations, and a clear perspective on the critical nature of research. It has certainly changed how I interact with the students, and has brought about a much richer learning environment — for me and them!

Of course, UM has been adopting new teaching approaches in all of its programmes. Of particular interest is the new Master of Teaching programme. The University is one of the primary suppliers of teachers to Victoria schools and has a close link with the State's Department of Education as a result. Just as with the new MD, the University has initiated an Australian first with its new clinical teaching programme.

A clinical teaching model enables the educator to focus in on the individual; to monitor their learning growth and to provide content appropriate to each individual student. The process must be evidence based and highly adaptive to different circumstances. Additionally, the clinical teaching model requires continual assessment by the teacher of the efficacy of their teaching techniques leading to ongoing improvements.

The true measure of such a clinical teaching programme is the impact on the ground. The principal at Koonung Secondary College, Peter Wright, made this clear in a recent speech:

> The impact on the ground at my school and others involved in delivering the MTeach model, was to open the door to classrooms, where team teaching, observations and visiting neighbouring classrooms and indeed neighbouring school classrooms is now commonplace.
>
> Experienced and graduate teachers sharing ideas, lesson plans, strategies and techniques used in the classroom are the norm and collegiality is powerful.

It is also noteworthy that with the introduction of the clinical teaching programme in education, UM has moved to #2 in the QS world rankings in the field of Education for 2014.

Creating an Integrated Biomedical Campus

In its current form, the Melbourne Biomedical Campus is quite extraordinary. Arguably, it rivals many international programmes that draw together hospitals, universities and research institutes and on many measures would sit in the top 5 in the world. Collectively, some 24 discrete entities are working together with UM; all of these are either within a short walk or drive from the main University campus. In terms of personnel, this means in excess of 10,000 scientists, clinicians and technical staff are engaged in a combination of biomedical and healthcare research, teaching and research training. More than 5,500 papers are produced annually and the University confers more than 7,000 undergraduate and graduate medical students. Students in the system benefit enormously from the shared knowledge provided by educators from our campus partners and from being immersed in these highly regarded structures.

There are strong levels of collaboration between various partners across the campus which has led to in excess of A$5 billion in public and private investment in recent years. The new Victorian Comprehensive Cancer Centre is an exemplar of how a specific disease-based partnership can work. The New Facility with over a billion australian dollars brings together the cancer research, education and clinical expertise of eight of Melbourne's leading institutions: the Peter MacCallum Cancer Centre, Melbourne Health (including the Royal Melbourne Hospital), UM, the Walter and Eliza Hall Institute of Medical Research, Royal Women's Hospital, Royal Children's Hospital, Western Health and St Vincent's Hospital Melbourne. The Doherty Institute for Infection and Immunity along with the Melbourne Brain Centre similarly draw together numerous partners to create internationally leading joint ventures.

Despite these joint projects, the Melbourne Biomedical Campus still lacks some of the cohesion that has been demonstrated internationally. It is important to note that there are significant differences between the governance structures that exist in Melbourne compared to those in some of the world's most highly regarded biomedical centres. For example, although the University has departments of medicine, surgery etc in the leading hospitals, it has no role to play in the governance of those institutions. They all have separate boards and CEOs and their funding structure is distinctly separate from the tertiary sector. Many of the research institutes are similarly distinct from the University, even though the University originally spawned these institutes. It could be readily argued that the distinct funding models of the medical research institutes, the hospitals and the University are set up in such a way as to force entities within each grouping and between the three groups to compete rather than collaborate. Any programme to draw together the tripartite mission requires onerous negotiations, but, with strength of leadership, is being achieved.

To this end, the University has a significant opportunity on its hands at present. The main Medical School building, constructed in the 1960s is no longer fit for purpose and no amount of internal modification will bring this facility to a standard where it can meet modern education and research needs. Its unusual "triradiate" shape carves out a very significant campus footprint whilst having limited actual relative floor space. The site is directly opposite the Royal Melbourne Hospital and the Walter and Eliza Hall Institute for Medical Research. Less than 100 meters up the road, the University also owns another site of similar size, this time across the road from the Victorian Comprehensive Cancer Institute (currently under construction). Collectively, these two sites represent some of the most critical healthcare and research real estate in Melbourne.

Town planning opportunities of this magnitude do not come about often, and the University is in a position to have a far more significant footprint in the precinct whilst providing the State Government with the means to address the growing healthcare needs of the population. We have also observed, a transition over recent years, the scale of collective endeavours that can be achieved in the Biomedical space. The Melbourne Brain Centre, focused on neuroscience, brought together the University, one hospital and a single closely affiliated medical research institute. The Peter Doherty Institute for Infection and Immunity brought together a very different group of organizations, again with the University leading the group, but this time with the addition of numerous government-funded agencies such as the Victorian Healthcare Associated Infection Surveillance System and the World Health Organisation Collaborating Centre for Reference and Research on Influenza. The VCCC (Victorian Comprehensive Cancer Centre) project on the other hand is a completely different beast. Bringing together the cancer clinical services of six major Melbourne hospitals along with the University and the Walter and Eliza Hall Institute means that eight distinctly governed entities, some of which are in competition, must work collaboratively to provide better cancer research, treatment and care.

What is being called the Gateway Health Sciences Project — which will involve the two University sites and the broader involvement they must have in the future of the entire Melbourne Biomedical Campus — is the next step in the level of complexity of the University's relationships with its partners. No longer can "closed door" facilities be built that are run by and for the University. These sites must be used to most effectively achieve the overall goals of the entire campus, with improved societal benefits as the vision for all involved. The University cannot undertake this mission alone. It must work closely with its campus partners, the community, and the local, State and Federal Governments to create a new Melbourne Biomedical Campus that can attract and retain the best researchers, educators and clinicians in the world. Ultimately, the impact we have is driven by the quality of the people we employ.

References

Angus. J.A. "From Hay, Corn and Horses to Building a World-Class Medical Precinct". Vernon Collins Oration, Royal Children's Hospital, October 2012.

Australian Government, Department of Infrastructure and Transport. "State of Australian Cities 2013".

Australian Government. "End of Year Summary of International Student Enrolment Data — Australia — 2013".

City of Melbourne. "A great place to study: International Student Strategy Draft 2013–17". Future Melbourne Committee Agenda item 6.7.

City of Melbourne. "Knowledge Melbourne — International Student Strategy Discussion Paper". September 2012.

City of Melbourne. "Melbourne — Australia's knowledge capital — The Contributions of Melbourne's universities to the City's economic, cultural and community development". May 2007.

City of Melbourne. "Retail and Hospitality Strategy 2013–17". 2012.

City of Melbourne. "Trends and Melbourne". August 2012.

Deloitte Access Economics. "The economic contribution of international students". February 2013.

McCamish, T. (2010). "The University of Melbourne — A Visitor's Guide". The Miegunyah Press.

Morrison. I. (1995). "The Accompaniments of European Civilization: Melbourne Exhibitions 1854–1888". *The La Trobe Journal*, No. 56.

Real Estate Institute of Victoria. Rental Market Snapshot. April 2014 (trend) <www.reiv.com.au>

Selleck, R.J.W. (2004). "Chancellor Barry", *The La Trobe Journal*, No. 73.

State Government of Victoria. Victorian Budget 2014–15. Budget Overview document.

University of Melbourne. (1993). "Change and Tradition: A Portrait of the University of Melbourne".

Victorian Heritage Database. (2012). "Former Northern cattle Market Reserve Wall".

About the Author

Shane Huntington is currently the Senior Policy and Strategy Adviser in the Faculty of Medicine, Dentistry and Health Sciences University of Melbourne.

Stephen K. Smith is the Dean, Faculty of Medicine Dentistry and Health Sciences at the University of Melbourne. Formerly Vice-President (Research) at the Nanyang Technological University.

APPENDICES

APPENDIX 1: CONFERENCE PROGRAMME

Co-Sponsors:

NANYANG TECHNOLOGICAL UNIVERSITY   金基氏李 LEE FOUNDATION

Pre-Conference: Sunday, 17th November 2013 (5 pm to 7.30 pm) Welcome Reception at Orchid @ Campus Clubhouse

Inaugural Conference on *"Univer-Cities' Strategic Implications for Asia"*

18th November 2013 at Nanyang Executive Centre, Nanyang Technological University, Singapore

Time	Programme (17th Nov 2013, evening)
5.00 pm–5.30 pm	• **Registration at Nanyang Executive Centre (NEC)** at **Level 2, Education Wing**, 60 Nanyang View, Singapore 639673 (Location Map)
5.30 pm–6.00 pm	• Welcome Reception at **Orchid @ Campus Clubhouse** with a NTU Welcome
6.00 pm–6.30 pm	• Short address and insights by **Professor Richard Bender** on 'Musings on 50-year Univer-Cities Evolution: Berkeley, Cambridge, Tokyo, New York City and CERN' — An introduction to the conference and future work on 'Univer-Cities', its history, the current explosion of interest and the emergence of some radical new forces that challenge thinking about the future.

Richard started his personal journey as a young architect at CERN (Conseil European pour la Recherché Nucleaire/European Organization for Nuclear Research).

6.30 pm–7.30 pm
- Cocktails Continue
- Good-nite

Co-Sponsors:

LEE FOUNDATION

Inaugural Conference on "Univer-Cities' Strategic Implications for Asia"

18th November 2013 at Nanyang Executive Centre, Nanyang Technological University, Singapore

- Conference Chairperson: **Mr Anthony SC Teo**, Adjunct Professor, Lee Kuan Yew School of Public Policy, Chevalier of the Ordre des Palmes Académiques
- Co-Chair: **Professor Barry Desker**, Dean, S. Rajaratnam School of International Studies, Nanyang Technological University
- Co-Chair: **Professor Stephen K Smith**, Dean, Faculty of Medicine, Dentistry and Health Sciences, University of Melbourne

Conference Day: Monday, 18th November 2013 (8.30 am to 9 pm)

DATE: 18th November 2013, Monday
TIME: 8.30am to 9pm
VENUE: Auditorium @ Level 2 Nanyang Executive Centre (NEC), Guest Wing
60 Nanyang View http://maps.ntu.edu.sg/maps#q:nec
Singapore 639673
NEC Contact Person: Mr Vincent Siew Telephone No: (65) 6790 6700   (65) 6790 6700 FREE

Central to this renaissance of the **New Silk Road** is the idea that new knowledge, technology and innovations can be created and re-defined by powerful city-centres with leading universities in greater Asia, Australasia and Pacific.

21st Century power which Univer-Cities have the potential to wield can be found in Tokyo, Hong Kong, Shanghai, Seoul, Melbourne, Mumbai and Singapore; and across to San Francisco, Palo Alto, Seattle and Vancouver.

With 50 percent of Asia set to become urbanites, cities in this region are engines of economies. Universities like KAIST, HKU, HKUST, IIT, IIS, Tsinghua University, Shanghai University, Tokyo University, NUS, NTU, University of Melbourne, *et al.*, hence have crucial missions to co-create the evolving concept of 'Univer-Cities' in Asia.

Conference Day: Monday, 18th November 2013 (8.30am to 6.30pm) – Conference at NEC

Time	Programme (18th Nov 2013)
8.15am–9.00am	• Registration: **outside NEC Auditorium, 2nd Floor Guest Wing, NEC**
9.00am–9.10am 	• Emcee **Ms Chye Shu Wen**, Editor, representing World Scientific Publishing • 'Welcome Address' by **Professor Bertil Andersson**, Nanyang Technological University President and Trustee, Nobel Foundation
9.10am – 9.15am	• Conference Chairperson's opening remarks and citation of Guest of Honour
9.15am–9.45am 	• Distinguished Key-Note Address by Guest of Honour, **His Royal Highness Raja Dr. Nazrin Shah**, The Regent of the state of Perak, Malaysia • Opening of Conference

9.45 am–11.15 am **Panel Session 1: Euro-American Niche Cities with Great Universities — Cambridge and Berkeley***

* UC Berkeley was ranked Number 1 in the latest US News and World Report rankings of public national universities, 10 September 2013

Chairperson: Univer-Cities Conference Chairperson **Mr Anthony SC Teo**, Chevalier of the Ordre des Palmes Académiques.

Mr Anthony SC Teo was NTU's Secretary to the University, an Ex-Officio member of the NTU Senate, and a member of the University Cabinet, until August 2010. Anthony served as the Advisor on Special Projects to the President, NTU till June 2012.

Panelist Presenters:

Professor Peter Carolin, pioneer of Univer-Cities, is Emeritus Professor of Architecture at the University of Cambridge where he was Head of the Department of Architecture. He is a Life Fellow of his College, Corpus Christi, University of Cambridge.

Professor Richard Bender is the former Dean of the College of Environmental Design and Chair and Professor of Architecture at UC Berkeley. He is a noted campus planner, with major involvement in university campus and related urban development in Asia, the americas, and Europe (also at the early developments at CERN).

Panelist Discussants:

AVC Emily Marthinsen is Assistant Vice Chancellor for Physical & Environmental Planning at the University of California, Berkeley with 30 years of relevant work experience at Berkeley and with design and planning firms in Berkeley, San Francisco, Washington, D.C. and Alexandria, Virginia.

Mr John Parman writes on urban development for *Architect's Newspaper and Arcade*, among other West Coast publications. He co-founded and published the award-winning journal, Design Book Review.

11.15 am – 11.30 am	• Networking and Refreshment Break
11.30 am–1.00 pm	**Panel Session II: Vice-Chancellors' Forum: East-West views of Univer-Cities**

Chairperson:

Dr Gordon Johnson, Fellow of The Royal Asiatic Society and President (2009–2012); and former Deputy Vice Chancellor, University of Cambridge.

Panelist Speakers & Discussants:

'UKM with Bangi, Federal Capital KL and Tiger Malaysia' by **Tan Sri Dato' Seri Professor Dr Sharifah Hapsah Syed Hasan Shahabudin**, Vice Chancellor, Universiti Kebangsaan Malaysia, and Chairperson, National Council of Women's Organisation, Malaysia.

Appendix 1: Conference Programme

'From the United Kingdom's Tyne to Eastern Australia's New South Wales and Asia—Re-linking the New Silk Road' by **Professor Caroline McMillen**, Vice Chancellor & President, University of Newcastle, New South Wales, Australia.

'The Architecture of Knowledge and the Knowledge of Architecture' by **Dr Roseann O'Reilly Runte**, President and Vice-Chancellor, Carleton University, Ottawa, Canada.

1.00 pm–2.30 pm	• Sit-down buffet Lunch with a talk given by **Dr Gordon Johnson**, titled "Becoming a Univer-City: From the Early Modern World to the 21st Century" **at the Atrium, Education Wing, NEC.**
	Historian Dr Johnson will share how Cambridge became an all-rounded Univer-City by the 16th century. A milestone was the establishment of Cambridge University Press, which has managed to thrive for nearly 500 years, and expanded internationally in the age of the internet and social media. Dr Johnson was the Chairman of the Press from 1981 to 2010.
	• Group photo taking

2.30 pm–4.00 pm

Panel Session III: The Singapore Case, Implications & Action for Univer-Cities Conference 2016

Chairperson:

Professor Stephen K Smith, Dean, Faculty of Medicine, Dentistry and Health Sciences, University of Melbourne

Panelist Presenter: "Conversations in Futures of Univer-Cities in the Asia Pacific: Singapore's Place and Education in the 21st Century".

By **Mr Harold Guida**, Senior Design Partner of Guida Moseley Brown Architects. Mr Guida has over 40 years of international experience on a wide range of architectural, interior design and urban design projects undertaken in Singapore, United States, Australia, South-East Asia, and China.

Panelist Discussants:

Professor Dr Cham Tao Soon, Chancellor, SIM University, Founder President of NTU and The Singapore Academy of Engineers. Professor Cham is the 2006 Recipient of the United Kingdom's Distinguished Engineering International Medal.

Appendix 1: Conference Programme

Professor Lap-Chee Tsui, OC, FRS, Vice Chancellor and President of The University of Hong Kong. Professor Tsui discoverer of the gene causing cystic fibrosis and is the former President of Human Genome Organisation.

Dr Ali Allawi, Senior Research Professor at the Middle East Institute of NUS, was former Finance Minister of Iraq. An MIT engineer, Harvard MBA, LSE city planner; and investment banker, he held Fellowships at Kennedy School, Oxford, Exeter, Princeton and the World Bank. He is a prolific writer, compelling speaker with a strategic view of the future of cities — originating from Mesopotamia's Eridu some 5,000 years ago.

Mr Andrew Donnelly is leading architect with Guida Moseley Brown Architects in Canberra, Australia, with extensive experience across a range of projects in both Australia and South-East Asia.

4.00 pm – 4.15 pm	• Presentation of Conference Mementoes to Speakers, Panelists and Sponsors
4.15 pm – 4.45 pm	• Adoption of Protocol to appoint Univer-Cities Conference Host 2016, Avenues for Research and Conference 2016 Theme.
4.45 pm – 5.30 pm	• Networking and Refreshment Break
5.30 pm – 6.30 pm	• Tour of NTU Campus (free and easy)

Farewell Dinner at President's Lodge, NTU

Time	Programme (18th Nov 2013, evening)
7.00 pm – 9.00 pm	• Farewell Dinner hosted by **Professor Bertil Andersson** at The President's Lodge, NTU (24 Nanyang Circle Singapore 639774) http://maps.ntu.edu.sg/maps#q:president's%20lodge
9.00 pm	• Evening concludes

Footnotes:

Readings — *Univer-Cities: Strategic Implications for Asia*	*Contributors*
(1) Setting the Conversation on Univer-Cities: Strategic Implications for Asia http://www.worldscientific.com/worldscibooks/10.1142/8816	Anthony SC Teo (Editor)
(2) Cambridge Futures: Enabling Consensus on Growth and Change	Peter Carolin
(3) Berkeley: Campus and Community	Richard Bender, Emily Marthinsen and John Parman
(4) Conversations in Futures of Univer-Cities in the Asia Pacific: Singapore — Place and Education in the 21st Century	Harold Guida and Andrew Donnelly
(5) Yunnan Gardens' Master Plan (with Postcripts)	Anthony SC Teo

Note: Extracts of other circulated papers will be provided.

Co-Sponsors:

NANYANG 金基氏李
TECHNOLOGICAL
UNIVERSITY LEE FOUNDATION

Univer-Cities Conference 2013 — Advisory Council

Advisory Council for *Univer-Cities' Strategic Implications for Asia Conference on 18th November, Singapore*

We are pleased to form the distinguished Advisory Council for the Univer-Cities Conference 2013.

Members include:

Professor Bertil Andersson, Nanyang Technological University President and Trustee, Nobel Foundation

Professor Dr Cham Tao Soon, Chancellor, SIM University, Founder President of NTU and The Singapore Academy of Engineers. Recipient of the 2006 United Kingdom's Distinguished Engineering International Medal.

Dr Gordon Johnson, Fellow of The Royal Asiatic Society and President (2009–2012); and former Deputy Vice Chancellor, University of Cambridge

Professor Dr Lilia Labidi, Visiting Research Professor at the Middle East Institute (National University of Singapore), and former Minister for Women's Affairs in the Tunisian cabinet post-Arab Spring

Professor John H McArthur, Dean Emeritus and George F. Baker Professor of Business Administration, Harvard Business School; Duke University Health System Board of Directors; Koç University Board of Overseers; Chairman of Asia Pacific Foundation of Canada; and Officer of the Order of Canada

Professor Dr Rudolph A Marcus, Arthur amos Noyes Professor of Chemistry, California Institute of Technology, Nobel Prize in Chemistry 1992

Tan Sri Dato' Seri Professor Dr Sharifah Hapsah Syed Hasan Shahabudin, Vice Chancellor, Universiti Kebangsaan Malaysia and Chairperson, National Council of Women's Organisation, Malaysia

Professor Lap-Chee Tsui, OC, FRS, Vice Chancellor and President of The University of Hong Kong, discoverer of the gene causing cystic fibrosis and past President of Human Genome Organisation.

I hope they will enjoy the fellowship — they will be appropriately acknowledged at the conference and its publications.

A bientôt, cordialement

Anthony SC Teo
Univer-Cities Conference Chairperson
Chevalier of the Ordre des Palmes Académiques
ascteo23@Univer-Cities.com

APPENDIX 2: OPENING REMARKS

INAUGURAL CONFERENCE ON "UNIVER-CITIES": STRATEGIC IMPLICATIONS FOR ASIA

18 November 2013 @ NEC, NTU

Conference Chairperson's Opening Remarks and Citation of Guest of Honour and HRH Royal Address at the Inaugural *Conference on* "Univer-Cities' Strategic Implications For Asia"
held at Nanyang Technological University (NTU)
By
Adjunct Professor Anthony SC Teo

Menghadap Duli Yang Maha Mulia Pemangku Raja Perak Darul Ridzuan (or Abode of Grace in Arabic), Raja Dr. Nazrin Shah or Your Royal Highness Raja Dr Nazrin Shah, The Regent of the state of Perak, Malaysia; may we thank you for so kindly consenting to be our Distinguished Guest of Honour of the inaugural international conference on "Univer-Cities: Strategic Implications for Asia" and the honour of your Royal Address.

Your Royal Highness, may we request a moment to welcome our international constituents here present. To our distinguished Conference Advisory Councillors, Your Excellencies, Trustees of NTU, leaders from academia, guests and delegates: welcome to this Inaugural International Conference on Univer-Cities — A strategic view of the future that Univer-Cities will redefine the New Silk Road, generously sponsored by NTU and the Lee Foundation.

Your Royal Highness, we started this conversation at the gracious audience in your Palace with our Conference Advisory Councillor, VC Tan Sri Dato' Seri Professor Dr Sharifah; and at the opening of your public health research and medical centre at your Royal Riding at Teluk Intan by the Perak River.

His Royal Highness represents the Government of Malaysia in the international arena as Financial Ambassador of the Malaysian International Islamic Financial Centre and as Malaysia's Special Envoy for Interfaith and Inter-Civilisational Dialogue. His Royal Highness is Pro-Chancellor of the University of Malaya; President of the Perak Council on Islam and Malay Customs; Eminent Fellow of the Institute of Strategic and International Studies, Malaysia; Royal Fellow of the Malaysian Institute of Defence and Security; Member of the Chancellor's Court of Benefactors, University of Oxford; Honorary Fellow of Worcester College, University of Oxford; and Honorary Member of Magdalene College, University of Cambridge. He is a Member of the Board of Trustees of the Oxford Centre for Islamic Studies, University of Oxford; Chairman of the Board of Governors of the Malay College, Kuala Kangsar; Royal Patron of the Kuala Lumpur Business Club; and Chairman of the 'Merdeka Award' Board of Trustees. His Royal Highness holds a B.A. in Philosophy, Politics and Economics from the University of Oxford; a Master in Public Administration from the Kennedy School of Government, Harvard

University; and a PhD in Political Economy and Government from Harvard University. His research interests are in the areas of economic and political development in Southeast Asia, economic growth in developing countries and economic history. He has written articles and spoken on a wide range of issues including constitutional monarchy, nation building, Islam, Islamic finance, ethno-religious relations, education and socio-economic development.

Ampun Tuanku, Perak Darul Ridzuan is unique. Unique for its pioneering devotion to educating and creating leaders at the Royal City of Kuala Kangsar — the 108-year old Malay College of which you are the incumbent Governor nurturing the motto to reality "Fiat Sapientia Virtus", Manliness through Wisdom. The tradition of excellence is for all to see: a rich and continuing legacy of alumni who achieve greatness: Yang di Pertuan Agongs, five in fact, Prime Ministers, Menteri Besars, Ministers, Captains of Industry, et al. In our presence is Professor Dato' Dr Mahmud Mohamed Nor, a surgeons' surgeon and Emeritus Dean of Medicine, Class of 1962. This tradition is reflexive of the "Academy of Isocrates" in Athens who trained leaders amongst Athenians and Spartans, and a few international talent like Prince Timotheus, of the Kingdom of Heraclea by the Black Sea near Georgia, who became King for a decade in Isocrates' lifetime.

Ampun Tuanku, as educator and Governor, you are wont to ensure that The Malay College leads; and at the newest and largest 12th Residential College that bears your Patronage and inspiration at the University of Malaya — Sister institution to our National University of Singapore — to inspire and exhort the challenges of the new age, new knowledge, new innovation and new attitudes. You speak with candour and recently, piognantly quoted Dante that "the hottest places in Hell are reserved for those who in time of moral crisis preserve their neutrality".

Ampun Tuanku, thank you once again for consenting to be our Distinguished Guest of Honour and delivering The Royal Address to inaugurate this Conference.

Distinguished Guests, Ladies and Gentlemen — to light the way ahead following our venture of the past 18 months of publishing the book on Univer-Cities and this inaugural conference, and the faith that pioneers do not fade away, they walk with history, it is my distinct privilege and honour to present to you, an educator, researcher, scholar à la Oxford and Harvard, leading light, representing a new genre of Prince who holds the promise — knowing no bounds — future philosopher-king in Plato's ideals; Crown Prince and Regent of Perak Darul Ridzuan, HRH Raja Dr Nazrin Shah.

Ampun Tuanku,

Demikianlah sahaja sembah ucapan patik. Patik dan seluruh warga NTU sekali lagi merafak sembah menjunjung setinggi-tinggi kasih atas keberangkatan Duli-duli ke majlis ini.

> Bertuah rumah ada tuannya
>
> Bertuah negeri ada pucuknya
>
> Elok kampung ada pimpinannya
>
> Elok negeri ada rajanya

Wabillahi taufiq walhidayah, wassalamualaikum warahmat

APPENDIX 3: PANEL SESSION III: THE SINGAPORE CASE

Univer-Cities: Panel III
Implications of Univer-Cities for Southeast Asia

at the

Inaugural Conference on "Univer-Cities' Strategic Implications for Asia" held at **Nanyang Executive Centre, Nanyang Technological University, Singapore on 18 November 2013**

By
Harold Guida and Andrew Donnelly

The recent experience of master planning at the Yunnan Garden Campus of Nanyang Technological University (NTU), host campus of the inaugural Univer-Cities conference, provided the basis for a broad discussion during Panel Session III. While the focus was on the Singapore experience, specifically the Campus Master Plan prepared for NTU by Guida Moseley Brown Architects, both Professor Lap-Chee Tsui and Dr Ali Allawi respectively provided contrasting lessons from Hong Kong and the Middle East, describing how purposeful collaborations between universities and the specificities of their place can be deepened to the mutual benefit of both institution and locality.

The Campus Master Plan for Yunnan Garden Campus responds not only to the pressing need for future housing and academic infrastructure, but to the broader environment in which NTU is situated. In part, this response was made possible due to the long-standing centralization of education policy in Singapore, which typically integrates the strategic direction of individual institutions with broader, national priorities. Universities are thus mindful of the bigger picture of which they are a part. Increasingly, this picture emphasizes the importance for universities of forging collaborative networks with complementary educational institutions overseas, drawing on a global marketplace of ideas for the intellectual capital upon which it is perceived Singapore's future well-being will heavily rely.

Pedagogical models are also changing rapidly. An important shift in Singapore, as elsewhere in the world, has been from a top down method of instruction to one whereby learning is achieved more independently, not always aligned with curricula promoted at a state or even institutional level. Students are finding innovative and diverse ways to gain and transfer new knowledge and skills, with collaboration and communications technology often increasingly important elements in their education. This in turn has implications for the environment in which they learn, and more universities in the region, including NTU, have responded with new programmes and new spaces in which such programmes can best flourish. As Hal Guida from Guida Moseley Brown Architects explained during *Panel Session III*, this was the context in which the Campus Master Plan at NTU evolved. Other important contributing elements to the Campus Master Plan arose through the university's new Strategic Plan, and importantly through extensive consultation both within the university community and without. Among the most repeated observations from a wide spectrum of people participating in the planning discussions was the high value placed on the natural environment of the Yunnan Garden Campus — the idea of a campus in a garden.

Accordingly, long-term planning goals were developed for Yunnan Garden Campus that sought to reinforce its prevailing natural systems, drawing on the qualities of the immediate environment — from its established Chinese garden, to the movement of water and fauna across the permeable campus boundaries. Importantly, these initiatives also coincided with wider government policy, especially those relating to improving environmental outcomes of water management, for example. Similarly, the wider recognition in Singapore of changing models for teaching and learning spaces — more varied and flexible in their planning than classrooms and lecture theatres typically allow — was adopted in the Campus Master Plan through its identification of spaces able to support new approaches to pedagogy: small group learning hubs, for example, and less formal spaces distributed throughout the campus' existing and proposed built environment for social and academic interaction between students and faculty.

Since its adoption, the Campus Master Plan has already proven an important element in establishing the parameters of new development on campus. A number of projects — both pending and underway — have taken its broad principles and long-term aspirations when responding to specific project briefs, each also interpreted in accordance with the contingencies of particular sites and building or landscape requirements.

Discussion of the recent campus planning experience undertaken at NTU during Panel Session III broadened in consideration of the differing potential models an institution might adopt in developing its relationship to place. NTU can be described as balancing two approaches: one where an institution occupies a defined, self-contained academic precinct largely distinct from the wider urban, semi-urban or rural environment in which it is situated, and another whereby the institution's physical infrastructure is in large measure dispersed throughout a region, locality or host city drawing on their physical, economic and cultural urban fabric to supplement or even establish the collegiality and identity of more physically fragmented campuses. The former tendency was supported in the Campus Master Plan's recommendations for improving the definition of the campus through recognizing the existing land-locked boundaries could be rendered more permeable through clearly marking points of arrival, and developing stronger entry sequences through the campus landscape, its precincts and built environment towards a more defined campus centre. The potential of partly adopting the latter model is nevertheless also accommodated by the location of several important NTU facilities, closer to the centre of downtown Singapore — the alumni, for example, already find benefit in occupying premises both on and off campus, while recently developed academic programmes in fields such as medicine are more ambitious still through their pursuit of collaborations with international academic partners overseas.

Other examples were discussed from both the Southeast Asian region and wider world, drawing for example on the long experience of universities in the Middle East, where it was argued that some degree of independence for a campus from its wider context is of value when urban, social or political environments are unable or unwilling to accommodate more dispersed models of campus planning. As well as cultural expectations as to what an academic institution might mean for a given society and how these might best contribute towards its education, and topography was similarly discussed as an important factor contributing to the character of a campus' design. This has clearly been the experience in Hong Kong, where the University of Hong Kong has achieved a high density of building form not dissimilar to the wider city context, and an internal street pattern responsive to the contours of the island's precipitous terrain. The example of Cambridge was also discussed: a long established institution that in some measure has been attempting to redefine itself through consolidation of physical infrastructure, recalibrating its relationship to the surrounding rural and urban environment so as to achieve agreater coherence than was possible with the prevailing model of more independent and discrete colleges.

In all examples, recognizing and accommodating the attributes of place is fundamental to achieving a campus with institutional coherence and meaning, whether its facilities be dispersed city-wide or restricted to a specific land allotment on its urban fringe. What is important to a place — culturally and economically, as well as physically — needs reflection and accommodation in institutions through considered planning and land management goals. For Southeast Asia in particular, the ideas raised in Panel Session III, reflecting upon and reimagining how the interests of a campus and city might best intersect, are timely given rapid and intensive urbanisation in the region. Singapore has the potential to evolve compelling models for collaboration between academic institutions, their physical infrastructure and host cities, whereby encouraging reciprocity of skills, knowledge and creativity could promote the free interchange of information, ideas and resources, bringing together civic and academic cultures in a manner instructive for other countries, regardless of the more specific goals expressed through particular education policies. The intent — as His Royal Highness Raja Dr Nazrin Shah succinctly proposed in the Royal Address — is to achieve a synthesis whose sum is larger than its parts. The beneficiaries would not least be prospective students, researchers and teachers, enticed to an institution by a physical environment encompassing both the tradition of intellectual independence associated with the campus, and the economic opportunities and social vibrancy evident in Asia's rapidly changing urban environment.

About the Authors

Harold Guida is a Partner Guida Moseley Brown Architects.

Andrew Donnelly is an Architect Guida Moseley Brown Architects.

INDEX

A

Academic enhancement, 147
Acclaro, 188
Adl-Dimnah, 234
Ahmed b. Muhammad al-Mihdar, 248
Alexander, Christopher, 69
Alexandria library, 15
Al-Kairouan hospital, 234
Amazon, 20
AMGEN, 20
Apple (industy), 2
Arab League, 238
Arab scholarly works, 249
Arab spring, 241
Architectural competitions, 149–151
Architectural space, 172
Architecture, new age of, 171–172
Architecture of knowledge, 161–163
Arizona State University (ASU), 19
Asia-Europe Meeting (ASEM), 94
Asian universities, 37
Association of Southeast Asian Nations (ASEAN), 94
Australian Agricultural Company (AACo), 96
Australian Government's *2013 National Workforce Development Strategy*, 108
Axiomatic Design (AD) theory, 177

B

Ballarat School of Mines, 114
Bangi campus, 84
Barnard, David T., 139
Batawa, 170–171
Battuta, Ibn, 244–245
Bay Area, 41–42
Beauregard, Robert, 144
Beit El Hikma Raqqada in Kairouan, 235
Bénard, Emile, 45–46
Bender, Richard, 39, 47
Berkeley, city government of, 41
Berkeley Architectural History Association, 48
Berkeley Large, 58–59
Berkeley Slow, 59–61
Berkeley Small, 57–58
BHP Steelworks, Newcastle, 100
Bimaristan, 234
Black Swan, 17
Bowker, Chancellor Albert, 47
Broken Hill Proprietary Ltd (BHP), 99, 103–104, 107
Building and Construction Authority (BCA) Academy, 109
Building industrial city, 97–98
Burnaby Mountain, 122, 128
Burnaby's Mountain Top to Vancouver and Surrey, 119–137
Bus rapid transit (BRT) system, 198

C

California, University of, 1, 44–47, 54–55
California Institute of Technology (Caltech), 242
Cambridge: beyond the univer-city, 67–80
Cambridge, from medieval market town to univer-city, 205–226
Cambridge Ahead (CA), 78
Cambridge Futures, 71–72
Cambridge Past Present and Future (CPPF), 73
Cambridge phenomenon, 70, 223
Cambridge Preservation Society, 73
Cambridge sub-region, 74–75
Cambridge University, 1, 4, 7–8
Cambridge University and city, 68
Cambridge University Press, 70
Campus and community, 39, 41–42
Campus Design Review Committee, 49
Campus master plan, 157
Campus Planning Office (CPO), 151
Campus Planning Study Group (CPSG), 43, 47–48
Campus Rally, 54
Campus revival, UC Berkeley, 47–49
Cam (river), 209
Canada's Carleton, 1
Canada's Model National Energy Code, 129
Cape of Good Hope, 95
Carleton University, 161–172
CBD (Central Business District), 109
Centre of international scholarship, Cambridge emerges as, 215–218
Chandler, Alfred, 2
Change agents, universities as, 34

Charting British Columbia's Economic Future, 134
Cheras medical centre, 84
Christensen, Clayton, 2
Chrysalis (La Chrysalide) (Algerian Aicha Lemsine), 236
Cities and universities, combining, 31
Cities as economic drivers, 32
City Southside Plan, 52
Civilization, my Mother!
   (La civilisation, ma Mère!)
   (Moroccan Driss Chraibi), 236
Collaboration, Leadership and Resilience: Sustainable Communities and Global Prosperity, 171
College Homestead Association, 44–45
College of California, 44
Collegiate university, 67
Commercial EV, 178
Community engagement, process of, 154
Community programmes, 105–106
Community Summit, 134
Competitions, 140, 149–151
Competitiveness, 208
Competitive RFP (request for proposal), 14
Complete communities, 156
Complete Communities: Directions Strategy, 146
Compressed natural gas (CNG) buses, 197–199
Comte, Charles, 236
Conference programme, "*Univer-Cities' Strategic Implications for Asia,*" 281 Appendix 1
Conseil, Ernest, 236

Conservatorium of Music, UON, 109
Co-presence, 248
Corpus Christi College, 210
Creative destruction, 40
Cross-cultural interactions, 93
CSIRO (Commonwealth Scientific and Industrial Research Organisation), 110
C4T (Carbon Reduction in Chemical Technology), 14
Curry, Joanne, 119
Cushing, Nancy, 93

D
Davis, Glyn, 271
"3-D" concept, 32–33
Democratic mass universities, 34
Density, characterizing the city, 32
Depression years, 46
Designing complex systems, 186–188, 190
Development Plan, 74
Disciplines, disputes within, 219
Disruptive innovation, 2, 6, 10, 13–14, 24–25
Distancing from city, universities, 39
Doctor of Medicine (MD), 273
Downing College, 213
Downtown Area Plan (DAP), 52
Downtown first policy, 144–145

E
Early Modern Cambridge, 211–215
Earthquake effect on UON, 107
East-west views of univer-cities, 83–91
Economic Transformation Programme, Singapore's, 33
Emanuel, Rahm, 54

Embracing city, universities, 39
Emergence of modern university, Cambridge, 218–220
Energy, environment, water, and sustainability (EEWS), 175, 183
Engaged univer-city, 6
Engaged university, 35, 131
Engagement process, 153
Engaging communities, 134
Engineers per 100,000 inhabitants, 239
Erickson, Arthur, 122, 126
Ethical university, 35
European Commission Communication, 111
European Enlightenment, 215
European Union (EU), 4, 94
Evans Hall, 47
Evolution of Berkeley Campus, 42–43

F
Factor X, 18
Farquharson, David, 45
Federation of Cambridge Residents' Associations (FeCRA), 73
Fen products, 209
Florida, Richard, 162
Forbes, John, 112
Foreign Students in French and British Universities, 238
Fort Garry Campus, 139, 142, 148–149, 151
Fragmentation, specialization leading to, 40

G
Gateway Health Sciences Project, 277
Gateway to the west, 143
Global context, univer-city in, 225–226

Globalization, 93
Global knowledge and innovation hub, UON, 109–113
Golden Gate, 45, 47
Gothic architecture, 166
Governance, 14
Great Bear Rainforest, 133
Great Recession, 40, 56
Green Belt, 74
Growth agenda, 72
Growth coalitions, 143
Growth machines, 143
Gum tree universities, 104

H
Hadrami Indian Ocean Trade Routes, 246
Hadrami settlement sites in E. African Coast, 247
Hakai Network for Coastal People, Ecosystems and Management, 132–133
Hammam, 234–235
Hawksmoor, Nicholas, 67
Hearst, Phoebe Apperson, 45
Hearst Memorial Mining Building, 46
Heroic leadership, 16
Higgs-Boson particle physics experiment, 163
Histoire de la médecine Arabe en Tunisie, 234–235
Historic buildings nominations of UC Berkeley, 48
Hong Kong, University of, 1
Howard, John Galen, 42–43
Human Development Index (HDI), 241
Hunter Medical Research Institute (HMRI), 110, 112–113
Hunter River, 95
Hunter Valley, 98
Huntington, Shane, 261
Huxham, Chris, 130

I
Idealized magnetic field flow of dual rail system, 195
Impact of universities on city of Melbourne, 268–271
Implications is interactivity, 37
Inaugural address, 1
Industry engagement, project of UON, 4–5
Initial engagement process, 153–154
Innovation, project of UON, 5
Institutional in nature, 37
Institutions, univer-cities as, 35–36
Integrated biomedical campus, creating, 275–277
Intergovernmental Panel on Climate Change (IPCC), 175, 177
Internal combustion (IC) engine, 176–177
International Urban Design Competition, 142
iphone, 2

J
Jameson, Graham, 110
Jameson Cell, 110
Japan Society for the Promotion of Science (JSPS), 242
Jeans, Paul, 107
John Galen Howard UC Berkeley Plan, 43
Johns Hopkins University, 1, 88
John H McArthur, 292

K

Kebangsaan, meaning, 86
Kelham, George, 46
Key performance indicators (KPI), 14
King, Governor Philip Gidley, 95
King's College, 218–219
Knowing, new ways of, 171–172
Knowledge, 161
Knowledge Eco-system, building, 87
Knowledge of architecture, 161–163
Korea Advanced Institute of Science and Technology (KAIST), 2, 15, 18, 175–200
Korean POSCO, 4
Kuala Lumpur, 83

L

Labidi-Teo essay, 13
Laboratories, 208
Langat River, 84
Lawrence, Paul, 2
Lay people, 151
LEED Gold, 129
Lee Foundation, 24, 296
Lee Kong Chian School of Medicine (LKCMedicine), 24
Lee Seng Tee, 226
Liberal Arts College, 220
Liddell Power Station, 111
Littlemore, Richard, 119
Living Building standard, 129
Local Agenda 21, 34
Local residents, 154–155
Lorsch, Jay, 2
2020 LRDP, 50
LRDP (Long-Range Development Plans), 9, 46–47

M

Madrasa, 234
Maghreb, 232
Magnetic field between underground power supply system, 195
Malaysia, Universiti Kebangsaan (UKM), 1, 6, 83, 86–87
Malaysia, University of Science (USM), 6
Malaysia, University of Technology (UTM), 6
Maqama dham al-dunya, 248
Marthinsen, Emily, 39
Massachusetts Institute of Technology (MIT), 1, 180, 191
Massey, Geoff, 123
Maybeck, Bernard, 42–43, 45
McLennan, Jason, 129
Mcmillen, Caroline, 93
Medical School, addition to UON, 106
Medieval Cambridge: religious origins, 209–211
Melbourne, colony to city, 262–268
Melbourne, univer-city of, 261–277
Melbourne, University of (UM), 261
Melbourne and its suburbs 1855, 263
Melbourne Biomedical Campus, 275
Melbourne College of Advanced Education, 266
Melbourne Model, 272
Michigan, University of (UM), 20–21
Microsoft, 20
Migration, principal routes of, 240
Milgrom, Richard, 139
Milky Way of universities, 167
Mitchell, David Scott, 101
Modelling good urban (design) behaviour, Manitoba, 139–157

Model of sustainability, 128
Morrill Act, 1, 45
Morris J. Wosk Centre for Dialogue, 124

N

NAFTA (North American Free Trade Agreement), 11
Naksa, 249
Nanyang Technological University (NTU), 14, 31
Nashar, Beryl, 105
National aspirations, UKM's responses to, 86–87
National Committee of Science and Technology (NCST), 184
National Committee on Green Economy (NCGE), 184
Nationalities with Highest Representation in French and British Universities, 238
National Transformation Initiatives, 87
National Transformation Programme (NTP), 86
Network, The, 133
Newcastle, origins of city of, 95–100
Newcastle, University of (UON), 1, 4–5
Newcastle College of Advanced Education, 115. *See also* Newcastle Teachers' College
Newcastle Institute for Energy and Resources (NIER), 110–112
Newcastle Region Art Gallery, 114
Newcastle's coal mining and industrial heritage, 96
Newcastle Teachers' College, 102
Newcastle Technical College, 101, 104
Newcastle University College, 103
Newcastle University Establishment Group, 103
New cultural and intellectual horizons, UON, 100–107
NeW Directions Strategic Plan, 113
New Economic Model (NEM), 85
New Silk Roads, 251
Newton, Isaac, 215–216
New York University (NYU), 22
Nicolle, Charles, 236
NIMBY factor, 72
Nobel Prize, 236, 242
NRF (National Research Foundation) of Singapore, 14
NSW State government, 109
NTI (Nanyang Technological Institute), 23. *See also* Nanyang Technological University (NTU)

O

OLEV bus system, 180
Olmstead Plan Sktech 1863, 44
Olmsted, Frederick Law, 45
One-stage competitions, 150
On-Line Electric Vehicle (OLEV), 2, 16, 18, 176, 181, 185, 195, 198–199
OPEC Oil crisis, 105
Open Foundation Program, 105
Opening remarks, "*Univer-Cities*' Strategic Implications for Asia," 295 Appendix 2
Organization for Economic Cooperation and Development (OECD), 238
Ottawa, University of, 164–165
OurWinnipeg, 145–146, 156
Outliers, 17
Oxford University, 217, 219

P

Panel session, Singapore case, "*Univer-Cities' Strategic Implications for Asia*," 299 Appendix 3
Pantun, 89
Parasitic urbanism, 144
Parman, John, 39
Pedagogy, 148–149
Pennsylvania, University of, 249
Permata Pintar programme, 88
Permata School for the Gifted and Talented, 84
Peter MacCallum Cancer Centre, 275
Petter, Andrew, 119
Phoenician trade routes, 232
Physical and programmatic engagement, SFU's, 137
Planning future campus, UC Berkeley, 50
Plan Winnipeg 2020, 144–145
Plugin electric vehicle (PEV) buses, 197–199
Pohang University of Science and Technology, 4
Porter, Michael, 2
Post-Great Recession, 54
Principia, 217
Punic period, 233

Q

Qarawiyyin University, 234
Quality of Australian Health Care study, 106
Quinn, Katrina, 93

R

Rasselas, 169–170
Reborn, Newcastle, 107
Reflux Classifier, 110
Reforming, university, 55
Regionality continuum of univer-cities:, 3–4
Regulating authorities, 156
Relative austerity, 41
Research and Innovation Clusters, 113
Reshaping Economic Geography (World Bank Development Report, 2009), 32
Richard, Michelle, 139
Rihla, 232, 244–245
Royal Commissions, 220
Royal Melbourne Hospital, 267
Rudolph A Marcus, 292
Runte, Roseann O'Reilly, 161
Rybczynski, Witold, 126

S

Sather Gate UC Berkeley, 50
2050 Scenarios, Berkeley, 61–65
Science, taste for, 233–241
Scientific research, 248
Search/solution space, 149
Seismic shift, from heavy industry to education, research and innovation, 107–108
Semester in Dialogue, SFU's, 132
Serendipity to strategy, 130–135
SFU Community Trust, 128–130
SFU faculty, 131
SFU Harbour Centre, 123
SFU Public Square, 134–135
SFU's Morris J. Wosk Centre for Dialogue, 135
SFU's Vancouver campus, 124
Shah, His Royal Highness Raja Dr Nazrin, 1, 31, 205

Shahabudin, Sharifah Hapsah Syed Hasan, 83, 91
Shanghai Cooperation Organisation, 94
Shantou University (STU), 17
Shaped Magnetic Field in Resonance (SMFIR), 16, 176–177, 181, 189, 192, 194, 196, 199–200
Silicon Fen, 80
Silicon Valley, US, 161
Silk Road, 94, 206, 233
Simon, Roger, 148
Simon Fraser University (SFU), 1, 119–120
Skottowe, Thomas, 96
Small and Medium Enterprises (SMEs), 88
Smith, Stephen K., 261
Societal engagement, 89–91
Sophia Jane, 96–97
South Hall, UC Berkeley, 46
Southwest for Garry Design Charrette (2004), 145
Southwood, 146–149
Space and place, 163
Space Education Precinct, 109
Specialization leading to fragmentation, 40
Strategic implications for developing Asia, 36–38
Strategic plan, Carleton University, 171
Strategic Planning Framework, 141
Strawberry Creek, 44–45
Structure follows strategy, 2
Surrey campus, SFU's, 125
Surrey Central Library, 126
Sydney University, 103

T

Talented Youth, Johns Hopkins University Centre for, 88
Taste for science, 233–241
Technical College at Tighes Hill, 102
The UON Research Associates Ltd (TUNRA), 105
Titan Manufacturing Company, 99
Together with city, university, 39
Toronto Dominion Bank, 124
Towards univer-city, 220–225
Town and gown, 137
Traditional academy, 121–122
Tram, Korea, 199
Transactional to transformative progression, 136
Transforming Australia's education landscape, 271–275
Trans-Saharan Trade, 234
Trinity College, 212, 215–216
Tudor sovereigns, 211
Tula Foundation, 133
Tunisian higher education, 237
Tunisian Scientists, arrived in singapore since 2010–11, 243
Tunisian Scientists, based in Singapore, routes taken by group of, 250
Tunisian scientists and new routes, 252
Tunisian scientists' experiences in Singapore, 231–254
Tunisian students and scholars in Europe, 240
Two-stage competitions, 150

U

UC Berkeley Campus, 1, 9, 39–65
UCLA campus, 46

UKM 3, 88
UKM location, 83
UKM Main Campus, Bangi, 84
United Nations Development Programme (UNDP), 2010, 241
Univer-Cities Conference 2013, 1
"*Univer-Cities' Strategic Implications for Asia*" conference programme, 281 Appendix 1
"*Univer-Cities' Strategic Implications for Asia*" opening remarks, 295 Appendix 2
"*Univer-Cities' Strategic Implications for Asia*" panel session, Singapore case, 299 Appendix 3
Univer-city, 210, 246
Univer-city, model sustainable development, 127–130
Univer-City Childcare Centre, 129
Univer-City of Melbourne, 261–277
Univer-City of Roosevelt Island, 22
Univer-city-region, Cambridge, 79–80
University and city, 67, 69–70
University-community engagement, 136
University constituencies, 155–156
University Library, 221
University of Manitoba (UofM), 139–140
University of Michigan-Ann Arbor (UM-AA), 20
University of Ottawa, 164
University's 1962 plan for Cambridge, 71
University town, 215, 221
UON building participation in higher education and univer-city, 108–109

UON identity, 104–107
UON Medical School, 106
UON Singapore, 109
UON's New Directions Strategic Plan, 110
Urban governance, 38
Urbanism, ecological implications of, 144
Urbanization, 38
Urbanization, drawbacks, 33
Useful university, 35
Utopia and campus master plan, 167–169
Utopias, 167–168

V

Vancouverism, 7, 126
Vancouverism spreads to Surrey, 125–127
VCCC (Victorian Comprehensive Cancer Centre) project, 277
Victorian Comprehensive Cancer Centre, 275
Video presentation, 9
Virtual university, 35
Visionary momentum, maintaining, 157
Visionary (re)generation competition, 151–152
2030 Vision for Cambridge Sub-region, 76

W

Wallis, James, 96
Wayne State-Detroit (WS-D), 20
Western Ontario, 21
Windsor-London, 21
Winnipeg context, 142–146

Women, representation in academic positions, 105
Women Scientists/Researchers from Maghreb, countries visited by, 252
World Economic Forum (WEF), 176
Wurster Hall, 47

Y
Yazami, Rachid, 242
Yi-Fu Tuan, 163, 167

Z
Zeuxis, 169
Zuweil, Ahmed, 242, 248–250

www.ingramcontent.com/pod-product-compliance
Lightning Source LLC
Chambersburg PA
CBHW071359300426
44114CB00016B/2121